Law and Gospel

Texts and Studies in Reformation and Post-Reformation Thought

General Editor
Prof. Richard A. Muller, Calvin Theological Seminary

Editorial Board
Prof. Irena Backus, University of Geneva
Prof. A. N. S. Lane, London Bible College
Prof. Susan E. Schreiner, University of Chicago
Prof. David C. Steinmetz, Duke University
Prof. John L. Thompson, Fuller Theological Seminary
Prof. Willem J. van Asselt, University of Utrecht
Prof. Timothy J. Wengert, The Lutheran Theological Seminary at
  Philadelphia
Prof. Henry Zwaanstra, Calvin Theological Seminary

Caspar Olevianus, *A Firm Foundation: An Aid to Interpreting the Heidelberg Catechism*, translated, with an introduction by Lyle D. Bierma.
John Calvin, *The Bondage and Liberation of the Will: A Defence of the Orthodox Doctrine of Human Choice against Pighius*, edited by A. N. S. Lane, translated by G. I. Davies.
Law and Gospel: Philip Melanchthon's Debate with John Agricola of Eisleben over Poenitentia, by Timothy J. Wengert.
Martin Luther: Prophet, Teacher, Hero: Luther's Function in the Life of the Church, 1520–1620, by Robert Kolb. (forthcoming)
Jerome Zanchi, *On the Christian Faith,* translated, with an introduction by John L. Farthing. (forthcoming)
Heinrich Heppe, *Reformed Dogmatics, Set Out and Illustrated from the Sources,* translated by G. T. Thompson, with a new introduction and corrections by Richard A. Muller. (forthcoming)
Theodore Beza, *Eternal Predestination and Its Execution in Time: Beza's* Tabula Praedestinationis *or* Summa totius Christianismi *(1555),* translated, with an introduction, notes, and appendices by Richard A. Muller. (forthcoming)
Benedict Pictet, *Christian Theology,* translated by Frederick Reyroux, revised, edited, and with an introduction by Martin I. Klauber. (forthcoming)

Law and Gospel

Philip Melanchthon's Debate with John Agricola of Eisleben over **Poenitentia**

Timothy J. Wengert

a Labyrinth Book

paternoster

Baker Books

A Division of Baker Book House Co
Grand Rapids, Michigan 49516

Published by Baker Books
a division of Baker Book House Company
P.O. Box 6287, Grand Rapids, MI 49516-6287

and

Paternoster Press
P.O. Box 300, Carlisle, Cumbria CA3 0QS
United Kingdom

Printed in the United States of America

Library of Congress Cataloging-in-Publication Data

Wengert, Timothy J.
    Law and gospel: Philip Melanchthon's debate with John Agricola of
Eisleben over poenitentia / Timothy J. Wengert.
      p. cm.
    Includes bibliographical references and index.
    ISBN 0-8010-2158-8 (pbk.)
      1. Repentance—Christianity—History of doctrines. 2. Law and gospel—
History of doctrines. 3. Melanchthon, Philipp, 1497–1560. 4. Agricola, Johann,
1494?–1566. I. Title.
BT800.W43   1997
234'.5'0922—dc21   97-38668

British Library Cataloging-in-Publication Data

A catalogue record for this book is available from the British Library.

For information about academic books, resources for Christian leaders, and all new releases available from Baker Book House, visit our web site:
http://www.bakerbooks.com

Table of Contents

Series Preface

The heritage of the Reformation is of profound importance to the church in the present day. Yet there remain many significant gaps in our knowledge of the intellectual development of Protestantism in the sixteenth century, and there are not a few myths about the theology of the Protestant orthodox writers of the late sixteenth and seventeenth centuries. These gaps and myths, frequently caused by ignorance of the scope of a particular thinker's work, by negative theological judgments passed on the theology of the Reformers or their successors by later generations, or by an intellectual imperialism of the present that singles out some thinkers and ignores others regardless of their relative significance to their own times, stand in the way of a substantive encounter with this important period in our history. Understanding and appropriation of that heritage can occur only through the publication of significant works—monographs and sound, scholarly translations—that present the breadth and detail of the thought of the Reformers and their successors.

Texts and Studies in Reformation and Post-Reformation Thought proposes to make available such works as Caspar Olevianus's *Firm Foundation*, Theodore Beza's *Table of Predestination*, and Jerome Zanchi's *Confession of Faith*, together with significant monographs on traditional Reformed theology, under the guidance of an editorial board of recognized scholars in the field. Major older works, like Heppe's *Reformed Dogmatics*, will be reprinted or reissued with new introductions. These works, moreover, are intended to address two groups: an academic and a confessional or churchly audience. The series recognizes the need for careful, scholarly treatment of the Reformation and of the era of Protestant orthodoxy, given the continuing presence of misunderstandings particularly of the later era in both the scholarly and the popular literature as well as the recent interest in reappraising the relationship of the Reformation to Protestant orthodoxy. In addition, however, the series hopes to provide the church at large with worthy documents from its rich heritage and thereby to support and to stimulate interest in the roots of the Protestant tradition.

Richard A. Muller

7

Preface

"During the inspection of churches [in 1527] we [Philip Melanchthon and law professor Jerome Schurff] discovered many kinds of ineptitudes. . . . When we tried to emend these things, I also got my ears boxed, so that afterwards others often attacked me."[1] So Philip Melanchthon described, some twenty-five years after the fact, the central events depicted in this book and their consequences for his later life. What seemed at the time a minor disagreement between two of Luther's foremost students, John Agricola and Melanchthon (Luther himself had described it as little more than nothing), Melanchthon remembered later as a watershed for his theology and his relation to the church. This monograph will probe the truth of that memory by analyzing the works and thought of the chief protagonists in this drama as they wrestled to understand the role of the law in the Christian's life, especially in connection with Christian *poenitentia*.[2]

After introducing the characters in this dispute and briefly examining the few scholarly pieces that touch upon it, this study will turn first to the exegetical contributions of John Agricola in the mid-1520s and then to the wealth of catechetical material produced by evangelicals, especially Melanchthon and Agricola, during this period. Is *poenitentia* the sorrow or terror that God's commandments evoke in the sinner? Or is it the new life of faith created by God's promise of forgiveness, a life in which no longer sinning is the highest form of *poenitentia*? Melanchthon's exegetical and catechetical contributions from this period make it clear that he not only disagreed with Agricola but, cognizant of the latter's position, pointedly refuted it, distinguishing it from his own approach, one grounded in his understanding of the movement from law to gospel and from terror to consolation.

The publication in 1527 of the so-called Visitation Articles, developed by Melanchthon in the course of his examination of Saxony's pastors, provoked Agricola's formal objection to Melanchthon's proposals

---

1. *MBW* 6654 (*CR* 7:1144f.), Melanchthon to George Buchholzer, dated 28 November 1552.
2. This term was alternatively understood as penance, penitence, and repentance. See p. 15 n. 1.

and led to a public confrontation between the two at the elector of Saxony's Torgau Castle, where Martin Luther played a mediatorial role. In the aftermath the participants, while adhering to Luther's compromise, continued to elaborate their own theological points of view. This led, on the one side, to Agricola's later confrontation with Luther during the first antinomian controversy of the late 1530s and contributed, on the other, to Melanchthon's developing the concept of a third use of the law (that is, a use of the law among believers as a guide for living). The question posed by the initial dispute, namely, the relation between the law and *poenitentia*, continues to be one of the central themes in Protestant theology and also continues to divide Christian, especially Lutheran, theologians. It is hoped that this examination of that theme's origins may provide the Reformers' heirs new insight and encouragement.

This book is the second volume reflecting my work on Philip Melanchthon's three commentaries on Colossians published between 1527 and 1534. That work began in 1991 as research conducted during four months at the Herzog August Bibliothek in Wolfenbüttel. I am especially grateful for that institution's financial support during that summer, and the encouragement and assistance accorded me by its fine staff, especially Sabine Solf and Gillian Bepler. I am also thankful for the conversations with other scholars which that time afforded me, especially with Robert Kolb and Irene Dingel.

Several portions of this work were first presented, respectively, at the Melanchthon seminar of the Eighth International Congress for Luther Research (St. Paul, 1993), the Sixteenth Century Studies Conferences (San Francisco, 1995), and the 1997 "Jubiläumstagung: Der Theologe Melanchthon," held in Bretten, Germany, to help celebrate the five hundredth anniversary of Melanchthon's birth. In addition, a preliminary version of a portion of chapter 2 was published as "Wittenberg's Earliest Catechism" in the *Lutheran Quarterly* (n.s., 7 [1993]: 247–60). I am indebted to all those who commented on these papers.

A special word of thanks also goes to David Steinmetz, who had the insight to realize in 1992 that my single manuscript on Melanchthon's interpretation of Colossians was in fact two separate works. (The first part of that project has been published as *Human Freedom, Christian Righteousness: Philip Melanchthon's Exegetical Dispute with Erasmus of Rotterdam* [New York: Oxford University Press, 1998].) Separating these two babies joined at the hip would not have been possible without the generous sabbatical leave provided me in 1995–96 by The Lutheran Theological Seminary at Philadelphia. The conversations with my colleagues there and the support of the dean, James Kenneth Echols, and the president, Robert Hughes, make it a joy to work at such an institution. I also want publicly to thank Richard Muller for his support in the later stages of this project and for seeing his way clear to accept the manuscript into the Texts and Studies in Reformation and Post-Reformation Thought series.

Finally, I want to recognize the wholehearted encouragement offered to me by my wife, Barbara Farlow Wengert. This work has often forced us to live our lives separated not only by oceans, but also by library walls and even by the ages as I have become more and more captivated by the sixteenth century. A heavy toll has also been exacted on my children, Emily Jane Wengert and David Hayworth Wengert, who, sad to say, grew all too accustomed to explaining to their friends their father's prolonged absences abroad, and who came to know Wolfenbüttel while waiting for their father to emerge each evening from the Duke August's *Zeughaus*. Yet their own developing vitality and eagerness to learn have encouraged and delighted me so much over the years that I proudly dedicate this work to them both, in the hopes that amid life's terrors they, like Master Philip, may find consolation in God's amazing promises.

Timothy J. Wengert
Philadelphia, Pennsylvania
16 February 1997, the five hundredth
anniversary of Philip Melanchthon's birth

¶ De Biblie
vth der vthlegginge Doctoris Mar
tini Luthers yn dyth düdesche
vlitich vth gesettet/ mit sun
dergen vnderrichtingen/
alse men seen mach.

Jnn der Keyserliken Stadt Lübeck
by Ludowich Dietz gedrücket.

M·D·XXXIII·

Law and Gospel
(title page from Luther's Bible)

Abbreviations

Anno. in Rom.	Philip Melanchthon. *Annotationes . . . in Epistolam Pauli ad Romanos unam. Et ad Corinthios duas.* 2d ed. Strasbourg: J. Herwagen, 1523.
Anzeygung	Philip Melanchthon. *Annotationes, oder Anzeygung . . . über die Andern Epistel S. Pauli zuo den Corinthiern verteütscht.* Nuremberg: H. Hergot, 1524.
Ap	Apology of the Augsburg Confession
ARG	*Archiv für Reformationsgeschichte*
Auslegung	Philip Melanchthon. *Auslegung der Episteln S. Pauls eine an die Römer vnd zwo an die Corinther . . . gedeudscht.* Translated by J. Agricola. Wittenberg: J. Klug, 1527.
Bindseil	Heinrich Bindseil, ed. *Philippi Melanchthonis epistolae, iudicia, consilia, testimonia aliorumque ad eum epistolae quae in corpore reformatorum desiderantur.* Halle: Gustav Schwetschke, 1874.
BKS	*Die Bekenntnisschriften der evangelisch-lutherischen Kirche.* 10th ed. Göttingen: Vandenhoeck and Ruprecht, 1986.
Buchwald	Georg Buchwald. "Lutherana: Notizen aus Rechnungsbüchern des Thüringischen Staatsarchivs zu Weimar." *ARG* 25 (1928): 1–98.
Cohrs	Ferdinand Cohrs. *Die evangelischen Katechismusversuche vor Luthers Enchiridion.* 4 vols. Berlin: A. Hofmann, 1900–1902.
Colosser	John Agricola. *Die Epistel an die Colosser, S. Pauls, Zu Speier gepredigt auff dem reychstage.* Wittenberg: S. Reinhart, 1527.
CR	Philip Melanchthon. *Corpus Reformatorum. Philippi Melanthonis opera quae supersunt omnia.* Edited by Karl Bretschneider and Heinrich Bindseil. 28 vols. Halle: A. Schwetschke and Sons, 1834–60.
HAB	Herzog August Bibliothek
HKJL	*Handbuch zur Kinder- und Jugendliteratur.* Edited by Theodor Brüggemann with Hans-Heino Ewers. 2 vols. Stuttgart: J. B. Metzler, 1982, 1987.
Jonas-*BW*	Justus Jonas. *Der Briefwechsel des Justus Jonas.* Edited by Gustav Kawerau. 2 vols. Halle: O. Hendel, 1884.
LC	The Large Catechism of Martin Luther
Luke 1525	John Agricola. *In Evangelium Lucae Annotationes.* Augsburg: S. Ruff, April 1525.

Luke 1526	John Agricola. *In Evangelium Lucae Annotationes*. Haguenau: A. Farcallius, 1526.
Luke 1529	John Agricola. *In Lucae Evangelium, Adnotationes*. Haguenau: J. Setzer, May 1529.
MBW	Philip Melanchthon. *Melanchthons Briefwechsel: Kritische und kommentierte Gesamtausgabe*. Edited by Heinz Scheible. 10 vols. to date. Stuttgart–Bad Cannstatt: Frommann-Holzboog, 1977–.
MLStA	Martin Luther. *Martin Luther: Studienausgabe*. 5 vols. to date. Berlin: Evangelische Verlagsanstalt, 1979–.
MSA	Philip Melanchthon. *Melanchthons Werke in Auswahl*. [*Studienausgabe.*] Edited by Robert Stupperich. 7 vols. Gütersloh: Gerd Mohn, 1951–75.
Roth	"Stadtschreiber M. Stephan Roth in Zwickau in seiner literarisch-buchhändlerischen Bedeutung für die Reformationszeit." Edited by Georg Buchwald. *Archiv für Geschichte des deutschen Buchhandels* 16 (1893): 6–246.
SA	Smalcald Articles
SC	The Small Catechism of Martin Luther
Scholia 1528	Philip Melanchthon. *Scholia in Epistolam Pauli ad Colossenses, recognita ab autore*. Wittenberg: J. Klug, 1528.
Scholia 1529	Philip Melanchthon. *Die Epistel S. Pauli zun Colossern durch Philip Melanchton ym latein zum andern mal ausgelegt*. Translated by Justus Jonas. Wittenberg: Michael Lotter, 1529.
Scholia 1534	Philip Melanchthon. *Scholia in Epistolam Pauli ad Colossenses iterum ab authore recognita*. Wittenberg: J. Klug, 1534.
SM	Philip Melanchthon. *Supplementa Melanchthoniana*. 4 vols. Leipzig: Rudolph Haupt, 1910–26.
*T*1, *T*2	Philip Melanchthon. *Melanchthons Briefwechsel: Kritische und kommentierte Gesamtausgabe. Texte*. 2 vols. to date. Stuttgart–Bad Cannstatt: Frommann-Holzboog, 1991–.
VD 16	*Verzeichnis der im deutschen Sprachbereich erschienenen Drucke des XVI. Jahrhunderts*. 19 vols. to date. Stuttgart: Anton Hiersemann, 1983–.
WA	Martin Luther. *Luthers Werke. Kritische Gesamtausgabe*. [*Schriften.*] 65 vols. Weimar: H. Böhlau, 1883–1993.
WABi	Martin Luther. *Luthers Werke. Kritische Gesamtausgabe. Bibel*. 12 vols. Weimar: H. Böhlau, 1906–61.
WABr	Martin Luther. *Luthers Werke. Kritische Gesamtausgabe. Briefwechsel*. 18 vols. Weimar: H. Böhlau, 1930–85.
WATR	Martin Luther. *Luthers Werke. Kritische Gesamtausgabe. Tischreden*. 6 vols. Weimar: H. Böhlau, 1912–21.

Introduction

This is a study of how Philip Melanchthon, during the time his theology first came under attack in the 1520s by another Wittenberg-trained Reformer, John Agricola of Eisleben, came to define the relation between *poenitentia*[1] and law. In one way, however, this little-known dispute originated in one of the most famous documents of the Reformation, the first four statements of Martin Luther's Ninety-Five Theses:

1. By saying "Poenitentiam agite" [Matt. 4:17], our Lord Jesus Christ wanted the entire life of the faithful to be *poenitentia*.
2. For the word cannot be understood concerning sacramental *poenitentia* (that is, confession and satisfaction which is administered by the ministry of priests).
3. But neither did he intend interior *poenitentia* alone; indeed, such interior *poenitentia* is nothing unless it produces various mortifications of the flesh.
4. Therefore *poena* [punishment for sin] remains as long as hatred of self (that is, true inner *poenitentia*) remains: right up to the coming of the kingdom of heaven.[2]

Here Luther used the results of his study of the Bible—especially Erasmus's interpretation of the Greek term *metanoia* in his *Novum Instrumentum* (the Greek New Testament and annotations of 1516)—and his developing evangelical theology to challenge the practice of indulgence selling and its relation to the sacrament of penance. The ensuing dispute and the rupture that it precipitated in the Western church have enjoyed meticulous investigation by countless scholars,[3] but almost always from the standpoint of the break between Wittenberg and Rome.

---

1. Because the word *poenitentia* and its German equivalent, *Buße*, may be translated "repentance," "penitence," or "penance" (and the phrase "poenitentiam agite [tut Buße]" translated "repent," "be penitent," or "do penance"), we will leave it untranslated throughout this work. Its meaning is key to the dispute studied here.

2. *WA* 1:233.

3. See especially Scott Hendrix, *Luther and the Papacy: Stages in a Reformation Conflict* (Philadelphia: Fortress, 1981), and the literature cited there; and, for the Roman side, David V. N. Bagchi, *Luther's Earliest Opponents: Catholic Controversialists 1518–1525* (Minneapolis: Fortress, 1991).

Either such studies have assumed that Luther and his party were united in their understanding of *poenitentia* and used the term consistently, or they have focused exclusively on Luther's own development as he moved steadily further away from the medieval understanding of the sacrament of penance until breaking with it altogether in his 1520 tract "The Babylonian Captivity of the Church."[4]

Yet Luther's statements on the subject may well have appeared ambiguous not only to his opponents but also to his followers. For example, despite his clarity in 1517 concerning the linguistic problem, he continued to use the ambivalent term *poenitentia* or *Buße*. Moreover, although he counted two proper forms of confession (to God and to one's neighbor), he also allowed and later even encouraged private confession to the priest.

Even more important and potentially confusing were Luther's statements on the highest form of *Buße* (*poenitentia*). In his "Discussion of *Poenitentia*" from early 1518, Luther insisted that there was more truth in the German proverb "Nymmer thun ist die hochste pusz" than in all the teaching about contrition.[5] He translated this phrase "the best *poenitentia* is the new life" and cited Galatians 6:15 in his defense. After John Tetzel attacked Luther's "Discussion of Indulgence and Grace,"[6] Luther responded in 1518 with "A Freeing of the 'Discussion regarding Papal Indulgence and Grace' against the 'Refutation.'"[7] In the midst of a demonstration of Tetzel's mishandling of the Scripture, Luther attacked the connection between *Buße* and the sacrament of penance, pointing to the nonsacramental use of the term by the laity in the adage "Nymmer thun ist die hochste puße."[8] When this aphorism became part of the papal bull of excommunication, Luther defended himself in the 1520 tract "Against the Bull of the Antichrist."[9] Luther confidently called in as judges the laity, who by inventing this saying had taught more accurately about *Buße* than had the pope. True contrition (*Reu*) cannot be bought.[10]

---

4. *WA* 6:543–49. This early rejection can be contrasted to his later praise for private confession and absolution.

5. "Sermo de poenitentia" (*WA* 1:321), which was a Latin reworking of his "Sermon von Ablaß und Gnade." Literally, the proverb reads, "Not to do a thing again is the highest *Buß*."

6. Tetzel's piece was entitled "Vorlegung . . . wyder eynen vormessen Sermon von tzwentzig irrigen Artickeln Bebstlichen ablas und gnade belangende." As the title implied, Tetzel's attack was directed against Luther's "Sermon von Ablaß und Gnade."

7. "Eine Freiheit des Sermons päpstlichen Ablaß und Gnade belangend . . . wider die Widerlegung" (*WA* 1:383–93).

8. *WA* 1:386.

9. "Widder die Bullen des Endchrists" (*WA* 6:614–29).

10. In some notes from the same time, Luther connected this use of *Buße* with his interpretation of Matt. 4:17. See *WA* 4:612.

In his more thorough refutation of the papal bull of 1521, Luther again took up the German saying and argued that "where contrition proceeds properly through God's grace, there a person is transformed at the same time into another person, heart, spirit, mind, and life; that implies that I no longer do [what I did before], and it implies a new life."[11] Contrition and a new life make up the best *Buße*. The pope, on the contrary, had to say that the best *Buße* was the remorse of Judas, which occurred apart from God's grace.[12] In the process of recounting biblical proofs for his assertion, Luther pointed out that the "new creation" of Galatians 6:15 begins with great attacks upon and fright to the conscience (the knocking of God described in Rev. 3:20), to which God at the same time adds grace and strength. Luther continued the metaphor of God's greeting: "For [God's] greeting is terrible at the beginning, but comforting at the end."[13] Like lightning that strikes a tree, first splitting it in two and then turning it toward heaven, "thus the grace of God at the same time terrifies, hunts down, and drives a person, and turns such a one to God."[14]

A related problem in Luther's thinking involved what Luther did not describe here: the means God uses to bring this splitting and turning grace to bear on the person. Luther explained that in another tract from 1520, "On the Freedom of a Christian."[15] It is the Word of God and more precisely the gospel that brings grace to the soul and creates faith.[16] Works are excluded because of the double nature of the Scripture. On the one hand, as command or law it teaches us what good works are, but it gives no power to do them and thereby proves that we are sinners and makes us afraid and humble. On the other hand, as gospel the Scripture then comes and invites us to faith in Christ, so that God's promises deliver what the commands demand.[17]

---

11. *Grund und Ursach aller Artikel D. Martin Luthers, so durch römische Bulle unrechtlich verdammt sind* (WA 7:308–457, here 361): "denn wo die rew recht angeht, durch gottis gnadenn, da wirt zugleich der mensch gewandelt ynn eyn ander mensch, hertz, mut, synn und lebenn, und das heysz ich nymmer thun und eyn new leben."

12. Luther later expanded this reference to make it clear that he was referring to the argument of Thomas Aquinas and others that attrition (sorrow for sin out of fear of punishment) is the only remorse a person in a state of sin can bring forth and thus suffices for the sacrament of penance. Their reasoning here is that at the point of absolution the grace that makes one acceptable is infused into the penitent and transforms attrition into contrition (sorrow for sin out of love of God).

13. WA 7:365: "Denn grewlich ist sein grusz ym anfang, doch trostlich am ende."

14. WA 7:365: "alszo die gnad gottes zu gleich den menschen erschreckt, iagt unnd treybt unnd zu sich keret."

15. "Von der Freiheit eines Christenmenschen" (WA 7:20–38).

16. WA 7:22.

17. WA 7:23–24. Note that Luther, unlike Paul Althaus, does not create a false distinction between *Gebot* and *Gesetz*. They are synonyms for him.

This distinction between law and gospel and its connection to true *poenitentia*—however straightforward they may seem to Luther scholars or Lutheran theologians today[18]—were not nearly as clear to Luther's students and readers. Questions over the nature of *poenitentia* and its relation to the law and to the sacrament of penance formed the basis of the first public controversy among Luther's students and profoundly shaped the nature of later Lutheranism by making the distinction between law and gospel one of its distinguishing characteristics. It is this controversy that the present study will investigate.

The Setting

In the mid-1520s, at the same time Melanchthon and Luther were doing battle with Erasmus's theology,[19] another opponent arose from what must have been for Melanchthon a much more unexpected corner. In 1527, for the first time in his career at the University of Wittenberg but certainly not the last, Melanchthon came under attack from someone within the evangelical camp itself. John Agricola of Eisleben had been a student of Luther since 1516, at which time he heard Luther deliver his lectures on Romans. When Melanchthon arrived in 1518, the two students became fast friends. In mid-1525, as part of Wittenberg's plans for the reform of Germany's educational system, Agricola moved with his family to Eisleben, his hometown, where he became rector of the Latin school.[20] In the same year, along with Justus Jonas, he was designated by Luther to write Wittenberg's first evangelical catechism.

The brief public dispute between Agricola and Melanchthon began with a letter from Agricola to Luther in August 1527 and concluded with a formal reconciliation at the end of November of the same year when Luther arranged a truce during a meeting at the Castle Torgau. At first glance, when compared to the battle with Erasmus, this confrontation, ostensibly over the definition of *poenitentia* in Melanchthon's Latin version of the Visitation Articles of 1527, may seem rather unimportant. Yet both in terms of its impact on Melanchthon's theology and in terms of its effect on the developing catechesis and doctrine of

18. Already the Lutheran confessional documents, all of which came into being after 1528, reflect little ambiguity on these points. Several do, however, bear the imprint of the dispute on which this study focuses.

19. See Timothy J. Wengert, *Human Freedom, Christian Righteousness: Philip Melanchthon's Exegetical Dispute with Erasmus of Rotterdam* (New York: Oxford University Press, 1997).

20. In May 1525 Luther and Melanchthon had accompanied Agricola to Eisleben to work out the details of his call. At nearly the same time Caspar Cruciger, Sr., moved to Magdeburg and Joachim Camerarius to Nuremberg as teachers in schools in those cities.

the emerging Lutheran church, the controversy between Agricola and Melanchthon concentrated Wittenberg's attention on the distinction between law and gospel by eliminating what would later be designated antinomian options for construing evangelical theology.

Secondary Literature

In this century several important studies have devoted space to an examination of the dispute regarding law and gospel. By far the most helpful work is still that of Gustav Kawerau, who in the course of his description of Agricola's theology devotes a chapter to what he calls "Das Vorspiel des antinomistischen Streites."[21] From that beginning two approaches to this issue have developed during the intervening century. On the one hand, some scholars have focused almost exclusively on the relation between Agricola and Luther in this earlier period as a way of explaining the so-called first antinomian controversy of the late 1530s. Joachim Rogge contributed to the discussion by comparing Agricola's early work to Luther's theology and investigating the first movements away from Luther's thought.[22] In his still useful reconstruction of the controversy itself, the focus is clearly upon Luther and Agricola. Nearly a quarter of a century later, Ernst Koch contributed a careful analysis of the earliest contacts between Luther and Agricola, especially the role of Luther's lectures on Romans.[23] At nearly the same time Steffen Kjeldgaard-Pedersen published his doctoral dissertation, also focusing on the theology of the young Agricola and containing a thoroughgoing critique of the approaches of Rogge and others.[24]

On the other hand, some scholars have attempted to explain the controversy regarding law and gospel by describing the development of various intellectual movements and theological positions in Wittenberg

21. Gustav Kawerau, *Johann Agricola von Eisleben: Ein Beitrag zur Reformationsgeschichte* (Berlin: Wilhelm Hertz, 1881), 129–53.

22. Joachim Rogge, *Johann Agricolas Lutherverständnis: Unter besonderer Berücksichtigung des Antinomismus* (Berlin: Evangelische Verlagsanstalt, 1960), especially B.II: "Die ersten offenen Auseinandersetzungen in der Frage des Nomismus und Antinomismus," 98–118.

23. Ernst Koch, "Johann Agricola neben Luther: Schülerschaft und theologische Eigenart," in *Lutheriana: Zum 500. Geburtstag Martin Luthers von den Mitarbeitern der Weimarische Ausgabe*, ed. Gerhard Hammer and Karl-Heinz zur Mühlen (Cologne and Vienna: Böhlau, 1984), 131–50. Koch also indicates the important role that Melanchthon's *Loci* and his "Epitome renouatae ecclesiasticae doctrinae" of 1524 played in the construction of Agricola's theological position (pp. 140–45).

24. Steffen Kjeldgaard-Pedersen, *Gesetz, Evangelium und Buße: Theologiegeschichtliche Studien zum Verhältnis zwischen dem jungen Johann Agricola (Eisleben) und Martin Luther* (Leiden: E. J. Brill, 1983), esp. pp. 173–212. Among the other approaches critiqued are those of Gustav Hammann and Susi Hausammann.

during this time. In an unpublished dissertation, Gustav Hammann characterizes the two approaches as nomianism and antinomianism.[25] A good portion of his work researches the differences between Melanchthon and Agricola on the basis of their various writings. Despite his useful attempt to fix the chronology of the controversy, Hammann's work is fundamentally flawed by his psychologization of the relationship between Luther and Melanchthon and by his dependence upon Wilhelm Neuser, who argued that Melanchthon derived his theology from a pre-Wittenberg humanism.[26] Further, Hammann has no useful explanation for Luther's behavior at the Torgau conference in November 1527, where Luther cannot seem to appreciate the differences between the positions of his two "friends." Moreover, Hammann reduces Melanchthon's theology to a kind of moralistic nomism.

Another work that examines the divergences between Agricola and Melanchthon is the analysis of *poenitentia* by Susi Hausammann.[27] She touches briefly on the controversy over the Visitation Articles, indicates the importance of Agricola's translation of Melanchthon's early commentaries on Paul, and generally portrays the two figures as offering opposing responses to Luther's original teaching on the doctrine of *poenitentia*.

In one sense all of the works mentioned have contributed to the understanding of the flap over the Visitation Articles of 1527 and form an important background to the material investigated here. However, they do not approach the subject matter in the ways employed in the present study.

First, with the possible exception of Kawerau, all are far more concerned about larger theological issues, such as nomianism versus antinomianism, and tend to fit the events of the period in question within the framework of that theological construct. This work, on the contrary, is self-consciously a history of the dispute.

Second, scholars have tended to place Luther and his theology in such a special position that his work becomes a kind of *regula fidei* by which the disputants in this controversy may be measured. It is true that without Luther's comments, as early as the Ninety-Five Theses, the dispute is unthinkable. However, this work concentrates on the princi-

---

25. Gustav Hammann, "Nomismus und Antinomismus innerhalb der wittenberger Theologie von 1524–1530," Ph.D. diss., Friedrich Wilhelms Universität, 1952.

26. See Wilhelm H. Neuser, *Der Ansatz der Theologie Philipp Melanchthons* (Neukirchen-Vluyn: Verlag des Erziehungsvereins, 1957). Hammann used the earlier dissertation on which the book was based.

27. Susi Hausammann, *Buße als Umkehr und Erneuerung von Mensch und Gesellschaft* (Zurich: Theologischer Verlag, 1974), 135–225. See the strong critique by Kjeldgaard-Pedersen throughout his book.

ples and investigates the struggle especially from Philip Melanchthon's perspective.

Finally, previous studies completely miss the rich possibilities that works edited after the controversy offer for insight into the positions of the two theologians and into their method of argumentation.[28] Neither have all the earlier sources for understanding this dispute been fully exploited. Kjeldgaard-Pedersen, who recognized some omissions, calls for a comparison of Agricola's and Melanchthon's commentaries on Colossians.[29]

Our interests in this controversy provide a different approach from what has come before. First, we are as much interested in the history of the controversy as in the theological types it may represent. Second, Luther will come into discussion only as events warrant. Granted, his early comments on the matter influenced all the participants, but although he was one of the judges in this case, he did not view the matter on the basis of something he had written ten years earlier. Third, the focus of this study will be Philip Melanchthon himself, because the controversy was engendered by his writings, focused on his theology not Agricola's, and came to influence later Lutheranism in that his reactions to this problem were enshrined in his later work. In this regard, Melanchthon's three editions of his commentary on Colossians, the *Scholia in Epistolam Pauli ad Colossenses*, published in 1527, 1528, and 1534, will provide an excellent window into developments within his theology and within the controversy itself.

Given the complexities of the events, however, no single document from the period contains the entire scope of this controversy. Therefore, to gain a proper perspective on what was written in any particular source, a wide range of evidence will be examined. By looking at John Agricola's exegetical work before 1527, chapter 1 uncovers how he expressed his position on *poenitentia* and the law before the public controversy. Chapter 2 examines the glut of evangelical catechisms from 1525 until 1527 and their widely divergent definitions and uses of the terms *poenitentia* and *law*. Chapter 3 investigates Melanchthon's exegetical battle with Agricola over Colossians and Melanchthon's statements in the Latin version of the Visitation Articles (1527) that directly fueled the controversy. The actual controversy takes center stage in

---

28. Particularly the commentary on Luke by Agricola and the commentary on Colossians by Melanchthon.

29. Kjeldgaard-Pedersen, *Gesetz, Evangelium und Buße*, 156 n. 1. Rogge, *Johann Agricolas Lutherverständnis*, 98, also mentions the necessity of a more thorough comparison of the two disputants, by which he means a theological comparison. We intend to investigate the historical relationship between the two and their exegetical and catechetical work.

chapter 4. While chapter 5 investigates in broad terms the effects of this controversy on the relation between these two theologians and their opinions of each other, chapter 6 looks more closely at a single important change in Melanchthon's commentary on Colossians (1534) and his development of the concept of a third use of the law.

1

Calm before the Storm: Agricola's Biblical Exegesis from 1525 to 1527

In the "Praefatio" to the first edition of the *Scholia* on Colossians (1527) Melanchthon wrote, "Nowadays many teach faith and the remission of sins, but they do not teach *poenitentia*. But without *poenitentia* faith is nothing but a foolish dream."[1] That the dedicatory epistle was written by the time the printer John Setzer left Wittenberg for Haguenau on 20 May 1527 and that he doubtless carried a manuscript of the *Scholia* with him[2] means that at least three months before Agricola complained to Luther about the understanding of *poenitentia* in the Visitation Articles, Melanchthon already knew of "many" dreamers who taught faith and remission of sins but not *poenitentia*. From Melanchthon's perspective, chief among them was John Agricola.

The Early Relationship between Melanchthon and Agricola

Joachim Rogge insists that in the time prior to the August 1527 dispute, the friendship between Melanchthon and Agricola had fallen on hard times, in large part because Melanchthon received the professorship at Wittenberg for which Agricola had longed.[3] This kind of speculation is unnecessary and unsupported by their correspondence. Their letters prior to the dispute bore all the characteristics of conversations between old school chums. The earliest, from 1520, recounted Melanchthon's unsuccessful attempt to get his new wife to let Agricola come and

---

1. *MSA* 4:212.29–31: "Nunc multi fidem et remissionem peccatorum docent, poenitentiam non docent. At nihil est fides sine poenitentia nisi inane somnium."
2. See *MBW* 547 (*MSA* 4:210f.) and *MBW* 550 (*CR* 1:867f.).
3. Joachim Rogge, *Johann Agricolas Lutherverständnis: Unter besonderer Berücksichtigung des Antinomismus* (Berlin: Evangelische Verlagsanstalt, 1960), 98–101. See also Gustav Kawerau, *Johann Agricola von Eisleben: Ein Beitrag zur Reformationsgeschichte* (Berlin: Wilhelm Hertz, 1881), 129ff.

live with them.[4] Beneath the exaggerated humanist prose of later letters lurked a true friendship.[5] What Rogge mistakes for desperation in Melanchthon's overblown expressions of affection is much more likely regret at separation couched in the typical excesses of humanist prose.

And separated they were. In the summer of 1525, Agricola moved to Eisleben to become the rector of the new Latin school there.[6] This move must be seen as a part of Wittenberg's attempt to establish *bonae literae* and the Reformation at the same time in Saxony's schools. Luther's appeal to the city councils, Melanchthon's declamations, and the establishment of a similar school in Nuremberg at nearly the same time were all parts of this attempt at reform. Luther and Melanchthon had accompanied Agricola to Eisleben in May 1525 in part to establish him in that position.[7] In a letter dated 20 December 1525, Melanchthon reported to Agricola his having turned down a newly created teaching post in theology at Wittenberg on the grounds of ill health. He also expressed the wish that Agricola get the post.[8] While in the next letter from Wittenberg to Eisleben, written at the beginning of January 1526, Melanchthon expressed regret at not having heard from Agricola, by January 15 not only had Agricola written, but, in answer to Melanchthon's question, had expressed a preference to stay in Eisleben for the time being.[9]

There was clearly a series of missed connections between the two in subsequent months, all coming after Melanchthon received a special professorship and hefty pay raise to teach in the faculties of both theology and arts.[10] In June Melanchthon did not stop in Eisleben on his way back from Nuremberg.[11] In October Melanchthon, who had come to Eisleben only to find that Agricola was away, could not stay until his return.[12] However, near Christmas of the same year

---

4. *MBW* 113 (*T*1:238), dated after November 1520. Melanchthon's wife resisted quite vehemently.

5. For example, *MBW* 419 (*T*2:346–48), dated 7 September 1525, in which Melanchthon insisted in a poem that, better than by wine or money, his cold could best be cured by friends, i.e., by Agricola now in Eisleben.

6. *MBW* 416 (*T*2:341–43), dated 24 August 1525.

7. See, for example, Melanchthon's letter to Joachim Camerarius from Bitterfeld, dated 16 April 1525, *MBW* 391 (*T*2:288–89).

8. *MBW* 432 (*T*2:364–65).

9. *MBW* 440 (*T*2:391–92) and *MBW* 443 (*T*2:394–96), respectively.

10. *MBW* 446 (*T*2:400–401), the Elector John of Saxony to Melanchthon, dated 13 February 1526.

11. *MBW* 468 (*T*2:429), dated around 20 June 1526.

12. *MBW* 507 (*T*2:502–3), dated 30/31 October 1526. The letter that follows, *MBW* 512 (*T*2:509), dated approximately 25 November 1526, included greetings to Alexander and Bartholomew Drachstedt and to William Rink, with whom Melanchthon must have met during his visit.

Melanchthon mentioned receiving a present of cloth.[13] Another missed connection occurred around 12 April 1527 with Melanchthon in Mansfeld and Agricola unable to come from Eisleben. The following letters indicated Melanchthon's concern that decisions regarding the Latin school not be made in Agricola's absence.[14] As late as 30 August 1527 Melanchthon wrote thanking Agricola for the comfort he extended to Justus Jonas upon the death of his son.[15] Difficulties? Yes. Strains? Perhaps. But the correspondence does not permit us to conclude that there was jealousy or breaks in friendship that caused Melanchthon to exaggerate his greetings.[16] The attack of Agricola had its origins somewhere else: in the exegetical and catechetical writings of the two men.

Agricola's Exegetical Work on the New Testament

Steffen Kjeldgaard-Pedersen describes well Agricola's early exegetical work and its relation to Luther's theology.[17] For our purposes we will use three of the many sources from the time prior to the controversy to sketch the theological background out of which it grew: Agricola's commentary on Luke, his sermons on Colossians, and his translation of Melanchthon's commentaries on Romans and 1–2 Corinthians.

In Evangelium Lucae Annotationes

In his commentary on Luke, Agricola produced a work that, in terms of both style and genre, reached the highest level of technical sophistication among all his writings. The bulk of his publications both before and after arose out of German sermons, or from his work at the Latin school in Eisleben, or as a result of controversy. Only the annotations on Luke of 1525, perhaps intended as a replacement for the commentary on the same Gospel produced the previous year by François Lambert, took on the commentary form found in the exeget-

---

13. *MBW* 516 (*T*1:514–15), dated 26 December 1526, and *MBW* 521 (*CR* 1:853f.), dated 1 January 1527. The greetings to Agricola's wife, Else, were a standard feature of all the letters during this period.

14. *MBW* 534 (*CR* 1:825), dated 12(?) April 1527. The following letters include *MBW* 535 (*CR* 1:825–26), 541 (*CR* 1:866–67), and 543 (Bindseil, 508).

15. *MBW* 581 (Bindseil, 508).

16. In fact, the exchange of friendly letters resumed within a year after the controversy (see p. 169). Only much later, during the bitter dispute over the Augsburg Interim, did their correspondence finally come to an end.

17. Steffen Kjeldgaard-Pedersen, *Gesetz, Evangelium und Buße: Theologiegeschichtliche Studien zum Verhältnis zwischen dem jungen Johann Agricola (Eisleben) und Martin Luther* (Leiden: E. J. Brill, 1983), 37–212.

ical work of other Wittenbergers at the time.[18] Its connections to lectures Agricola may have given in Wittenberg cannot be ascertained from the preface to George Spalatin, who had clearly encouraged Agricola's work.[19] The annotations afford us insight into two crucial parts of Agricola's theology: the definition of law and the function of *poenitentia*.

Agricola's commentary contains a lengthy preface entitled "What Is Required from the Sacred History? (*Quid ex sacra historia requirendum sit?*)," which was translated into German and published separately under the title "A Short and Lovely Report on How One Should Read the Holy Scripture, and to What One Should Pay Attention in the Reading, What One Should Search for and Inquire after."[20] The commentary itself and its preface were revised by the author and published in Haguenau the following year.

The changes between the first and second editions, taken into consideration by neither Gustav Hammann nor Kjeldgaard-Pedersen, show just how much Agricola was concerned at this time with the law and its claim on human affairs. Unlike other Wittenberg commentaries of the same time, Agricola did not begin with the distinction between law and gospel, but with a discussion of the *cognitio* crucial for every Christian. The Scripture everywhere adumbrates two natures: that we are born children of Adam and hence of wrath, and that we are brought forth as children of Abraham by the promise.[21] Thus, Agricola's beginning point was not law but sin and the nature of the human being. From there he proceeded to describe the effects of original sin.[22]

Only after describing sin did Agricola introduce the category of law. Here the 1526 version added the title "For What Purpose the Law Was Given, and What Are the Powers of the Law."[23] Because original sin re-

18. For details of Wittenberg's work on New Testament commentary, see Timothy J. Wengert, *Philip Melanchthon's "Annotationes in Johannem" in Relation to Its Predecessors and Contemporaries* (Geneva: Librairie Droz, 1987), 31–42.

19. For the exact description of Agricola's exegetical works, see appendix 1. Here we are using the annotations published in April 1525 (*Luke* 1525, [A1]v°): "Credebas tunc plane ex re orbis Christiani fore, ut meas in Lucam annotationes aederem." The work was reprinted almost immediately (July 1525) in Nuremberg by John Petreius.

20. "Wie man die Heilig geschrifft lesen/ vnd wess man in der lesung der Euangelischen histori acht haben/ Was man darinn ersuchen vnd forschen soll/ Ain kurtze vnd Schöne Bericht."

21. *Luke* 1525, 1v°: "Scriptura in universum duas naturas adumbrat. Alteram, qua ex Adam nascimur quotquot posteritas Adae censemur. Et qua ex semine Abrahae promisso gignimur, alteram."

22. *Luke* 1525, 1v°–2r°: At this point the 1526 edition adds the title "PECCATVM ORIGINALE unde uires acceperit."

23. *Luke* 1526, 4v°: "AD QVID LEX DATA SIT, & quae sint legis vires."

sults in blindness, the law of Moses was given to uncover (*retegere*) this mortal wound to our eyes. As a result of encounter with the law, the human is condemned to hell, "unless one would change one's heart."[24] In both versions an explanation of the Ten Commandments followed. However, what in 1525 had been a diffuse and unmarked section of the introduction was in the 1526 version rewritten, expanded, transposed, and given titles to cover each commandment in order.[25] Agricola presented the law exclusively as unfulfillable demand. Unless human beings fulfill the law, they stand condemned.

In 1526 Agricola emphasized the law's demands further by explaining each commandment more fully. God, who was referred to only indirectly in the material covering the first commandment in 1525, became in the 1526 edition the supreme *Legislator*. God gave the law so that we might be aware that he, who is touched by our cares and from whom we can expect whatever we need, holds us in his hands. Proper use of God's name, which in 1525 was linked to prayer and praise, in 1526 was tied directly to salvation. In 1525 Agricola took the command to honor the Sabbath as a prohibition of human traditions; in 1526 he strengthened his explanation by giving the reason for the prohibition: "so that [people] may remember that not they but God in them lives and works for his good will."[26]

Agricola also expanded his explanation of the second table of the law, stressing obedience in his explanation of the fourth commandment and adding the sixth commandment, which for him implied not only proper behavior but also "conversatio honesta."[27] To comments on the eighth commandment, which in 1525 included speaking honestly before one's superiors and defending widows, Agricola added consoling the sick and generally not hoping for gain.[28]

The summary of the commandments, similar in both editions, gave heightened stress to their demands by excluding all forms of provocation in the Christian's life. Agricola concluded, "For the law always goes forth, not ceasing to drive us to desperation, unless we were to do

24. *Luke* 1525, 2r°f.: ". . . nisi cor mutauerit homo."

25. In 1525 Agricola composed a single sentence of thirty-four lines beginning with a description of the blindness of original sin and ending with the fifth commandment. The sixth commandment was completely ignored, and references to several commandments came out of order (second, fifth, fourth, third, fifth).

26. *Luke* 1526, 5r°: "ut recordetur, non se, sed Deum in se uiuere & operari pro bona uoluntate sua."

27. The fifth, ninth, and tenth commandments remain basically the same with the addition of some material linked originally with the first commandment.

28. *Luke* 1526, 6r°. There are similarities throughout to Luther's 1520 treatise on good works.

freely what it commands."[29] To prove his point, in a section entitled in 1526 "The Struggle between the Law and the Conscience Not Yet Imbued with Christ's Spirit" Agricola described the law's effect on human beings, how it puts dread in the conscience until people become like Proteus, fighting the law's yoke and blaming God for their problems. As examples of the terrors of the law, Agricola took the description of the giving of the law in Exodus 20 as well as several references from classical literature. The human plight under the law is so horrible that only God can remedy this evil pestilence of nature "by some new kind of cure."[30]

Agricola summarized his argument: "The source of sin is produced from Adam; that inborn power certainly runs through all the children of Adam. The law has been added, *not so much to restrain or remove that congenital blemish*, as to increase and reveal it, and so that sin may receive power (as the apostle says, the conscience is incited by the power of the law)."[31] Here Agricola played down any positive role for what Melanchthon later called the first use of the law (a civil force for the restraint of sin). But even the second use of the law was thought of not so much as driving to Christ or mortifying as making the human situation even worse; hence the title for this section stressed the fight between law and conscience for those *not yet* imbued with Christ's Spirit.

Only in a final sentence of the summary did Agricola give any positive sense to the law: "In this is the whole of Moses and the prophets, that people acknowledge their sin and deplore it, despair of themselves, and finally expect the help of that great prophet [Deut. 18]."[32] But even this last sentence and the explanation that followed make clear that for Agricola the "expectation of the great prophet" did not arise so much from despair brought on by the commands of God as from the Old Testament promises themselves. At the same time, Agricola defined the gospel in such a way as to attribute all transformation to it, even the

29. *Luke* 1525, 2v°: "Eo usque enim lex progreditur [1526: usque progreditur lex], non cessans nos solicitare ad desperationem, nisi hoc quod iusserit liberaliter fecerimus." Except for the addition of further titles, the two versions were almost identical in the rest of the preface.

30. *Luke* 1525, 5r°.

31. *Luke* 1525, 6r° (emphasis added): "Peccati fons ex Adam producitur, decucurrit nimirum genialis illa uis in omnes filios Adae. Lex addita est non tam ut coerceret labem congenitam aut tolleret, quam ut augeret & reuelaret, atque ut peccatum uires acciperet (sicut Apostolus ait) ui legis irritata conscientia."

32. *Luke* 1525, 6r°: "In hoc totus est Moses, omnes prophetae, ut peccatum suum agnoscat & deploret homo, de se desperet, tandemque expectet prophetae illius magni auxilium."

28

transformation of the law into something desirable.[33] Here Agricola expressed the notion introduced earlier, of doing the law freely, in terms of deepest human desires. Agricola's understanding of the law was marked by the tension between something which does no good and something which is the highest good.

The negative definition of Moses and the law continued within the commentary itself. The transfiguration provided Agricola an opportunity to discuss the role of the law again. God wanted to have a peculiar people in whom he could show his power. According to Galatians 3:24, he made Moses the "governor and guide (*rector et paedagogus*)" for these people "so that, pressed and terrified by the law, they might acknowledge their error and try to avert punishment by entreaty."[34] The prophets reproached people for their sins and predicted the coming of Christ. With Christ's coming the need for a special people or for Moses and the prophets ceases, as the phrase in Luke 9:36 ("relicto Iesu solo") proves.

Whereas the introduction to Luke's Gospel gave a glimpse into Agricola's developing understanding of the law, the commentary itself provided several places where he connected this teaching to *poenitentia.* Luke 3, which describes the appearance of John the Baptist in the desert, provided Agricola with the perfect text to discuss *poenitentia* and the gospel. In a section labeled "On the Reason for *Poenitentia*," he insisted that John bears a type of the gospel and is a "witness (*auspex*) of the New Testament." This gospel has two offices: to condemn whatever is exalted and stands against true worship of and faith in God, and to announce the remission of sin in Christ.[35] Just as Agricola earlier noted that the law had little positive role to play, here the gospel itself takes over all salvific functions by both condemning and making alive. Similarly, in comments on Luke 16:16 Agricola insisted that, unlike John, "the law shows and increases sin; it says nothing about help."[36] The law as Agricola defined it had no role to play in the life of the believer.

---

33. *Luke* 1525, 10r°: "Vides itaque fructum esse Euangelij summam, ut transformemur in nouitatem quaedam uitae, per gratiam illius qui uocauit nos Iesus Christus, sitque nobis lex, quam antea summe detestabamur, desiderabilis super aurum & obrysum [refined], dulcior melle & fauo, id est, nuper omnes uoluptates."

34. *Luke* 1525, 89v°: "ut lege pressi & territi, errorem agnoscerent, & poenam deprecarentur."

35. *Luke* 1525, 20r°: "Deinde Euangelij, cuius typum gerit Ioannes, noui testamenti auspex, duo esse officia, alterum, damnare quidquid est excelsum, sublime sanctum, breviter denotiri amone altitudine erigentem, & iactantem se, contra uerum cultum dei, id est, contra doctrinam fidei. . . . Alterum nunciare remissionem peccatorum per Christum."

36. *Luke* 1525, 122v°: "Lex peccatum ostendit & auget, auxilium tacet."

In the discussion of Luke 3, Agricola defined John's call for *poenitentia* by associating it with what Christ calls the cross and Paul the death of the old creature, giving as an example for that mortification Ephesians 4:28 ("Let the one who stole steal no more"). This meant, of course, that *poenitentia* is a mark of the new creature, not of the old. Thus Agricola wrote: "Consequently, if *poenitentia* is an appellation for the new creature, which is being renewed daily, then death, whose symbol is baptism, completes it."[37] This makes sense of Agricola's reference to Ephesians 4:28: the new creature no longer sins, in this case steals, because baptism completes the process of mortification.

Agricola then cemented this identification of *poenitentia* with the new creature: "Without a doubt you may understand that 'to do *poenitentia*,' 'to be justified,' 'to have a change of heart,' is solely a work of God, not of human powers, *and that as many as divide the reckoning of poenitentia most ineptly into attrition, confession, and satisfaction err to the highest heaven.*"[38] Here Agricola showed that because *poenitentia* and justification are God's work they cannot be divided into human categories that imply human works. This also means that for Agricola the law had nothing to do with the gospel. The medieval division of *poenitentia* simply masked a form of works-righteousness. Clearly Agricola's concern was to protect the gracious action of God.

Agricola's other important discussion of *poenitentia* came in comments on the Zacchaeus story. Here again Agricola defined *poenitentia* in terms that exclude any human activity:

> In Zacchaeus is adumbrated some truly living form of *poenitentia*, of which Paul, too, reminds us in the last chapter of Ephesians [Eph. 4:28], "Let the one who stole no longer steal," which is what we say in German, "The highest *Buße* is never to do it again." Furthermore, this freedom of the soul, this progress into another life, does not begin with the recording of sins, with simulated thought of the human heart, but with the blessing of God, which the heart senses that God has imparted to it, when he draws and attractively calls to himself and invites.[39]

---

37. *Luke* 1525, 23rᵒ: "Proinde si est nouae creaturae uocabulum poenitentia, quae in die in diem innouatur, donec mors eam consummauerit, cuius symbolum baptismus." Both "quae" and "eam" could refer either to the new creature or to "poenitentia."

38. *Luke* 1525, 23vᵒ (emphasis added): "Procul dubio intelliges poenitere, iustificari, mutare cor, solius dei opus esse, non uirium humanarum, errareque toto caelo, quotquot poenitentiae rationem, in attritionem, confessionem & satisfactionem ineptissime partiti sunt." The use of the term *attrition* (sorrow for sin out of fear of punishment) is no accident.

39. *Luke* 1525, 144vᵒ: "In Zachaeo adumbrata est uiua quaedam uere poenitentiae forma, cuius & Paulus meminit ult. cap. Ephe. Qui furabatur iam non furetur, id quod Germanice dicimus, Nimmer thun ist die hochste buß. Porro haec libertas animi, hic progressus in aliam uitam, non incipit a recordatione peccatorum, a simulata cordis humani

Here the outlines of Agricola's definition of *poenitentia* become clear. True *poenitentia* involves a new life, not counting sins. Ephesians 4:28, linked to the German saying, provides the correct way of understanding the true penitent's behavior. It arises not out of the law or the thoughts of the human heart—here Agricola was thinking of contrition and confession—but from the gospel and benefits of God.

Agricola identified gospel with a word that kills and causes *poenitentia*. Thus, in a section added to the annotations in 1526 he wrote that when Christ speaks of the grain of wheat dying (John 12:24), he signifies that new life comes "after the flesh has been put to death by the word of the gospel, that is, the word of the cross."[40] This does not mean, however, that judgment itself, as in Luke 3:17, comes from the gospel. What pertains to the gospel is the revelation of judgment, not judgment itself. For Agricola the gospel contained within itself the power to put to death in order to make alive. Any judgment that remains judgment belongs outside the gospel in the law.

A similar contrast between gospel and law is to be found in Agricola's introduction to the passion story, where he discussed unleavened bread. A new law must come to drive out the old leaven, that is, to mortify us so that our joy is not simulated but from the heart. To this work of the gospel Agricola contrasted the old law: "The whole law makes liars and hypocrites; on the contrary, the gospel makes sincere, honest, and truthful people."[41]

This narrow meaning of the law and its practical exclusion from the life of the Christian had direct consequences for Agricola's understanding of Christian freedom. Thus he wrote (in German) that a person who thinks that only virtuous people, and not the impure, should be in the church has abandoned the gospel. "For God uses such a stratagem (that one is an angel today and a devil tomorrow) . . . so that he can make the world look foolish."[42] This rejection of a moralistic Christianity stemmed from Agricola's rejection of a positive use for the law and also from his emphasis on a particular theology of the cross. Unlike

---

cogitatione, sed a beneficio Dei, quod sentit cor sibi impartiri Deum, cum allicit & blanditer ad se uocat atque inuitat." Agricola's dependence on Luther's language and examples is clear. This construal of *poenitentia* and its removal from the work of the law became the crux of the debate with Melanchthon.

40. *Luke* 1526, 59v°: "postquam mortificata fuerit caro uerbo Euangelij, quod est uerbum crucis."

41. *Luke* 1525, 161r°: "Lex tota, menaces facit & hypocritas, Euangelium rursus synceros facit, candidos et ueraces."

42. *Luke* 1526, 69v°: "Dan Got braucht darumb solchs kampffstuck das eyner heut eyn engel/ morgen eyn teufel sey. . . das er die welt zu narren mache."

Melanchthon, who discussed the cross primarily in the context of sanctification of the believer, Agricola delighted in portraying it as the basis of Christian freedom.

Die Epistel an die Colosser . . . gepredigt

Melanchthon's prefatory letter to Alexander Drachstedt for the *Scholia* of 1527 began, "Since very well written commentaries on the Epistle to Colossians exist, there was good reason why we would not publish these our *Scholia*."[43] At that time the only evangelical commentary to which he could have been referring was the sermons on Colossians by Agricola.[44] During August 1526, while serving as a preacher for Elector John of Saxony at the Diet of Speyer, Agricola had delivered an entire series of sermons on Colossians.[45] If Melanchthon's preface was indeed referring to these sermons, then they probably appeared in print within the first four months of 1527. Kjeldgaard-Pedersen offers a thorough look at all aspects of this commentary.[46] We are interested in what it may add to our understanding of Agricola's developing theology of good works and *poenitentia*.[47]

If the Gospel of Luke gave Agricola opportunity to discuss the law, Colossians permitted him to explore how works relate to the life of the believer. An eighteen-page discussion of Colossians 1:3–9 closed with a four-page examination entitled "What Purpose Do Good Works Serve?"[48] The text of Colossians seemed to support the notion of merit. To oppose this interpretation Agricola stressed on several occasions that works of love done for one's neighbor are "lauter notwerck (pure works of necessity)."[49] They must occur, but they earn nothing.

---

43. *MSA* 4:210.3–5.

44. Johann Bugenhagen's brief annotations on the Pauline corpus and Erasmus's paraphrase need not be considered.

45. A reference in *Colosser*, C.vii.r°, to Agricola's sermon on Luke 18:9–14 indicates that a good portion of the sermons on Colossians must have been given after 12 August 1526. Since they close with the "Valete vnd letzter abschied von Speier" (R.ii.r°–R.vii.r°), the series of sermons on Colossians must have ended before his return to Eisleben in mid-September. For a list of the printings, see appendix 1.

46. Kjeldgaard-Pedersen, *Gesetz, Evangelium und Buße*, 173–212.

47. Outside of our particular interest, there do seem to be some indications that Agricola was dependent to some extent upon Bugenhagen's brief annotations on Paul's letters (Ephesians through Hebrews), published in 1524. For example, in discussing Col. 1:4 both exegetes define faith and love in similar ways and refer to the parable of the vineyard. A portion of Agricola's commentary, containing his polemic against the mass, was published with rather vulgar annotations in 1547 as part of an attack on Agricola's role in introducing the Augsburg Interim.

48. *Colosser*, C.i.v°: "Wozu dienen denn gute werck?"

49. *Colosser*, C.i.v°: "Vnd hie sihestu/ das der dienst vnd die werck die dem nehsten geschehen/ lauter notwerck sind die geschehen mussen/ vnd doch nichts verdienen."

After citing the text of Romans 2:6 as supposed proof for the meritorious nature of good works, Agricola responded, "You have now just heard that all works we do are *not werck*."[50] This assertion did not quite satisfy Agricola, so he added that good works also serve to instruct each person how close to or far from God one is. Loving someone who hates in return means that "you then have a living witness . . . that God dwells in and with you." Contrariwise, lacking such love, "then you are dismayed in yourself and fear before God. Cry out to him . . . for you have not yet discovered in your heart how great the treasure and riches of grace are."[51] Here Agricola put an interesting twist on the practical syllogism and undermined the very certainty of salvation so important for the Reformers in Wittenberg.[52] Moreover, because these works lie outside the individual's control, that is, because they occur by necessity, there is no direct way to receive comfort. The one who lacks these works is separated from God; the only recourse is to be frightened and beseech God for help.

In later sermons Agricola came back to the theme of works, but now from the perspective of Colossians 2:8ff. and the division between human philosophy and Christian truth. Again he sought to avoid completely any notion of merit. In comments on Colossians 2:16f. he used what might best be described as Platonic imagery to make his point. Since God is spirit, and the soul is spirit, what can they have to do with the body and temporal works? He even cited favorably the Latin saying of pagan philosophers who realized that "the finite is not in proportion to the infinite."[53] "The eternal and the temporal," he translated, "body and spirit, never more fuse together." The gospel brings light into our spirits. Although the soul is supposed to rule the body, when it becomes bound to all kinds of human ordinances and practices, it becomes temporal, or corporeal, and dies. God takes from it its eternal inheritance, as in the case of Adam.

Into this description of human nature and the fall Agricola now fit good works. The work that the Spirit works in us through the eternal Word is "faith apart from all works." Then Agricola drew this revolutionary conclusion: just as the soul can live without the body, so this

---

50. *Colosser,* C.ii.r°: "du hast ytzund gehort/ das alle werck die wir thun/ not werck sind."

51. *Colosser,* C.ii.r°–v°: "So hastu ein lebendiges zeugnis . . . das Got bey vnd ynn dir wonet. . . . So erschrick fur dir selbs vnd furchte dich fur Gott/ klage es ym . . . denn du hast noch nie ynn deinem hertzen empfunden/ wie gros die schetze vnd reichtum is[t] der gnaden."

52. See Susi Hausammann, *Buße als Umkehr und Erneuerung von Mensch und Gesellschaft* (Zurich: Theologischer Verlag, 1974), 187.

53. *Colosser,* K.viii.r°: "finiti ad ifinitum [*sic*] nulla proportio." It is precisely the rejection of this philosophical presupposition that shapes later Lutheran understanding of the natures of Christ and the Lord's Supper.

faith can live without works, like the thief on the cross.[54] To be sure, Agricola distinguished a reasonable soul from a rough, wild one. However, just when it seemed that law might have a place in his system to tame wild souls, he concluded by saying that faith, wherever it is present, can never be hidden. "Since it is spirit and an eternal thing, it needs no instruction on how it ought to bear [fruit] and work."[55]

As radical as the polemic seems, Agricola's point was far tamer. He used the distinction between soul and body (and between faith and works) to introduce a long attack on various ceremonies practiced in the church.[56] He derived this distinction and polemic especially from Colossians 2:8ff., where Paul also attacked the notion of human ceremonies and traditions, but Agricola always went back to the particular word "Philosophey" of Colossians 2:8, a word that to him implied human, temporal things.[57]

How deeply this division between spirit and flesh had penetrated Agricola's thought becomes clear in the section following the attack on ceremonies. Commenting on Colossians 3:1, Agricola noted that Paul divides the believer into two parts: one seated in heaven with Christ at the right hand of God, and the other living on earth, destined to die. This means that the believer's life entails, as Paul describes, both dying, putting off the earthly nature, and rising, putting on the heavenly nature. Against the assertion of philosophy that what lives, lives, the Christian stands with the Crucified and claims that what lives dies and what dies lives.[58] Under this radical reversal, the pope's understanding of the church and of the importance of externals stood condemned.[59]

At the same time, Moses also has no part in the Christian life. Commenting on Colossians 3:5–7, Agricola exclaimed, "How completely different is the teaching of Moses, the law, human ordinances, worldly tra-

---

54. *Colosser*, L.i.r°: "der glaube on alle werck." The opposite of course is not true; that is, no work without faith pleases God.

55. *Colosser*, L.i.r°: "Also auch wo der glaube ist/ da kan er sich nicht bergen/ Syntemal er ein geist vnd ewiges ding ist/ vnd bedarff keiner leer/ wie er gebaren vnd wircken sol."

56. *Colosser*, L.i.v°–N.i.r°. Agricola would venture far more daring conclusions ten years later.

57. For a comparison with Melanchthon's discussion in the *Scholia* of 1527 see pp. 80–89.

58. This practical application of a theology of the cross was matched by insistence on an understanding of the atonement that stressed Christ's victory over sin, death, and the devil (*Colosser*, E.vi.r°) as opposed to Melanchthon's stress on Christ's satisfaction for sin. Agricola also emphasized the hidden wisdom of the Trinity (D.vi.r°) and the scandal of the kingdom of God's being brought in by the incarnate Christ (H.vi.r°): "Gott richtet sein reich vnd weisheit auff mit thorheit."

59. *Colosser*, O.ii.v°. Agricola described for his audience Augustinian Cardinal Giles of Viterbo traveling through Italy at the behest of Pope Julius II and crying out, "Bon Tempo! Bon Tempo!"

ditions, and philosophy regarding the doing of good works from that of the apostle through the gospel."[60] Here all commandments fall on one side, while the gospel stands on the other. Once more Agricola strictly excludes any positive role for Moses in the life of a Christian. He would again defend this point of view at the Torgau in the actual controversy with Melanchthon.

How consistently Agricola divorced the law from the Christian life may be seen in his comments on Colossians 2:21–23. He gave his hearers the advice that when they sin, they are to run to Christ and shake their sins off on him. At the same time, any good works are not theirs, but his. According to 1 Timothy 1:9, Christians need no law; they travel on a "Mittelstrassen," free from good and evil works. Evil works do not harm their blessedness, nor do good works help their righteousness. "Grace, grace it is that does not pay attention to sin nor look upon good works."[61] Later he repeated the same position in an even more fundamental way: "[Good or bad] works do not condemn me, lack of faith does. If you believe, you become holy even in sin."[62] In his summary of this sermon[63] Agricola again contrasted "philosophia," which looks into God's Word and determines that God is pleased by good works, with "God's Word and the freedom of the Spirit," which say that only by grace does one become blessed, while remaining an unworthy servant (Luke 17:7–10):

Philosophy says, "When you sin, you are condemned; be afraid!" God's Word says, "When you sin, be happy. It is to have no consequence. Sin does not condemn you; good works do not save you, but rather faith in Jesus Christ alone." For this reason, then, there is in the congregation forgiveness of sins without ceasing.[64]

At this point two caveats are in order. First, it would be incorrect to draw a direct line from such a statement to the antinomian controversy

---

60. *Colosser*, O.iii.rº: "Wie gar viel anders leren gute werck thun/ Moses/ das gestze [*sic*]/ menschliche ordnung/ weltliche satzung/ philosophey/ vnd die Apostel durchs Euangelion."

61. *Colosser*, J.vi.rº: "Gnade/ gnade/ ist es/ die die sunde nicht achtet/ noch guete werck ansihet." At the same time Agricola rejected all human rules, statutes and ceremonies, including the decrees of Nicea.

62. *Colosser*, J.vii.rº: "Wercke verdammen mich nicht/ sonder der unglaube/ gleubstu/ so wirstu auch ynn der sunde selig."

63. The sermons on Colossians are peppered with such summaries, a technique Agricola also used in his commentary on Titus and to a lesser extent in the annotations on Luke.

64. *Colosser*, J.vii.vº: "Philosophia sagt/ Wenn du sundigest/ so bistu verdampt/ furchte dich. Gottes wort sagt/ Wenn du sundigest/ so sey frölich/ Es sol nicht not haben/ Sunde verdammen dich nicht/ gute werck seligen dich nicht/ sonder der glaube an Jhesu Christ alleine/ denn darumb ist ynn der gemeine/ vergebung der sunden on vnterlas."

of the 1530s. Agricola here is simply using his rhetorical skills to underscore his rendering of the Reformation's central dogma of *justificatio sola fide et gratia*. Second, we ought not ask to what degree such a statement represents Luther's theology. Spalatin, surely no neophyte when it came to Luther's theology, was likely in the audience which heard this sermon and did not, as far as we know, object. The sermons were published with the rather cryptic remark "looked over by Dr. Martin Luther (*Durch D. Martinum Luther vbersehen*)" on the title page. There can be little doubt, as Kjeldgaard-Pedersen has shown, that similar statements can be found in the young Luther. But the developing controversy was not between Luther and Agricola, but between Melanchthon and Agricola. Such statements clearly contradicted much of Melanchthon's understanding of good works and *poenitentia* and quite likely contributed both to the pointed way in which he formulated his definitions in the Visitation Articles and to certain comments within the *Scholia* itself.

Agricola's sermons on Colossians also afford us another look at his developing view of *poenitentia*. Colossians 1:10 gave Agricola a chance to discuss growth in the Christian life. This growth comes in two forms: first, one holds more firmly to God's Word, teaching, and work; second, one's knowledge of one's self increases. Every person who has been called to faith in God through the gospel learns what is proclaimed therein: "*Buße* and forgiveness of sins."[65] Only from the light of the gospel can Christians learn where they have been (under the rule of darkness), where they are (so that they condemn their previous life), and where they are headed (to God who alone can help). Temptations function to drive a person still closer to God. "Thus we now see," Agricola concluded, "how *Buße* and forgiveness of sins are to be practiced throughout life and without stopping. *Buße* kills; forgiveness of sins comforts and makes alive. *Buße* reveals sins; forgiveness of sins heals them."[66] This passage, taken out of context, might seem at first glance to fit nicely into Melanchthon's theology. However, the entire discussion of *poenitentia* excluded both the work of the law and any other human work. *Poenitentia* and forgiveness are both functions of the gospel, not of the law.

Nowhere did Agricola better lay out his understanding of *poenitentia* than in a discussion of Colossians 1:24 and the meaning of dying and being buried. He insisted that there are two kinds of dying, exemplified respectively by Judas and Peter. Both fell into sin at the time of Christ's

---

65. *Colosser*, D.vi.r°.

66. *Colosser*, D.v.r°: "So sehen wir nu/ wie die Busse vnd vergebung der sund geubet sol werden/ weil wir leben/ vnd nicht auffhoren/ Busse die todtet/ vergebung der sunde trostet/ vnd macht lebendig/ Busse eroffnet die sunde/ vergebung der sund heylet sie."

passion. Both died. But Judas remained dead, while Peter was made alive. In cases like Peter's, baptism is the perfect sign of Christian righteousness because, while the body is bathed in water and will die, the soul is promised comfort. As soon as the conscience, out of its need, turns itself around and thinks only on the Word, a light shines in its heart, and the resurrection draws near.

The difference between Peter and Judas rests in the fact that only Peter heard a word of promise from Christ, namely, that although the disciple would deny his master, Christ had prayed for him that his faith would not fail. Peter returned because of this promise. Judas had no such word, could not see beyond the punishment for his sin, and remained in his sin eternally. Peter could see beyond his sin to the light of the gospel and therefore wept. Judas confessed his sin to the priests, but without any promise he could only go out and hang himself.

From these examples Agricola concluded that *poenitentia* is the result of the gospel: "However, whenever the forgiveness of sins (the watchword of Christ's kingdom) descends into *Buße*, baptism, and the heart of the sinner, so that such a one begins simply to consider it, then the resurrection comes near."[67] Only in the light of the gospel can the heart condemn its own nature and uphold God's grace. Here the root of the controversy is exposed. Were Agricola to be told that *poenitentia* must be thought of in terms of contrition and confession, as preparation in the human being for the gospel, it is not hard to imagine his reaction.

Auslegung der Episteln S. Pauls . . . gedeudscht

On 20 January 1527 Agricola completed a short preface to his translation of Melanchthon's annotations on Romans and 1–2 Corinthians. In it he complained about the earlier translations and explained that he had to use more words to bring into German what Melanchthon had said more briefly in Latin.[68] Agricola was putting it mildly. In point of fact, his translation, unlike the earlier ones from 1523 and 1524, represented a paraphrase to which Agricola had added pages of his own com-

---

67. *Colosser*, G.vii.v°: "Wenn aber nu die vergebung der sunde/ die losung des reichs Christi/ felt in die busse/ ynn die tauffe/ ynn des sunders hertze/ also das er beginnet nur daran zugedencken/ so nahet es sich zur aufferstehung."

68. For the printing history, see appendix 1. The earlier translations used the second edition of Melanchthon's annotations, published by John Herwagen of Strasbourg in January 1523. Agricola used a second edition that was published by Herwagen on 15 January 1524 and again in July 1525; it also contained Luther's preface to Romans from his translation of the New Testament. Similar complaints about the verbosity of German appear in Luther's own comments on translating the Bible and in Justus Jonas's comments about translating Melanchthon's *Scholia*.

mentary, hardly the simple "notelchen" to which he referred.[69] What makes this translation particularly important for our purposes is those places where Agricola, finding an understanding of *poenitentia* or law different from his own, was inclined to change Melanchthon's text to agree with his own theology.[70]

Before looking at any texts in detail, we must say a word about the method used to compare Melanchthon's original and Agricola's translation. The source of the changes in the translation has been debated in the secondary literature. Whereas Susi Hausammann simply assumes Agricola's hand and states that what is found in the sermons on Colossians may also be found in this work,[71] Kjeldgaard-Pedersen challenges this assumption and wonders what it means to say, as Hausammann implies, that the annotations on Romans (of Melanchthon) and the sermons on Colossians (of Agricola) agree.[72] A thorough comparison of Melanchthon's annotations and Agricola's translation goes beyond the scope of this work. However, in order to take some of the difficulties of comparing a translation with the original into account, we have also examined the translation of 1524. In point of fact, Kjeldgaard-Pedersen's concerns are unfounded. The amount of material that comes from Agricola's hand is so great as to make this commentary as much his as Melanchthon's.[73]

We begin with the understanding of law and gospel. Sometimes Agricola faithfully rendered Melanchthon's text according to its original meaning. Where Melanchthon wrote that the gospel has two offices—il-

69. The preface, *Auslegung*, 2r°, reads in part: "Die weil . . . die auslegunge meins lieben freundes Philippi Melanchthon vber die selbe Epistel also zuuor gedeudscht ist, das sie mehr nach lateynischer denn deudscher art redet, habe ich mich der mühe nicht verdriessen lassen, die selbige nach vnser gemeynen sprache zu deudschen, den zu gut die nicht lateyn können. Ich habe auch vnterweilen vmb klerers verstands willen ein klein notelchen hynzu gesetzt, denn was ym lateyn kurtz geredt wird, müssen wir deudschen villeycht das wir sein noch nicht gewonet sind, vnd viel ein ander art haben mit viel worten reden."

70. In the latter part of 1526 the work was already well on its way through the presses. On 5 January 1527 Gregory Borner wrote to Stephen Roth, "Darczu [woldeth mir verschaffen] . . . dy zcwu Episteln zcun Romern vnnd Corynthern" (cited in Buchwald, 55, no. 103). A letter from George Rörer in 1527 (63, no. 129) requests Agricola's annotations on Luke with an index.

71. Hausammann, *Buße als Umkehr*, 185–89, esp. 186.

72. Kjeldgaard-Pedersen, *Gesetz, Evangelium und Buße*, 176f.

73. To name just one example, in comments on Romans 1:18f. Agricola added two pages to the discussion of the difference between faith and unbelief. This kind of free translation deserves its own study, especially since Agricola had heard a portion of Luther's lectures on Romans. See Ernst Koch, "Johann Agricola neben Luther: Schülerschaft und theologische Eigenart," in *Lutheriana: Zum 500. Geburtstag Martin Luthers von den Mitarbeitern der Weimarische Ausgabe*, ed. Gerhard Hammer and Karl-Heinz zur Mühlen (Cologne and Vienna: Böhlau, 1984), 146.

lumination so that we know God's mercy and will ("voluntas Dei"), and protection against God's judgment ("iudicium")—Agricola gave a faithful rendition except that he left out the words "voluntas Dei" and translated "iudicium" as "zorn (wrath)."[74] Were such the only kind of changes Agricola made, a comparison would make very little sense indeed. But Agricola's additions and subtractions penetrate much deeper in other places.

On Romans 1:1 Melanchthon discussed the differences between law and gospel. Where he wrote simply "what is the difference between law and gospel (*quid intersit inter legem & Euangelium*)," Agricola added "what purpose each serves and what each effects (*wo zu ein iglichs diene/ auch was ein iglichs wircke*)," certainly well within Melanchthon's meaning, but an expansion nevertheless. Where Melanchthon then gave one example of law ("Love God above all else and your neighbor as yourself"), Agricola added prohibitions from the Ten Commandments. Melanchthon summarized the effect of the law briefly: "Therefore the law is an odious discourse, because it commands impossible things, accuses, and terrifies all people."[75] This did not satisfy Agricola, who wrote:

This law sounds almost evil in human ears, for it is impossible that any person can do or allow it. Nature experiences no greater love than the love for itself, out of which it then reckons to those it does not love. The law wants to restrain this love in nature and directs nature that it should love something other than itself and be loving to that which it hates. Therefore it is a hostile sermon: "You shall love God more than yourself or else you must die." Through this, too, terror and despair are forced upon all people. Therein every person is stuck and is not helped out.[76]

Here we can easily recognize Agricola's modus operandi. He paraphrased Melanchthon's work and, after adding his own excursus, re-

---

74. Cf. *MSA* 4:52 with *Auslegung*, 214r°. (Except where the second edition, which Agricola used for his translation, differs from the first, we will cite the edition of 1 and 2 Corinthians in *MSA* 4.) The translation of 1524 includes the phrase "oder des göttlichen willens" and the term "gericht gottes" instead of "zorn." As we have seen, Agricola's understanding of the gospel entails a different set of functions.

75. *Anno. in Rom.*, 4r°: "Est ergo Lex odiosus sermo, quia impossibilia imperat, & reos agit, et terret omnes homines."

76. *Auslegung*, 6v°f.: "Diese gesetz stymmen/ klingen fast vbel ynn der menschen oren/ denn es ist vnmöglich/ das sie yigend ein mensch möge thuen odder lassen/ Natur empfind kein grösser liebe/ denn die sie zu yhr selbst hat/ daraus sie sich rechent an den sie nicht liebet/ Diese liebe wil der natur das gesetze weren/ vnd weiset der natur etwas anders das sie lieben sol denn sich/ vnd hold seyn dem das sie hasset/ Derhalben ists ein feindselige predigt/ Du solt Gott mehr lieben denn dich/ odder must sterben/ dadurch auch ynn alle menschen schrecken vnd verzagen getrieben wird/ darynne es yederman stecken lest/ vnd hilfft nicht eraus."

turned to the text. However, in this case he left out the phrase "reos agit (accuses)." Instead, he showed just what this accusation involves. Nature loves itself, but the law wants to turn human nature away from self-love toward loving what nature naturally hates. The law is, then, a "feindselige predigt" resulting in "schrecken vnd verzagen," which leave a person stuck with no chance for rescue. Accusation, which for Melanchthon led to *poenitentia* and forgiveness, led for Agricola to anger.

In just such subtle ways Agricola shaped Melanchthon's exegesis to his own ends. Whereas Melanchthon moved from the accusation of the law to the forgiveness of sins, Agricola viewed the law as a dead end from which there is no escape. This same shift may be seen in a later part of the same passage. Where Melanchthon described the conscience as frightened and made anxious ("terreri & angi") by the law, Agricola added that the conscience is "burdened (*beschwert*)" by the law—"how it sneers at and struggles against the law (*wie sichs rümpfft vnd weret widder das gesetze*)." Melanchthon's gospel, comfort for terrified consciences, disappeared before a conscience sneering at and fighting against the law.

In comments on Romans 4:15, Agricola appeared almost to correct Melanchthon. Melanchthon had written, "Therefore [God] gives the law, not just so that sin may be increased, but so that it may be recognized, so that [such] known [sin] may humble and invite the humbled ones to seek the grace of Christ."[77] The sense is clear. The law has a positive purpose. It was not given just to increase sin but to make it known, so that that knowledge may humble and invite the humbled to the grace which must be sought from Christ. This positive view of the law received correction from Agricola: "For this reason God gave the law: that it may increase sin, so that each person recognizes one's own trespasses. For a person does not see what is small, and when it becomes enlarged, everyone sees it. So that when each person sees one's own misfortune, that person is humbled and has reason to search for help elsewhere."[78] The care that Melanchthon took in identifying two subtly different purposes of the law ("so that sin may be increased" and "so that it may be recognized") was lost in the translation of Agricola, who assumed simply that the more sin there is, the more likely it is to be

---

77. *Anno. in Rom.*, 25rº: "Ideo legem [Deus] dedit, non quidem ut augeretur, sed ut cognosceretur peccatum, ut cognitum humiliaret, & ad gratiam Christi quaerandam inuitaret humiliatos."

78. *Auslegung*, 73vº: "Gott hat darümb das gesetze geben, das es die sünde heuffete, auff das ein yeder seine gebrechen erkente. Denn was wenig ist, das sihet man nicht, vnd wens gros wird, so sihet es yederman. Auff das wenn yemands sein vnglück sehe, gedemütiget werde vnd vrsach habe anderswo hülffe zu suchen."

seen. Even the phrase "to search for help elsewhere" pales in comparison with the very positive notion of Melanchthon, who assumed that knowledge of sin drives a person to seek Christ's grace.[79]

Agricola's unwillingness to attribute any positive function to the law can be found as well in his independent introduction to Romans 1:18, where he explained the two works of God in terms of Isaiah 28. God first must perform the alien work of killing in order to do his proper work, because no one desires grace. Agricola added the German adage, "No one cries until he is lacking something (*Es schreyet niemand dwe/ es feyle ihm denn etwas*)."[80] Now Melanchthon's comments on Romans 1:18 had insisted that God "causes all people to be unjust and sinners through the law." Agricola omitted the phrase "per legem" and translated: "Thus, when God promises through the gospel, through the preaching of his Son, grace, help, and eternal life, it [the gospel] has no place unless it also proclaim the wrath of God come down from heaven, . . . by which they become worn down and desire to participate in Christ's righteousness. . . . As Christ says . . . 'I am not come to call the righteous but sinners to *Buße*.'"[81] Now the gospel itself has even become responsible for bringing sinners to *poenitentia*. Once again, the law has no positive function to play in Agricola's understanding of *poenitentia*; it capitulates all of its usefulness to the gospel.

Within this context Ernst Koch's critical analysis of Agricola's translation is convincing.[82] He points out that in Agricola's translation of the annotations on Romans 7:6 Melanchthon's comment "The gospel is not spirit (*Euangelium non est spiritus*)" is completely lacking and that the rest of the remarks have been changed as well. Where Melanchthon wrote, "The law is not spirit, the gospel is not spirit; but the *affectus* loving the law, the *affectus* constantly believing the gospel, is spirit," Agricola disturbed the parallelism and translated, "The law is not spirit. The desire which approaches the law from the heart, and that one believes

79. This is not to say that Agricola completely rejected Melanchthon's exegesis. For example, he quite accurately rendered the conclusion to Melanchthon's arguments (74r°): "Summa. Das gesetze zeyget die sünde an/ vnd tödtet/ Christus vergibt die sünde/ vnd macht lebendig." Melanchthon had written: "In summa, Lex ostendit peccatum et mortificat; Christus medetur & vivificat."

80. *Auslegung*, 22v°.

81. *Anno. in Rom.*, 9r°: "omnes homines causatur iniustos & peccatores esse per legem"; *Auslegung*, 22v°: "Also wan Gott durchs Euangelion/ durch die predige von seynem son/ gnade/ hulffe vnd ewiges leben verspricht/ so hat es [=Euangelion] keynen raum es verkundige denn auch den zorn Gottes/ von hymel herab/ . . . auff das sie mürb werden/ vnd Christus gerechtigkeit begeren teylhafftig zu werden/ . . . alse Christus sagt . . . ich byn nicht kommen/ die gerechten zu beruffen/ sonder die sunder zur busse." The final phrase, "zur busse," is not in the Latin text.

82. Koch, "Johannes Agricola neben Luther," 140–45.

the gospel—that is spirit."[83] The *affectus* is no longer connected to faith in the gospel; gospel is no longer excluded from spirit.

Like Melanchthon's interpretation of Romans, his comments on 2 Corinthians also gave Agricola the opportunity to correct the understanding of *poenitentia*. In an experiment with his developing *loci* method of biblical interpretation, Melanchthon had used a rather long discourse on *poenitentia* to introduce 2 Corinthians 2 and its discussion of the congregation's acceptance of a sinner.[84] Some of the changes Agricola introduced were quite small. Melanchthon talked about "the fallen *(lapsi)* who are *poenitentes*." While the earlier translation rendered this phrase "die gefalnen die püß thuon (the fallen who *Buße tun*)," Agricola avoided the ambiguity of the word *poenitentes* and translated, "Die da gefallen seyn/ vnd bekennen es (those who have fallen and acknowledge it)."[85] Any reference to a sacrament was thereby removed.

But Agricola also broke the connection between contrition and *poenitentia*. Melanchthon had written, "Therefore the fallen person is justified at that time when one truly is sorry and trusts the gospel that absolves."[86] But Agricola could not bring himself to mention this kind of feeling (after all Judas had felt bad, too) and translated instead, "Therefore the fallen person is righteous when he believes and trusts the gospel that forgives him."[87] The phrase "cum uere dolet" disappeared.

Agricola's peculiar understanding of the role of the gospel in *poenitentia* came to expression in the way he treated Melanchthon's comments on the Scholastic term for mortification. In a quite evenhanded way, Melanchthon writes, "Fifthly, the Scholastics call mortification contrition, but mortification alone does not justify unless you believe your sin is forgiven."[88] Clearly for Melanchthon mortification was a necessary preliminary to faith. For Agricola, faith preceded mortifica-

---

83. *Anno. in Rom.*, 36rº: "Lex non est spiritus, Euangelium non est spiritus, sed affectus amans legem. Affectus constanter credens Euangelio, Spiritus est"; and *Auslegung*, 101rº: "Das gesetze ist nicht geist/ Die lust/ die zum gesetze von hertzen gehet/ vnd das man dem Euangelio gleubet/ das ist geist."

84. Already in the *argumentum* Melanchthon defined *poenitentia* as one of the *loci communes* of the Corinthian correspondence. Moreover, in the preface to the Latin text of 2 Corinthians, published for the lectures on which the *Annotationes* were based, Melanchthon also insisted that this letter defined the "form of *poenitentia*." See *MBW* 172 (*T*1:358.14f.), dated September/October 1521.

85. *MSA* 4:95; *Anzeygung*, b.iv.vº; *Auslegung*, 261rº.

86. *MSA* 4:96: "Ergo tum iustificatur lapsus, cum uere dolet & confidit Euangelio se absoluenti." The *Anzeygung* includes the words "warhafftig sich beschmertzt."

87. *Auslegung*, 261vº: "Darümb wird/ der gefallen ist gerecht/ wenn et [*sic* =er] gleubet vnd trawet dem Euangelio/ das yhn löset."

88. *MSA* 4:96: "Quintum mortificationem contritionem vocant Scholae, sed mortificatio sola non iustificat, nisi credas remitti peccatum."

tion. Thus he translated, "Fifth, the Scholastic teachers call mortification contrition. However, mortification does not make righteous where you do not believe in the gospel."[89] The word "sola" is missing, and the language implies that faith must at very least accompany and perhaps precede mortification. In the context of Agricola's example of *poenitentia* from the passion story (see pp. 36–37), the translation and correction of Melanchthon make perfect sense.

Where Melanchthon discussed confession itself, the gulf between him and Agricola appears even wider. Melanchthon distinguished between confession to God and confession to other human beings. Among human beings, furthermore, there were three kinds of confession: public exclusion of sinners; private confession with public *poenitentia* (as in the punishment of a murder in the Latin West, a practice that, Melanchthon admitted, had stopped among the Greeks), and private confession.[90] In regard to the second kind of confession, Agricola omitted the examples given by Melanchthon and simply wrote, "Dis hat auch affgehöret (this, too, has ceased)," although Melanchthon made the point that it had not.

Agricola then completely reshaped Melanchthon's discussion of private confession to conform to his own criticism of this sacrament. Melanchthon had described it in a neutral manner. Private confession represented a third type. Formerly it was free as to whom, when, and which sins one confessed. One consulted the saints in the congregation and heard from them the absolution and the "sententia Dei." This type of confession was mentioned in Basil's booklet on the monastic institutes and perhaps in James 5:16.[91]

The discussion of the types of confession having been the seventh point in a longer list, Melanchthon continued with the eighth point: whether confession is required according to divine law (*de iure diuino*). He answered that only the first kind of confession, when one is accused before the whole church, is required. Then one must confess and be reconciled to the injured party. His ninth point followed from this. If a person amends one's ways, so that ecclesial correction becomes unneces-

---

89. *Auslegung*, 261v°: "Zum fünfften/ Die Schullerer heissen die tödtung/ rewe/ aber die tödtung macht nicht gerecht/ wo du nicht gleubest/ dem Euangelio." The *Anzeygung*, c.i.r°, reads: "doch die ertödtung alleyn macht nit rechtfertig/ nur alleyn du glaubst dann/ das dir nachgelassen vnnd vergeben werden die sünd." The order from mortification to faith is clearly preserved.

90. *MSA* 4:96f.

91. *MSA* 4:97: "Tertium genus, est confessio priuata, quae quondam talis erat, ut liberum esset cuiuis confiteri, cum vellet & confitebantur, quoties conscientia angebat, consulebant sanctos, & absolutionem, & dei sententiam de se audiebant. Huius confessionis Basilius meminit in libello de institutis Monachorum, & huc pertinere uidetur, quod est apud Iacobum, confitemini alter alteri peccata."

sary, then there is no "ius diuinum." Finally, the tenth point added that "absolutio priuata" is as necessary as baptism, because it is a testimony that one's sins are forgiven. This absolution may even be requested without a listing of one's sins.[92]

Agricola's conviction that there was no place in the church for the third kind of confession is evident in his rendering of Melanchthon's comments:

> There is a third kind of confession, also secret, in which one has the free-dom to confess to whomever one wishes. The only thing one should pay attention to is the absolution, which the brother gives as if from God. The first two forms of confession are public. The first God wants to have from Christians as long as they live. The second James talks about. When someone harms another in body, honor, or property, that person must publicly confess. Basil also refers to this, and it also is necessary. The third is optional; only, as has been said, it must have God's word, which I can receive, and I retain the freedom whether or not I confess my short-comings.[93]

No longer was private confession as necessary as baptism. No longer did it retain the proof texts of James 5:16 or Basil. No longer was there any discussion of self-correction without the intervention of the church. While Melanchthon expressly envisioned private confession for the distressed conscience, Agricola narrowed the concern to absolution alone. Whereas Melanchthon did not require the listing of sins (*recensio peccatorum*), Agricola was even more open—one's sins need not be mentioned at all. He no longer emphasized absolution, which implied confession of sin and which Melanchthon called a "testimony that your sins are forgiven you," but God's word—just what Peter needed in order to experience true sorrow for sin and confess.

92. *MSA* 4:97: "Octauum, ergo si quaeratur V[trum] Iure diuino exegatur confessio? Respon[deo]. Solam primam esse iuris diuini, confiteri si accuseris coram ecclesia. Item reconciliari fratri tuo, quem leseras. Nonum, si ultro emendes te, ita ut ecclesiae correp-tione non sit opus, non exigit ius diuinum confessionem. Decimum, Absolutio priuata necessaria est, sicut baptismus. Nam priuata absolutio, quae tibi fit, est testimonium quod tibi propria peccata condonata sunt, & illam sine recensione peccatorum petere possumus."

93. *Auslegung*, 262r°: "Die dritte beycht is auch heymlich/ mit freyheit zu beychten/ wem man wölle/ allein das man acht habe auff die absolution/ wilche von dem bruder als thet es Gott/ geschicht/ Die ersten zwo beycht sind öffentlich/ Die erste wil Gott haben von den Christen/ dieweyl sie leben/ Von der andern sagt Jacobus/ Nemlich wo einer den andern/ an leib/ ehre vnd gutt geschadet hette/ das er öffentlich bekennet/ Bekennet eynander ewer sünde/ Auch gedencket yhr Basilius/ vnd ist auch von nöten. Die dritte ist frey/ alleine wie gesagt ist/ das sie Gottes wort hat/ das ich hole/ vnd stehet bey mir/ das ich yhm sage odder nicht sage meinem gebrechen."

As if this were not enough, Agricola also changed Melanchthon's comments under "Satisfactio" as well. Both agreed that, as Agricola put it, "in sum: either we must deny Christ, or we must let our satisfactions be nothing."[94] However, Agricola simply omitted Melanchthon's explanations of 2 Corinthians 2:5, in which he corrected Erasmus, and of 2 Corinthians 2:6, where he gave this summary: "The conclusion of this topic: from this text you may infer an argument regarding the restoring of the fallen after baptism, the abolition of satisfactions, the power of absolution, the snares of the devil, etc."[95] It is hard to understand why Agricola overlooked this particular text. As we shall see in the following chapters, however, the questions of restoring the lapsed and the power of absolution, as well as the division of *poenitentia* into three parts, became the subjects of intense debate between these two men in the late summer of 1527.

Agricola's exegetical argumentation on the question of the law and *poenitentia* is now clear. In his three major writings just prior to the controversy he consistently expressed a low estimation of the law and its function. Instead the gospel itself, as promise, creates the basis for death and resurrection in the Christian's life. This view of law and gospel meant that *poenitentia*, too, underwent a radical redefinition. No longer a sacramental act based upon the inner affections of the individual, *poenitentia* occurs only in the light of the promise itself. Contrition, defined by Agricola as *attritio* (sorrow over sin out of fear of punishment), can occur in anyone's life, even Judas's. But true death and resurrection come about only from the promise of baptism itself. Thus, one does not move from an anxious conscience to absolution, but from the promise of God to sorrow over sin and, better still, to refraining from sin completely. Where this movement does not occur, God himself must have abandoned the sinner—a cause for real anxiety. Where it does occur, it must be seen as the work of God alone.

---

94. *Auslegung*, 262v°: "Summa/ Entweder wir müssen Christum verleugnen/ odder müssen genugthuen nichts seyn lassen."

95. *MSA* 4:98: "Epilogus huius loci. Ex hoc textu colliges argumentum de restituendis lapsis post baptismum, de abolendis satisfactionibus, de vi absolutionis, de insidiis diaboli, etc."

2

The Flood of Catechisms
(1525–27)

The struggle to define the relation of law and *poenitentia* played itself out on another front besides commentaries, namely, the evangelical catechisms produced in Wittenberg from 1525 to 1527. Without a discussion of this explosion of catechisms, one would be hard-pressed to understand why a simple set of instructions to local pastors, the Visitation Articles published in 1527, could have created such a furor in the first place. Moreover, one would have to posit that Melanchthon and Agricola were studying one another's exegetical writings with the same intensity afforded to them by twentieth-century historians. By examining the catechisms of the time, we discover, first, that questions about *poenitentia* and law concerned others beyond simply Melanchthon and Agricola, and, second, that another important source for Agricola's thought, to which Melanchthon probably had access, appeared shortly before the publication of the *Scholia* on Colossians. Eisleben's catechisms could easily have precipitated Melanchthon's criticism of those who preach the gospel without true *poenitentia*.

The Impetus for the Wave of Catechisms

Almost without exception, previous studies of the early catechisms have rested upon the encyclopedic work of Ferdinand Cohrs, who at the turn of the twentieth century published four volumes of evangelical catechisms appearing before Luther's.[1] Thirty years later, Johannes Meyer used Cohrs's work as the basis of his own careful analysis of Luther's catechisms.[2] Even John Michael Reu, who was mainly interested in cat-

---

1. Cohrs 1–4. This dependence is true even of the work of Ingrid Hruby in *HKJL* 2:190–244.
2. Johannes Meyer, *Historischer Kommentar zu Luthers Kleinem Katechismus* (Gütersloh: C. Bertelsmann, 1929).

echisms produced after 1529, owed a tremendous debt to Cohrs's work.[3]

Cohrs examined all catechisms, regardless of their provenance. We will focus more narrowly on what Wittenberg's own presses produced and in the process examine several oversights in Cohrs's work, which point to the possibility that several of Wittenberg's catechisms were in direct theological, to say nothing of—from the printer's perspective— economic, competition.[4] Yet even this small glimpse into an otherwise extremely complicated story rests upon Cohrs's formative work.

Two events caused the wave of catechisms in Wittenberg. The first was the publication of a book that was not thought of as a catechism at all. In 1522 Martin Luther and his eager assistants at Grünenberg's print shop published his "Betbüchlein."[5] In its original form it was not a catechism, but stood instead in a long line of medieval prayer-books designed to assist especially the laity in their devotional life. Luther's preface placed the book squarely within the tradition of these "para-dise" books and "gardens of the soul." While Luther was unsure whether to ban such books altogether or to reform them, he claimed his book was merely a beginning, a simple Christian form to pray the Lord's Prayer and the Ten Commandments.[6]

The book itself was made up of excerpts from Luther's previous ser-mons and translation work. Its forty leaves contained material already published separately in 1520 in "Eine kurze Form" of the Command-ments, the Creed, and the Lord's Prayer,[7] additions from 1522 on ways to pray and the Ave Maria, as well as a selection of psalms and a trans-lation of Titus, which only in later editions conformed to the *September Testament*. Ten separate printings in 1522 alone, according to the Wei-mar edition of Luther's works, bespeak its popularity.

These early printings show the printers' concern to make additions to

3. John Michael Reu, *Dr. Martin Luther's Small Catechism: A History of Its Origin, Its Distribution and Its Use* (Chicago: Wartburg, 1929). Albrecht Peters's posthumous work on the catechism, *Kommentar zu Luthers Katechismen*, 5 vols. (Göttingen: Vanden-hoeck and Ruprecht, 1990–94), is more theological than historical and depends heavily upon all three scholars for its historical conclusions. Nevertheless, it represents an im-portant contribution to the research. See also Peters's article "Die Theologie der Kate-chismen Luthers anhand der Zuordnung ihrer Hauptstücke," *Luther-Jahrbuch* 43 (1976): 7–35.

4. See appendix 2.

5. *WA* 10.2:355, printing "A," entitled, "Eyn bett buchlin | Der tzehen gepott. | Des glawbens. | Des vatter unßers. | Und des Aue Marien. | D. Martini Lutheri. | . . . ."

6. *WA* 10.2:375.15–17: "Und yn des zum anfang diße eynfeltige Christliche form und spiegel die sund tzuerkennen unnd tzu beten fur hallten nach den tzehen gepotten und dem vatter unßer."

7. *WA* 7:204–29.

the work.[8] A major change in the form took place only one year later at the hands of Nicholas Schirlentz. With the appearance of the *September Testament*, this Wittenberg publisher, perhaps under Luther's supervision, turned the "Prayer Booklet" into a 156-page New Testament reader, adding Romans, 1–2 Timothy, 1–2 Peter, and Jude.[9] The book had now taken on the form of a lay Bible. Still, we cannot call this work a catechism.

While the "Prayer Booklet" provided an important model, it was a second event or, rather, series of events that broke the dam.[10] In 1523, Nicholas Hausmann, pastor in Zwickau and comrade-in-arms with the Wittenberg theologians, sent to the court of the elector a request that a visitation of the churches in Saxony be instituted. Elector Frederick delayed. At the end of 1524, Hausmann turned to Wittenberg itself and in a now-lost letter to Luther reiterated the need for a visitation. In this connection he must have asked that Luther also address the problem of instructing the young. To this second matter Luther replied on 2 February 1525 that Justus Jonas and John Agricola had been asked to write a catechism.[11] A little more than a month later, on 26 March, Luther told Hausmann that a catechism had been demanded from them.[12] Hausmann sent a second request to the court, this one dated 2 May 1525, the time of Elector Frederick's death, and again asking "what kind of lessons should be held for the unlettered small children."[13] In the same month Agricola was making preparations to move to Eisleben to become rector of the Latin school. That, coupled with the death of the Elector Frederick and the Peasants' War, had placed Hausmann's request on the back burner for many in Wittenberg and at the court. Thus, on 23 August 1525 Hausmann wrote to Stephen Roth, then an assistant at the Wittenberg city church: "On account of the departure of [John Agricola of] Eisleben, to whom the catechism had been committed, I am ignorant [of the situation]. O that it would be supplied and quickly published by [Justus] Jonas; from him I expect great progress."[14] At nearly the same time he must have written to Luther,

---

8. For details see *WA* 10.2:366–69.

9. *WA* 10.2:356f., "L," entitled: "Eyn Bett= | buchlin vnd | leße büchlin, | Mar. Luth. | gemehret vnd ge= | bessert. | . . . ." Schirlentz also prepared a second edition in the same year (not in the *WA*).

10. See Cohrs 4:247ff.

11. *WABr* 3:431.

12. *WABr* 3:462.

13. Cited in Cohrs 4:247: "was für Übunge mit den unverständigen kleinen Kindern solle gehalten werden."

14. Cited in Cohrs 4:248: "Catechismus propter discessum Eislebii cui sit commendatus, ignoro. Utinam a Jono suppleretur citoque ederetur in lucem, sperarem profectum inde maximum."

whose response on 27 September 1525 indicated that Luther himself intended to write a catechism.[15]

Hausmann also sought a revision of the worship service and its translation into the vernacular. In order to secure a copy by Christmas 1525, he even sent his own messenger to Wittenberg.[16] Whether he succeeded or not is unclear. Certainly the new order of the "Deutsche Messe" was used in Wittenberg on Christmas 1525. Whether it was also used in Zwickau on that date is unknown. On 4 January 1526, Luther wrote as if he had not yet finished the editing of the work, but by 2 February 1526 he seemed surprised that no copies had yet reached Erfurt.

In his preface to the "Deutsche Messe," written during this period, Luther also discussed the need for a simple, straightforward catechism on the three chief parts, that is, a book in question-and-answer format covering the Ten Commandments, Creed, and Lord's Prayer.[17] He added, "One could take such questions out of our *Betbüchlein*, where the three parts are briefly explained, or could write another himself."[18] Two things are clear. First, Luther offered his own "Prayer Booklet" as a source for catechization. Second, he invited others to write their own. Luther then speculated about what such a catechism might contain, using the well-known picture of two little purses (faith and love), each with two pockets (sin and salvation, and love for others and the cross for ourselves, respectively). Into these purses Luther suggested placing Bible verses, golden ones for faith and silver ones for love.

At the same time, Luther described the fuller religious life of the city churches, where there were more than simply Sunday services. Here he suggested that early on Mondays and Tuesdays a service of readings be held in German covering the Ten Commandments, the Creed, the Lord's Prayer, baptism, and the sacrament (of the altar). These days were to be set aside for inculcating the catechism "in its proper understanding."[19] For the first time, the five chief parts of the catechism were mentioned in connection with the word *catechism* itself. Luther proposed a second level of catechetical instruction based upon this broader subject matter.

We have seen several causes for the publication of catechisms. Catechisms arose from the need for new prayer books and personal edification. Their production was stimulated by a lone pastor's single-minded effort to institute evangelical congregational life in Zwickau. They met the

---

15. *WABr* 3:582.
16. See *WA* 19:51.
17. As Peters, "Die Theologie," 13, points out, this matches the transformation of auricular confession into preparation for the Lord's Supper.
18. *WA* 19:77.11–13: "Solch fragen mag man/ nemen aus dem unsern betbuchlin, da die drey stuck kurtz ausgelegt sind, odder selbs anders machen."
19. *WA* 19:79.17–20: "ynn seym rechten verstand."

evangelical demand for material with which to instruct both children and those unfamiliar with the Christian faith. Their form arose out of the Reformer's call for instruction in faith and love and out of the church's three traditional teaching sources, now expanded to include the sacraments.

The Onslaught of Catechetical Literature

This multifaceted demand for catechesis resulted in a storm of publications, all intended to instruct the common folk in the faith.[20] From 1522 to 1529, sixty-two printings of thirteen different instructional booklets were produced in Wittenberg.[21] We begin our survey with Luther's "Prayer Booklet," which in 1525 was produced in its third Wittenberg edition, this time at the hands of Hans Lufft.[22] In this edition the Scripture completely disappeared, except for the material from the Psalms and the newly added Prayer of Manasseh. Also included were portions of Luther's sermons on prayer, the cross, baptism, the Lord's Supper, penance, and death.[23] The 40 leaves of 1522 had grown to 164, larger than the lay Bible published by Schirlentz only two years before. The stuff for a catechism was here; the book had a clear pedagogical intent, but it also maintained its edificatory tone.

Luther's "Prayer Booklet" was not alone. Already in 1524 a German translation of the questions and answers of the Bohemian Brethren had been published in Wittenberg, perhaps by Grünenberg. It was followed in 1525 by a *Niederdeutsch* edition printed by Hans Barth and Hans Bossow.[24] Luther could actually have been referring to this kind

20. The amazing success of these booklets places in question the common opinion that Luther's and Lutheranism's influence among the simpler folk waned after the Peasants' War. If anything, it increased as the Reformers themselves developed media for getting their particular message across, something they had not done in a consistent, organized manner heretofore.

21. The total number of printings throughout Germany of just these catechisms was at least 176. With the exception of Luther's "Prayer Booklet," these printings occurred between 1524 and 1529. Eight of the thirteen booklets were intended specifically for children. Three others claimed to derive their content directly from the Scriptures. All were meant to bring to the people the basics of evangelical teaching in the simplest possible form.

22. *WA* 10.2:358, "V," entitled simply "Eyn Bett= | büchlin. | Mar. Lut. | Wittemberg. | 1525." This may well be a reworking of "N," a *Niederdeutsch* edition published in Hamburg.

23. The sermons on prayer, baptism, penance, the Lord's Supper, and preparation for death match material in the *Kirchenpostille*; see *WA* 2:136–42, 175–77, 685–97, 727–37, and 15:481–505.

24. See Joseph Müller, ed., *Die Deutschen Katechismen der Böhmischen Brüder* (Berlin: A. Hofmann, 1887), 4, 158. The German editions are titled "Eynn Schöne | Frag vnd Ant= | wurt, den jungen kindern. Zuo | vnderweysen, Gott tzuoerkennen | . . . " and "Eyne schon= | nye vorklarynghe/ des | kynder bückelins/ Wo müse/ | in dem rechten louen/ vß war= | cken/ leren schal/ yn be= | wys/ der hylgen sch= | ryfft gegründet." For a more complete list of printings, thirteen in all and as many as three from Wittenberg, see *HKJL* 2:1104–6.

of book when he called for the use of questions and answers in catechetical instruction.

From John Toltz, a schoolmaster in Plauen, we have "Eyn kurtz handbuchlyn fur iunge Christen souiel yhn zu wissen von nöten."[25] He sent the booklet to the University of Wittenberg for its approval. The rector, Herman Tulich, who was about to depart with Agricola for Eisleben, gave it to Johann Bugenhagen, who wrote his approval on 18 December 1525: "And [I] say that in my estimation I know nothing else than that this booklet is godly and useful."[26] The sixteen-leaf booklet was published by George Rhau in 1526.[27]

In 1527 Christopher Hegendorfer wrote an explanation of the three chief parts of the catechism, "Die zehen gepot/ der glaub/ vnd das Vater vnser/ für die kinder/ kürtzlich ausgelegt"; it was published once in Wittenberg by George Rhau.[28] Two years later its Latin translation, first published in Haguenau by John Setzer and perhaps edited by George Rörer, appeared as an appendix to a Latin version of Luther's "Prayer Booklet."

George Rauth from Tresen published a small booklet in Wittenberg that claimed to cover in seventeen articles everything in the entire Scriptures that the Christian needed for comfort. Stephen Roth, perhaps in part spurred on by Nicholas Hausmann's requests, served as editor for some of the editions, which were published in Augsburg, Leipzig, and Wittenberg (two times).[29] Such books very clearly filled the need for books of edification, connecting the Scriptures to the comfort of the gospel.

Two similar sets of articles, which had their origin outside of Wittenberg, also stimulated new publications. Benedict Gretzinger, probably from Augsburg, published in 1523 a short work of important Scripture texts with an explanation of how to use them in case of persecution.[30]

---

25. Cohrs 1:243–60. A second book, which was a necessary second step in catechesis after the child had memorized the *Laienbibel* (see Cohrs 4:31), was not published in Wittenberg. Toltz was formerly the rector of the academy in Wittenberg and city pastor. He died in 1573.

26. Cohrs 1:247: "Vnd [ich] sage, das ich nach meynem vorstande anders nicht weys, denn das dis Buchlyn Gottlich vnd nutze sey."

27. According to Cohrs, four reprints followed—one in Leipzig, one in Wittenberg, one unidentified printing, and one *Niederdeutsch* printing from Rostock or Lübeck, dated 16 February 1526. It was also printed three more times before 1530, once in Wittenberg and twice in Nuremberg, as part of Toltz's *Tropi biblici*.

28. Cohrs 3:359; HAB call no. 1222.98 Th. 8°. Rhau's initials appear in a shield on the title page.

29. These editions are not in Cohrs; see appendix 2 for the titles.

30. *VD* 16: G 3248–68 lists nineteen printings of this book, including one in Wittenberg in 1524. In addition, there were Wittenberg *Niederdeutsch* editions for two printings that were edited by Stephen Roth in 1525 and 1526.

In 1525 Stephen Roth published a new edition of this work for Wittenberg. At the same time (the title page bears the date 9 March 1525), Urbanus Rhegius published a new edition of his explanation of the Creed and the chief articles of the faith.[31] These two works would not fall within our purview were it not for the appearance in 1525 of a booklet that was based upon them. Published by the end of 1525, it was entitled "A Comforting Disputation Put in Question-and-Answer Form between Two Artisans, and Touching on Faith and Love and Other Christian Doctrines; Also the Form of How One Person Should Instruct Another in a Christian Fashion, Very Useful for the Articles of Doctor Urbanus Rhegius and Gretzinger."[32] Between 1525 and 1528 this work, ostensibly a dialogue between two artisans, appeared at least eighteen times in at least three different editions and in a *Niederdeutsch* translation; it was published in Wittenberg (eight times), Leipzig (five times), Augsburg (once), and Nuremberg (four times). While it was advertised as a supplement to the works of Rhegius and Gretzinger and is often found bound with one or both of those books, it was in fact an independent catechetical tract in the very question-and-answer form Luther had called for in the preface to the "Deutsche Messe."

Given Stephen Roth's reworking of Gretzinger's text, it is possible that he had something to do with the Wittenberg revisions of the "Disputation between Two Artisans" as well. In fact, when Agricola left his post as catechist at the Wittenberg city church, it seems that Roth may have filled those duties until he left for Zwickau in 1527.[33] We have already seen that he edited two catechetical pieces. Furthermore, once Agricola had left for Eisleben, Hausmann appealed to the native from Zwickau regarding the proposed catechetical work of Jonas and Agricola. Indeed, we find yet another 1525 booklet that could very well have been the work of either Jonas or Roth or both. (Certainly in its later editions, Roth played a special role.) That is "Eyn buchlin fur die leyen vnd kinder."

---

31. *VD* 16: R 2024–56 lists thirty-one printings of this work, including six in Wittenberg (of the new edition only). One of the six is in *Hochdeutsch* (1525) and the other five in *Niederdeutsch* (three from 1525, two from 1526).

32. "Ein trostliche disputation, auff frag vnd antwort gestellet: Von zwayen Handtwercks mennern den glauben vnd die liebbe auch andere Christliche leer betreffen, auch form wie einer den andern Christenlich vnterweysen sol, gantz nützlich zu den artickeln Doctoris Vrbani Regij vnd Gretzingers." Two editions of this booklet are mentioned by Cohrs 4:155, "German B & C," but only because these two printings contain Luther's five questions on the Lord's Supper. For a complete list of printings see appendix 2. Because the Nuremberg printing stated that it was "new corrigiert vnd gemert," there is good reason to assume that there were earlier editions.

33. Roth was called a "Hülfsprediger" already in 1524; see the *Allgemeine Deutsche Biographie* (1907 ed.), 53:564–67. He married Ursula Krüger, sister-in-law of the Wittenberg printer George Rhau, on 11 May 1524.

"Eyn buchlin fur die leyen vnd kinder"

In his work on the evangelical catechisms before Luther's, Cohrs argues that "Eyn buchlin" was first published in *Niederdeutsch*, probably by Johannes Bugenhagen of Pomerania, the new pastor of the city church of Wittenberg.[34] This theory is fraught with difficulties. It does not explain why all *Niederdeutsch* editions contain a separate booklet of titles that is not found in any *Hochdeutsch* version. Nor does it clarify why the second edition of the catechism appeared only in *Hochdeutsch*. Moreover, it sheds no light on why in 1527 printers in Strasbourg and Basel reprinted a *Hochdeutsch* version of what Cohrs presumed was the *Niederdeutsch* first edition—a version, however, that followed word for word the renderings of the *Hochdeutsch* second edition.

By positing the existence of an earlier *Hochdeutsch* edition, all the problems in Cohrs's theory disappear. The *Niederdeutsch* version would be a translation to which someone added the booklet of titles. The printers in Strasbourg and Basel would have used this first *Hochdeutsch* edition as the basis of their reprinting. The *Hochdeutsch* edition of which Cohrs was aware would have been a revision of the earlier *Hochdeutsch* printing. We need not speculate about such a printing, however, since in fact it exists, published by Nicholas Schirlentz in 1525.[35]

The complicated history of publication began with Schirlentz's printing of the book, probably in September or October 1525. The alphabet was followed by a "Lay Bible," the chief parts of the catechism, including (in order) the Ten Commandments, the Apostles' Creed, the Lord's Prayer, a proof text from Mark 16 for baptism, and the Words of Institution. The booklet then presented an excerpt from Luther's sermon "Eine kurze Form der zehn Gebote, etc." (*WA* 7:204, 214–20), which it called "Eyn unterweysung." There followed a series of prayers, including a morning order of blessing, the *Benedicite* and *Gratias* for meals, and a blessing from Psalm 63 for bedtime. After an excerpt from Luther's 1519 "Auslegung deutsch des Vaterunsers für die einfältigen Laien" (*WA* 2:128–30), the booklet concluded with a short discussion of *Buße*, for which no parallel exists in Luther's works.

Shortly after this first printing appeared, a *Niederdeutsch* edition, to which had been added the booklet of titles, rolled off the presses of Hans Weiß.[36] All other portions followed the Schirlentz edition. Be-

---

34. Cohrs's argument is taken over in the bibliography of *HKJL* 2:1088–90.

35. HAB call no. QuH 132.7 (5). This book does not appear in Cohrs (see appendix 2) or in *VD* 16. Given Rhau's later strong commitment to the work, it would not be surprising if he too had published a first edition.

36. Cohrs 1:187, "German a"; *VD* 16: B 6329; HAB call no. J 149.8° Helmst. (8). This kind of title booklet has a history of its own. It included ways to address the emperor, princes of various sorts, and the pope, cardinals, bishops, priests, abbots, and other clerics. The catechism is reprinted without the title booklet in Cohrs 1:200–236.

fore the end of the year, a Latin version appeared from the presses of George Rhau.[37] This printing included a table of contents, a conclusion to the Ten Commandments (*WA* 7:207), passages from 1 Corinthians 11 and Psalm 67, a new explanation of the Lord's Prayer (*WA* 7:220–29/*WA* 6:11–19) in place of the original (*WA* 2:128–30), and an explanation of *poenitentia* to which had been added material from Luther's sermon on the subject (*WA* 15:482.15–483.26), a reference to Melanchthon's *Loci*, and a discussion of auricular confession. Several passages from the Bible were appended at the end, including Matthew 6 (as found in Melanchthon's "Enchiridion"),[38] and Psalms 127, 122, and 128. The work concluded with a list of roman and arabic numbers.

Probably around the same time a short excerpt for young children appeared from some press in Wittenberg; it was reprinted by Jobst Gutknecht in Nuremberg and bore the title "Eyn Buchlyn daraus man die iungen knaben lernet lesen."[39] It contained the ABCs, the Lord's Prayer, the Ave Maria, and an explanation of the Creed.

Around the New Year, 1526, George Rhau published a second *Hochdeutsch* edition.[40] It contained from the Latin version the conclusion to the Ten Commandments, the added material on *Buße*, and a portion of Matthew 6. The words of institution now conformed to the version in the "Deutsche Messe." These three editions—*Niederdeutsch*, Latin, and second edition *Hochdeutsch*—were printed several times from 1526 through 1528.[41] In 1527 a new twist was added by the Strasbourg printer Hans Preüssen. He took Schirlentz's original edition and added to it a German translation of Melanchthon's "Enchiridion." This was reprinted in Basel and Strasbourg in the same year.[42]

37. Cohrs 1:189, "A"; HAB call no. 1250.7 Theol. (1). Not listed in *VD* 16, this version is reprinted in Cohrs 1:200–238.

38. See Cohrs 1:17–64.

39. Cohrs 1:192; *VD* 16: B 9113 and B 9114; HAB call no. QuH 161.26 (6).

40. Cohrs 1:190, "German A"; *VD* 16: B 9115. The date on the cover is 1525, but in the colophon, 1526.

41. *Niederdeutsch*, 1526: 1. Cohrs 1:187, "German b"; *VD* 16: B 6331 (Nicholas Schirlentz); 2. Cohrs 1:188, "German c"; *VD* 16: B 6332 (Hans Weiß); 3. *VD* 16: B 6330; HAB call no. QuH 169.4 (1) (Erfurt: Loorsfeld). *Niederdeutsch*, 1527: Cohrs 1:188, "German d"; *VD* 16: B 6333 (Erfurt: Loorsfeld). *Niederdeutsch*, around 1527: *VD* 16: B 6334; HAB call no. QuH 132.3 (1) (George Rhau). *Hochdeutsch*, 1526: Cohrs 1:190, "German B"; *VD* 16: B 9116 (George Rhau). *Hochdeutsch*, 1527: Cohrs 1:190, "German C"; *VD* 16: B 9117 (George Rhau). *Hochdeutsch*, 1528: Cohrs 1:190, "German D"; *VD* 16: B 9118 (Joseph Klug).

42. The original was printed on 11 May 1527; see Cohrs 1:22, "German C" (=*SM* 5.1:cxxvii, no. 2). The second printing was by Thomas Wolff in Basel on 1 June 1527; see Cohrs 1:22, "German D" (=*SM* 5.1:cxxvii, no. 3). The third printing occurred on 12 July (1527) by Wolff Köpphel; see Cohrs 1:23, "German E" (=*SM* 5.1:cxxviii, no. 5).

A completely new edition of "Eyn buchlin" appeared in 1528, this time from Zwickau itself, from the presses of Gabriel Kantz.[43] Cohrs surmises that this is the work of Nicholas Hausmann himself, but one cannot help thinking that Stephen Roth, the newly hired *Stadtschreiber*, might also have had his hand in this revision.[44] It began with letters, names, and common words; continued with the "Unterweysung" (*WA* 7:204), the five chief parts of the catechism, and the Ave Maria; and added biblical texts for baptism and infant baptism. After quoting John 13:34, it gave an expanded list of prayers and Luther's "Vermanung und kurtze Deutung" (*WA* 19:95.22–96.19) of the Lord's Prayer. It concluded with biblical material used in the liturgy (*Magnificat, Nunc dimittis, Benedictus*), and a collection of Luther's hymns, including some hymns from the "Deutsche Messe." There was no mention of confession in this work at all.

Just before this Zwickau catechism was to come off the presses, George Rhau wrote to his brother-in-law, Roth, about his plans for this very book. On 7 November 1527 he reported, "My prayer booklet, which you have prepared for me, I want—God willing—to start printing."[45] Three months later, on 10 February 1528, Rhau wrote: "You should also know that Dr. Martin has permitted me to print my prayer booklet (the one you put in order). And when I otherwise have nothing more to print, then I will typeset it. Already now I am having the illustrations prepared."[46] This letter proves that, at least at this stage, Stephen Roth served as editor, that George Rhau viewed the book as his, and that Martin Luther had approved its printing. Rhau did not publish just one version in 1529, but three: one in *Hochdeutsch* with an entire series of woodcuts, one in *Niederdeutsch*, and one in Latin.[47] Besides the new

43. Cohrs 1:191, no. 1; *VD* 16: B 9119.

44. Cohrs 1:180.

45. Roth, 66, no. 138: "Mein bettbuchlein, wilchs yhr mir zugericht habt, wil ich, ab gott wil, anheben zu drucken."

46. Roth, 70, no. 149: "Wisset auch das mir der Doctor Mart: erleubet hat mein Bett-buchlein (so yr mir yn ein ordenung gestellet habt) erleubet hat zu drucken, vnd wenn ich sonst nicht mehr zu drucken hab, so wil ichs aufflegen vnd ich lasse itzt die figuren dazu schneiden." Rhau's "prayer booklet" should not be confused with Luther's own, printed in this same period by Hans Lufft.

47. *Hochdeutsch*: Cohrs 1:191, "2A"; *VD* 16: B 9120. *Niederdeutsch*: Cohrs 1:188, "German e"; *VD* 16: B 6335; HAB call no. J 151.8° Helmst. (1). Latin: Cohrs 1:189, "B." In 1530 Joseph Klug reprinted the *Niederdeutsch* (Cohrs 1:189, "German f"; *VD* 16: B 6336) and George Rhau the Latin (Cohrs 1:190, "C"). The Latin and *Niederdeutsch* editions were basically reprints of the material from 1525. Besides the editions listed above, there are also a *Niederdeutsch* edition from Erfurt in 1531 (*VD* 16: B 6337) and one from Rostock in 1561 (*VD* 16: B 6338). An unidentified Wittenberg printing from 1534 (Cohrs 1:190, "German E"; *VD* 16: B 9121), which reproduced the 1526 *Hochdeutsch* edition, may also have come from Joseph Klug's press.

woodcuts, the new *Hochdeutsch* edition contained an expanded set of prayers and the "Kurtze deuttung" of the Lord's Prayer that is found in the Zwickau edition (*WA* 19:95.22–96.19). It also added a section entitled "Eine christliche weise zu beichten" and Melanchthon's "Etliche Sprüche."

As direct competition to Rhau's book, Hans Lufft reprinted Luther's "Prayer Booklet" of 1525, now including a calendar and a "Passional" with fifty woodcuts.[48] In the same year he also published a Latin version, including Melanchthon's paraphrase of the Lord's Prayer, a Latin version of Luther's Small Catechism, and an expanded version of the table of duties.[49]

Both editions from Rhau and Lufft in 1529 straddled the border between prayer book and catechism. With the addition of woodcuts and prayers, these books now defined much more clearly their edificatory purpose without giving up their pedagogical one. Edification and pedagogy were also intended in 1547 when near the end of his life George Rhau once again published a prayer book, called "Hortulus Animae," with a wealth of woodcuts, including one of the new evangelical saint, Martin Luther. In a poignant preface to his five daughters, Rhau described his duty as an evangelical father: "Now I have brought you to Christ and through others allowed you to be brought in that you received baptism and almost all of you memorized your catechism, as our dear lord and father Dr. Martin composed the same with a short explanation in question-and-answer form."[50] Rhau still retained Luther's paraphrase of the Creed from the original text of "Eyn buchlin."[51] He viewed this prayer book as fostering a second stage of evangelical piety to begin after baptism and the memorization of Luther's Small Catechism.

We have spent much time on "Eyn buchlin" because, as Cohrs himself asserts, it "is the most important publication of the catechism literature from the same period. It contains for the first time the five evangelical chief parts, which from now on are more and more generally accepted and through Luther's 'Enchiridion' are sanctioned. In this the

---

48. *WA* 10.2:359, "Z." This was reprinted immediately by Lufft in 1530.

49. *WA* 10.2:361, "m." This version is 16°, not 8° as indicated in the *WA*.

50. "HORTVLVS ANIMAE. I [red] Lustgarten der See= I [red] len: Mit schönen lieb= I [red] lichen Figuren. I [woodcut of Christ's resurrection] I [red] 1548." 4°. Colophon: "Gedruckt zu Wit= I temberg durch I Georgen I Rhaw. I [Leaf] I [Decoration]." A woodcut of Rhau appears on G.iii.r°. The quotation is from A.ij.v°: "Nu hab ich . . . euch zum Herrn Christo gebracht, vnd durch andere bringen lassen: Also das jr die Tauffe empfangen, vn[d] auch fast alle ewren Catechismum, wie denselbigen vnser lieber herr vnd vater D. Martinus mit einer kurtzen auslegung jnn Fragestücke gefasset, auswendig gelernet."

51. See Cohrs 1:207ff.

booklet forms a milestone in the history of the oldest evangelical cate-chisms."[52] Also included were prayers for mealtimes and a discussion of penance, which also form a portion of Luther's Small Catechism. The text, most likely prepared by a student and catechist from Wittenberg, interwoven with Luther's own words, and laced with Melanchthon's catechetical material in later editions (for which Melanchthon himself may have been asked to write new material), demands attention be-cause it depicted a very different understanding of *poenitentia* and law from Agricola's. If "Eyn buchlin" represented one attempt at catecheti-cal writing, stemming perhaps from half the team originally asked to write such a book, Agricola's work offered an opposing view.

The Catechetical Contributions of Melanchthon and Agricola

Within this crush of catechisms Melanchthon's and Agricola's contri-butions took their places. Melanchthon's early attempts were really quite insignificant compared to the enormous success enjoyed by the works of his friend from Eisleben. In 1523, at the same time Setzer began printing Melanchthon's *Annotationes in Johannem*, a small book-let appeared from the same press, "In caput Exodi XX Philipi Melanchth. Scholia."[53] This kind of material may well have originated not in formal lectures at the University of Wittenberg, but rather in lec-tures before Melanchthon's *schola privata*. From the same source we have his paraphrases of the Lord's Prayer that were used by Christopher Hegendorfer in 1526 and in the Latin version of Luther's "Prayer Book-let" in 1529.

In late 1523 Melanchthon published another catechetical work, again meant for young Latin students and perhaps coming from his *schola privata*, and more than likely published without his permission. An undated version appears with the title "Enchiridion elementorum puerilium. Vuittemberge."[54] This was almost immediately translated and, under the auspices of Jobst Gutknecht in Nuremberg, appeared with the title "Philipps Melanchthons Handtbüchlein, wie man die

---

52. Cohrs 4:249.

53. "IN CAPVT I EXODI .XX. PHILIPI I MELANCHTH. I SCHOLIA." 8°. [4] leaves. In *SM* 5.1:cxxv, Cohrs mistakenly counts this as a sixth printing. It was in fact the first and soon after its initial appearance was reprinted with other material. In 1523 Ulrich Morhard of Tübingen published it with Melanchthon's short commentary on Genesis (*SM* 5.1:cxxiii, no. 1). In 1524 it appeared in Nuremberg with the second edition of Luther's "On the Freedom of the Christian," and with Melanchthon's speech "De officio sacerdotali" (*SM* 5.1:cxxiv, no. 2). It also appeared three times in translation in 1525 (*SM* 5.1:cxxv f., nos. 1, 2, and 3), one of which (no. 3) was printed in Wittenberg.

54. *SM* 5.1:cxxvii, no. 8 (cf. also nos. 1 and 3, which I take to be references to the same printing). Joseph Klug reprinted this work in 1527 under the same title (*SM* 5.1:cxxvi, no. 4). Perhaps he was the original printer.

kinder zuo der geschrifft vnd lere halten sol. Wittenberg."[55] The printer's preface bore the date 26 December 1523. In January 1524, Simprecht Ruff, the Augsburg printer, combined the Latin version with a tract of Ulrich Zwingli.[56]

A third kind of material, which may also have arisen out of Melanchthon's attempts to catechize young students, was printed in 1527 under the title "Some Passages in Which the Entire Christian Life Is Contained, in All Ways Beneficial to Keep in View and to Consider."[57] Cohrs fixes its publication date as late 1527 and sees it as a response to Agricola's open attack in August and October of the same year.[58] However, a *Niederdeutsch* translation by Ludwig Dietz from Rostock or Lübeck that bore the date 1527 on the frontispiece and the words "Printed by Ludwig Dietz on 14 February" in the colophon makes this late dating impossible.[59] Cohrs was right, as we shall see, to interpret this work as Melanchthon's response to Agricola's understanding of *poenitentia* and law, but it was issued six months *before* the public dispute, not while it was going on![60]

While Melanchthon had entered the lists three times between 1523 and 1528,[61] Agricola was also busy with some entries of his own. Having earlier received from Luther the task to produce a catechism for Wittenberg, Agricola now set about completing the project as the newly installed rector of the Latin school in Eisleben.[62] The first result came with a Latin piece entitled "Elementa pietatis congesta," first published by Jo-

---

55. *SM* 5.1:cxxvii, no. 1; cf. *VD* 16: M 3173, where the printer is identified. This work reappeared in the three versions of "Eyn buchlin" published in Strasbourg and Basel in 1527 (*SM* 5.1:cxxvii f., nos. 2, 3, and 5; see n. 42). It was published separately, perhaps by a Wittenberg publisher, in 1529 (*SM* 5.1:cxxviii, no. 4).

56. *SM* 5.1:cxxvi, no. 2; *VD* 16: M 3168. This Latin version was reprinted shortly thereafter (*SM* 5.1:cxxvii, no. 9; *VD* 16: M 3172).

57. *SM* 5.1:cxxix: "Etliche spruch l darynn das ga= l ntz Christlich leben l gefasset ist, nutzlich l allweg fur augen l zu betrach= l ten/ l Philip. Melanch. l Wittemberg l 1527 l."

58. *SM* 5.1:cxxvii, cxix.

59. See *VD* 16: M 3320. The title reads: "Etlike spro l ke dar jnne dat gan= l tze Christlyke leuent l geuatet ys/ nutlick alle= l wege vor ogen tho heb l bende vnde tho be= l trachtende. l Philippus Mela[n]chthon l M.D.XXvij." 8°. [12] leaves.

60. Also mitigating against a publication date late in 1527 for "Etliche Sprüche" was its inclusion in Luther's "Prayer Booklet" printed in 1527 in Nuremberg by Jerome Formschneyder (*WA* 10.2:358f., "X"; *SM* 5.1:cxxx, no. 3). George Rhau included it as a separate part of his 1529 edition of "Eyn buchlin" (*SM* 5.1:cxxx, no. 2; *VD* 16: M 3316 and E 4083).

61. For discussion of the unfinished catechism of 1528 see pp. 146–48.

62. The teaching plan for the school (worked out in conjunction with Melanchthon?) proposed bringing the children to fear of God, to faith, and to good morals: "Et ut acuatur cura discendorum sacrorum in pueris non sufficiet his multa praelegisse. Sed cogentur ediscere orationem Dominicam, Symbolon Apostolorum, Decalogum, lectissimos psalmos et certos alios locos scripturae, qui ne e memoria excidant, exiget tanquam pensum diei Dominici praeceptor, ut recenseantur ordine memoriter" (Cohrs 2:3).

seph Klug in 1527.[63] At the same time a slightly expanded German version was also published by George Rhau under the title "Eine Christliche kinder zucht, ynn Gottes wort vnd lere, Aus der Schule zu Eisleben."[64] The prefatory letter to this version was dated 11 November 1526.[65] We know that it appeared very early in 1527 because on 17 February 1527 the preacher George Buchholzer (or as he put it, the "elected bishop" in Schönau) wrote a letter asking Stephen Roth to send him the *"kinder czucht* Ißlebij deusch (the 'Kinderzucht' of [John Agricola of] Eisleben in German)."[66] This book was an immediate success. In 1527 and 1528 we find it reprinted in Zwickau, Augsburg, and Nuremberg.[67] In Erfurt a small section of the work was published by Wolfgang Sturmer.[68]

Agricola, or perhaps his wife Else, who was possibly a teacher at the girls' school, quickly discovered that the "Kinderzucht" was too complicated for the capacities of beginning students. To remedy this problem, and also (it turned out) to attack directly Melanchthon's understanding of *poenitentia* and the law, Agricola reworked the piece into a question-and-answer form entitled "Hundert vnd Dreissig gemeyner Frage stücke/ für die iungen kinder/ ynn der Deudschen Meydlin Schule zu Eyssleben (130 Common Questions for the Young Children in the German Girls' School in Eisleben)." The preface, dated 18 November 1527, was written at the very height of the controversy with Melanchthon. The book first appeared early in 1528, published by George Rhau.[69] Its immediate success can be judged by the number of reprints: three in *Hochdeutsch* in 1528 and one in *Niederdeutsch*; two in an expanded edition in 1528; three in the same second edition in 1529.[70] Ten printings

63. Cohrs 2:12, "A"; *VD* 16: A 973. This was reprinted in Haguenau by Amandus Farcal in the same year (Cohrs 2:12, "B"; *VD* 16: A 972).

64. Cohrs 2:12, "German A"; *VD* 16: A 975 and 976 (two printings were made in this year).

65. Cohrs 2:18.

66. Roth, 56, no. 108. The fact that Buchholzer specified the German version may imply that the Latin was also available.

67. Zwickau: Gabriel Kantz, 1527 (Cohrs 2:13, "German B"; *VD* 16: A 977); (Augsburg: Philip Ulhart, Sr.) 1527 and 1528 (Cohrs 2:13, "German C and E"; *VD* 16: A 974 and 979, where the printer is identified); Nuremberg: George Wachter, 1528 (Cohrs 2:13, "German D"; *VD* 16: A 980). *VD* 16: A 978 lists an unidentified printing from 1528.

68. Cohrs 2:14; *VD* 16: A 981.

69. Cohrs 2:266, "German A"; *VD* 16: A 996. See also *HKJL* 2:210–22.

70. The "130 Questions" was reprinted in 1528 by John Stüchs in Nuremberg (Cohrs 2:267, "German B"; *VD* 16: A 992); by George Wachter in Nuremberg (Cohrs 2:267, "German C"; *VD* 16: A 993); by Gabriel Kantz in Zwickau (Cohrs 2:267, "German D"; *VD* 16: A 997); and in *Niederdeutsch* by John Weiss in Wittenberg (Cohrs 2:268, "German a"; *VD* 16: A 989). The "156 Questions" was printed in 1528 by Jobst Gutknecht in Nuremberg (Cohrs 2:268, "German E"; *VD* 16: A 991); by (John Knoblauch) in Strasbourg (Cohrs 2:268, "German F"; *VD* 16: A 995); in 1529 by Hans Lufft in Wittenberg (Cohrs 2:269, "German G"; *VD* 16: A 998); by George Wachter in Nuremberg (undated) (Cohrs 2:269, "German H"; *VD* 16: A 994); and by Melchior Sachssen in Erfurt (*VD* 16: A 990).

in two years! However, except for a Latin translation appearing in Berlin, Agricola's new home, in 1541, it was never printed after 1529, because a far more successful set of catechisms authored by Martin Luther himself began rolling off Wittenberg's presses at that very time.

Poenitentia in Wittenberg's Catechisms

With Luther's attack on the sacrament of penance already in "The Babylonian Captivity of the Church" (1520) and in his tract on private confession in the same year, the question of the positive role of this sacrament and its parts was up for grabs. In his *Loci communes* of 1521 Melanchthon still maintained the threefold division of the sacrament, but was careful to place it under baptism and to connect it with Christian freedom.[71] In 1524 a new phase of the discussion started with Luther's Palm Sunday sermon on the subject, which was immediately printed.[72] It was then quickly included in the Lenten portion of the *Kirchenpostille*, first published in 1525.[73] At the same time, the entire sermon found a place in Luther's "Prayer Booklet" of 1525, and a portion of it ended up in the second edition of "Eyn buchlin." Thus Luther's position affected the catechetical tradition from the start.

Luther's "Betbüchlein"

To begin with, in the sermon on *poenitentia* found in the "Prayer Booklet," Luther made the point that confession ought not be forced with threats, as the devil did under the papacy. He distinguished three kinds of confession. The first occurs before God, as David prays in Psalm 32, and involves the admission of our sinfulness. This kind of confession is of the highest necessity and marks the entire life of the Christian. The second kind occurs before one's neighbor and arises from love, in the way the first arises from faith. This second kind is described in James 5:16: we confess to our neighbor to whom we have done harm. Like the previous kind of confession, this, too, is commanded and thus is a necessary fruit of faith.

The third kind is auricular confession, on which Luther concentrated his remarks. It is not commanded by God; the pope, however, had made it mandatory and thus martyred many consciences. This

71. *MSA* 2.1:149–55.
72. See *WA* 15:439f. for the printing history of the sermon and *WA* 15:481–505 for the text. Within two years it was printed four times in Wittenberg by three different printers, including George Rhau.
73. *WA* 10.1–2: XV–XXI; *WA* 17.2:246f. This Postil was published eight times separately (including the famous theft by the Regensburg printer Paul Kohl) and seven times (before 1530) with the Advent and Christmas Postil.

kind of confession has to occur freely, because God wants people to come to him of their own free will. Moreover, although one cannot be forced to come, this kind of confession is good, because it contains in it the absolution of the gospel. Whenever a preacher opens his mouth, out comes the gospel promising forgiveness to those who believe. This comment introduced Luther's practical advice: when going to the priest, do not be as concerned about confessing as about hearing the absolution.

Confession, like the Lord's Supper, holds this advantage over preaching the gospel: it is completely personal. We would go to the ends of the earth to hear an angel, and yet the Scriptures prove that God himself speaks the absolution through the priest. Moreover, even if confession did not involve the word of God, it would still afford the opportunity to seek counsel and support from a Christian brother. While Luther refused to make it mandatory that a Christian go to confession before the Lord's Supper, still he urged his listeners that they receive God's word as often as possible.

Luther's conclusion stressed the centrality of the absolution and contrasted evangelical confession to that of the past, where a person was forced to perform works of satisfaction. A closing paragraph gave practical advice concerning how one should confess. Whereas confession in the past had been characterized by references to the seven deadly sins or the Ten Commandments in an effort to discover one's sins and by related pressure to remember all one's sins, Luther countered with the simple advice to confess only those sins that bother the conscience.

All in all, Luther's view of auricular confession was very positive. He sought to tread a fine line between the freedom of confession and the importance of the gospel. He did not emphasize the law as a means of discovering one's sins or of forcing confession. On the other hand, he also did not exclude sorrow over sin—especially from the first and second kinds of confession. He turned private confession into an opportunity for receiving a personal gospel, even more direct than a sermon. A crucial point for the later debate is that Luther saw faith as the origin of the first kind of confession, love as the origin of the second, and the gospel as the origin of the third. Faith in Christ, sorrow over sin, law and gospel all have their place in this sermon as reproduced in the "Prayer Booklet."

"Eyn buchlin fur die leyen vnd kinder"

On the question of *poenitentia* and confession, "Eyn buchlin" presented two different views. In the only part of the first edition without a parallel in Luther's extant writings, the author placed the discussion of confession at the very end of the work.[74] He spoke of two different kinds of confession. The one, which is demanded by God and without which we cannot become holy, flows from faith. We confess that we are eternally lost, that our works mean nothing to God, and that only through pure grace and mercy can we become righteous. There followed a series of proof texts, including Psalm 32:5b and a sizable portion of the parable of the tax collector and Pharisee (Luke 18), which concluded that Christ absolved the one and damned the other. This kind of confession must occur without hypocrisy or self-made thoughts, and from the "bottom of one's heart." Where this occurs, God's grace is surely present. This kind of confession is performed every time we recite the Lord's Prayer. So far this edition of "Eyn buchlin" matched Luther's discussion of the first type of *poenitentia*.

The second kind of *poenitentia* is to one's neighbor. However, what the author had in mind was not Luther's second kind of confession, but the third, except that it was not understood as a sacrament. This kind, unlike the first, is not necessary, but is useful and comforting, since the neighbor has God's word and can impart the gospel to the one confessing. There is no better way to plague the devil and bring peace to the conscience than through this kind of confession. Here the author cited Matthew 18 as proof that as Christians and coheirs of Christ we have authority to forgive one another.

In the first edition of "Eyn buchlin" the author presented a view of *poenitentia* completely severed from the sacramental life of the church. One is to go to a neighbor who has God's word. It is significant that the closing remarks omitted any reference to the role of the priest and instead viewed confession in terms of the priesthood of all believers.

In the Latin edition of "Eyn buchlin," published shortly before the end of 1525, the editor left out the section on the two kinds of confession. At the beginning of 1526 it was also omitted from the second *Hochdeutsch* edition. Instead, a small portion of Luther's sermon on confession, drawn from his "Prayer Booklet" and dealing with the three kinds of confession, was inserted, both in the opening paragraph and as

---

74. See Cohrs 1:176–78 for his theory that the material stems from "Eyn sendebrieff | herrn Johan Bugenhagen | Pomern/ Pfarrer zu | Wittemberg/ vber | eyne frage vom | Sacrament. | Item eyn vnter | richt von der beycht vnd | Christlichen absolution. | Wittemberg | MDXXV." The letter is dated at the end: "Geschriben zu Wittemberg am midwochen fur Epiphanie Domini [4 January] M.D.XXV." 4°. [6] leaves. [Rhau-Grünenberg.] There were some parallels in words and phrases, and the letter, like the booklet, did divide confession into two, rather than three, kinds. It was less a source than representative of the teaching in the Wittenberg city church at that time. Someone familiar with the letter, such as Stephen Roth, could easily have used it as the basis for his own explanation of confession.

a replacement for the section on the two kinds of confession. At the end of the *Hochdeutsch* edition, the editor added, "Read more about this in the *Prayer Booklet* of D. Martin Luther."[75] In the Latin, the reference is even more instructive: "Read the remaining things in either the *Loci communes* of Philip or in the booklet of Dr. Martin concerning confession."[76] So in later editions of "Eyn buchlin" the compiler placed himself squarely on Melanchthon's side.

However, the actual editing had a different effect. From the first edition both the section that discussed the origin of confession (it arises out of a faith that admits to being eternally lost save for God's mercy) and the reference to Jesus' parable were retained. But the editor cut Luther's discussion of the kinds of confession short, including practically everything on the first two kinds,[77] and leaving next to nothing on the third. He mentioned the fact that auricular confession was commanded by the pope, not by God, and that thereby many souls had been martyred. All of the positive things Luther had to say about auricular confession completely disappeared into a footnote sending the reader to other books. The asacramental position in the first edition now bordered on the antisacramental. This differed sharply even from the Latin edition, which contrasted the practice of confession under the pope ("conscientiarum carnificina") to the anguished conscience' need to seek spiritual counsel and the consolation of the word of God.[78] Whether the omission of Luther's positive assessment of auricular confession was intentional cannot be shown from the text. The various editions of this text did demonstrate, however, that the understanding of *poenitentia* and confession was very fluid in Wittenberg, and could include positions that downplayed or omitted the sacrament altogether.

Other Catechetical Material

Other instructional material produced in Wittenberg before Agricola's *Elementa pietatis* generally expressed very positive assessments of *poenitentia*. Question 67 of the "Kinderfragen" asked whether confession might still be practiced. The author answered quite confidently, "Yes, confession may be practiced," but then reminded the children that only the passion of Christ, not confession, rosaries, psalms, and other works, frees from sins.[79] Proper confession has a different basis, namely the conscience that, being filled with fear before the

---

75. Cohrs 1:236: "Dauon lies weytter yn dem Bettbüchlyn D. Mart. Luth."
76. Cohrs 1:236: "Reliqua lege vel in Locis communibus Philippi, vel in libello D. Martini de Confessione."
77. *WA* 15:482.23–484.18.
78. Cohrs 1:236.
79. Müller, *Deutschen Katechismen*, 181f.

judgment of God, comes to trust in Jesus Christ.[80] This is what Paul meant by cleansing out the old leaven and bringing in the new creature. Having been cleansed of sins by God's grace, we then turn from evil desires to good ones, presenting our bodies as living sacrifices (Rom. 12) and forgiving our neighbors. Here this positive assessment stopped short of a discussion of the sacrament itself. The author discussed instead what Luther described under the first two kinds of confession: the penitent moves from fear of God's judgment to faith in Christ's forgiveness.

John Toltz's catechism reflected Luther's assessment of confession quite clearly. He wrote that in the Scriptures God commands two kinds of confession from the believer. The one occurs in God's presence and involves admission of one's sins and the request for God's mercy. The other occurs when one confesses to a neighbor whom one has injured. The third form of confession, in use for a long time, has not been commanded by God but by human beings. Toltz went on to counsel that this form of confession is not unfruitful, since one can use it freely to seek counsel and admit one's sinfulness.[81] Despite the generally positive view of this third kind of confession, the centrality of the gospel, so crucial to Luther's argument, is completely lacking in Toltz's explication. He even neglects to mention the importance of Christ's death and God's mercy in the first two kinds of confession.

The "Comforting Disputation between Two Artisans" expresses the most favorable understanding of confession. When the work was re-edited for Wittenberg's presses, the section on confession, which fell near the back of the Nuremberg edition, was brought to the front to conclude a discussion of good works. The initial question in this part of the dialogue tried to clear up a misconception about the evangelical position on confession. One artisan observes, "They say I should not go to confession."[82] The answer begins by criticizing the mandatory nature of auricular confession. The author continues, "First, however, I want to tell you about contrition (*Reu*), then about confession, and finally about *Buße*."[83] This very traditional threefold division, where *Buße* is understood as penitential satisfaction, would in 1527 spark Agricola's dissatisfaction with the Visitation Articles.

---

80. Müller, *Deutschen Katechismen*, 182: "Ouerst bote möte wy dön, Na einer anderen wyse, Nömelyken also, wenner wy vnse sünde bekennen, so vorschercket sick vnse conscientie vör dem rechten gerychte Gades. . . ."

81. Cohrs 1:255.

82. *Disputation*, B.v.v°: "Man sagt ich darff nicht beichten."

83. *Disputation*, B.vi.r°: "Erstlich aber will ich dir sagen von der rew/ darnach von der beicht/ yn letzt von der puß." Here the author separates the subject into the traditional medieval divisions of contrition, confession, and satisfaction.

The author of the "Artisans' Disputation" placed his discussion of contrition within a dialogue about how God makes a righteous person out of a sinner. Because we are joined with Christ who died and rose, we, too, must undergo death and resurrection. "First God terrifies the person with the law, so that the person has an anxious conscience in the face of the knowledge of one's sin." Then God comes "and sweetly comforts the person by means of the gospel."[84] This effects such a fundamental change in penitents that they come to abhor their previous life and through the Spirit willingly put to death all carnality out of love for righteousness. Such mortification of the flesh and renewal of the spirit is called contrition (*Reu*) and comes not from human powers but as a gift of God.

The discussion of contrition leads directly to the question of confession itself. Here auricular confession is the presumed context, and receiving the gospel the purpose. "In confession this divine word is spoken: Your sins are forgiven you."[85] The point is not the recitation of sins and one's past life, but the future life. God has set up three kinds of confession in the Scriptures. The first occurs before God alone, when a person confesses one's sins. Without this confession sins cannot be forgiven. "Christ is not Christ for you unless you confess that you are sick."[86] The second form of confession is to one's neighbor and is called "brüderliche beicht."[87] "The third kind of confession occurs when one accuses oneself not only before God but also before other people, because for a true Christian, auricular confession is not difficult but good."[88] Two things should motivate a Christian to this form of confession: "the holy cross, that is, shame and disgrace, and second, the comforting promise of God."[89]

After practical examples of how to frame confession to a priest, there followed a discussion of *Buße*, here understood as satisfaction. Nowhere in the Scriptures is satisfaction demanded of us for sin. Only the precious holy death of Christ makes satisfaction. Accordingly, Christ

---

84. *Disputation*, B.vi.v°: "Von ersten erschreckt er [Gott] den menschen mit dem gesetz/ das der mensch ein engstigs gewissen hatt vor erkentnis seiner sunde. . . . Vnd [Gott] tröst den menschen süssiglich durch das Euangelion."

85. *Disputation*, B.vii.r°: "Ynn der beicht wird diß Göttliche wort gesprochen/ Dir werden vergeben deine sunde."

86. *Disputation*, B.vii.v°: "Christus ist dir nicht Christus/ denn allein du bekennest dich kranck."

87. *Disputation*, B.viii.r°.

88. *Disputation*, B.viii.v°: "Die dritte beicht/ wenn sich der mensch nicht allein daheym fur yhm selbs Gott beklagt sondern auch fur andern leuten/ Denn einem rechten Christen menschen ist die oren beicht nicht schwer/ sondern gut."

89. *Disputation*, B.viii.v°: "das heilig creutz/ das ist/ schand vnd scham/ das ander das tröstlich verheissen Gottes."

did not demand satisfaction of the woman taken in adultery; "it was enough not to do the thing again."[90]

Here we have encountered the most positive assessment of confession. Although the author recognized the abuse of forced auricular confession, he clearly derived all three kinds of confession from the Scripture. He used the medieval division of *poenitentia* into contrition, confession, and satisfaction, criticizing only the third part and replacing it with the satisfaction made by Christ on the cross. He retained the movement from death to resurrection in contrition and forgiveness, and connected it both with Christ's death and resurrection and with law and gospel. He also connected the phrase "nymmer thue" with "puß," not as a way of defining *poenitentia* as a whole, but as a way of eliminating medieval understandings of satisfaction.

The Law in Wittenberg's Catechisms

Luther's "Betbüchlein"

From its first appearance in 1522, Luther's "Prayer Booklet" contained "Eine kurze Form der zehn Gebote, Eine kurze Form des Glaubens, Eine kurze Form des Vater unsers" from 1520.[91] Three things a person needs to know to become holy: first, what to do and what to avoid (Ten Commandments); second, where to turn for help upon realizing that one cannot through one's own power do and avoid what is commanded (Creed); third, how one then ought to search for and obtain such help (Lord's Prayer). Luther compared these three parts of Christian knowledge to a sick man's need to know what the sickness is, then what the remedy is, and finally where the remedy is to be found. "The commandments teach people to recognize their sin, so that they see and sense what they can and cannot do or refrain from doing, and so that they recognize themselves to be sinners and evil human beings."[92] We begin with the commandments, Luther continued, for this reason: "to teach and recognize our sin and evil (that is, spiritual sickness), through which we do not do or refrain from doing as we ought."[93]

Luther then worked through each commandment, showing first how they are broken and then how they are fulfilled. He concluded that the

90. *Disputation*, C.ij.r°: "gnügen das man nymmer thue."

91. *WA* 7:204–29 (= *WA* 10.2:376–407).

92. *WA* 10.2:377.4–6: "Alßo leren die gepot den menschen seyn kranckheyt erkennen, das er sihet/ und empfindet, was er thun und nit thun, lasszen und nit lassen kan und/ erkennet sich eynen sunder und boßen menschen."

93. *WA* 10.2:377.15f.: "zu leren und/ erkennen unßere sund, boßheyt, das ist geystliche kranckeyt, da durch wyr nit thun noch lassen, wie wyr wol schuldig seyn."

commandments, as Augustine had already said, forbid self-love and are fulfilled only through love of God and neighbor. What we learn from the commands, Luther summarized, is that human beings do not live well. In the Creed we discover where we can get that which we need to live well and fulfill the commandments.[94]

Here we discover a very positive approach to the law. Without any second thoughts Luther saw the commandments as providing human beings crucial knowledge about themselves and their positions, and as revealing the depth of the illness so that they can seek help from God's mercy. He did not foreshorten the law's work. The law is not made irrelevant by the gospel, nor does it cause resentment against or increased dread of God and his judgment.

"Eyn buchlin fur die leyen vnd kinder"

A portion of the section on the commandments found its way from Luther's "Prayer Booklet" into "Eyn buchlin." In three short sentences the editor rephrased Luther's opening remarks regarding the three things needed for salvation. On the commandments the editor wrote simply, "First, the Ten Commandments teach so that individuals know what they should do or refrain from doing. Second, when they now see that they cannot from their own powers do or refrain from doing these very things . . . ."[95] Despite the fact that this is the only statement in "Eyn buchlin" about the law, the main point of Luther's exposition remained intact. The commandments tell us what we are to do and what we are to avoid. When we see that we can neither do what we ought nor avoid sin by our own powers, God provides the Creed and Lord's Prayer.

The Works of Gretzinger and Rhegius

Although neither Gretzinger nor Rhegius discussed *poenitentia*, both made comments on the law. The work of Gretzinger as edited by Stephen Roth contained this straightforward statement: the law shows that it is impossible for human beings from their own powers to fulfill the law. Our hope and comfort lie in Christ. When asked why the law was given, Gretzinger described the fall and human weakness and stated that the law "brings us to a knowledge of ourselves and our sin and makes us ashamed and completely doubting of ourselves."[96] We have recourse only in Christ.

---

94. *WA* 10.2:385.14–19 and 388.15–18.

95. "Eyn buchlin" (Schirlentz, 1525), A.vii.r°: "Zum ersten/ das er wisse/ was er thun und lassen sol/ das leren yhn die Zehen gepott. Zum andern/ wen er nu sicht/ das er das selbige nicht thun noch lassen kan/ aus seynen krefften/. . ."

96. Gretzinger, A.vi.v°: ". . . vns bringt zu erkentnis vnser selbs/ vnd vnser sund/ vnd vns zu schanden mach/ vnd an vns selbs lere verzweifflen."

Rhegius also dealt with the meaning of law. Law is a judgment, so that "one commands the good and forbids the evil."[97] This law is spiritual and seeks out the desires of the heart. It can be fulfilled only by the Spirit. As a result, "with the law people come no further than into terror and recognition of their sin and damnation."[98] Under his discussion of the gospel, Rhegius returned to the law, describing how it frightens human beings and shows their misdeeds. Contrariwise, "the gospel comforts the individual and shows one the physician."[99] Under the rubric "Christian Freedom," Rhegius returned again to the question of the law, this time indirectly, warning that Christian freedom is such that not the law but human beings are changed.[100] To say that one has faith is no excuse for not doing good: "This is not right. One ought not make a cover for villainy."[101]

Rhegius, unlike the catechisms we have examined so far, stressed the law's effect on us. He also tried to prevent an interpretation of Christian freedom that would lead to license. He alluded to the Augustinian metaphor of sickness used by Luther, but made the gospel the place where we discover not the cure, but the physician.

"The Disputation between Artisans"

The discussion of law in the "Artisans' Disputation" echoed the works of Gretzinger and Rhegius. In his discussion of contrition, the author described how God terrifies the human being with the law. He tied the work of the law to mortification, something that comes not from our powers, but from the Holy Spirit.

Curiously, several sections of the Nuremberg second edition were left out of the Wittenberg editions, including a more thorough discussion of mortification and its links to baptism and the preaching of the law. This included Rhegius's claim that the law is spiritual, but we are carnal; the description of the new birth in baptism as taking place through law and gospel; and the entire discussion introduced by "Dear brother, tell me how the death of the old creature and the life of the new occur."[102] This section had described how the law terrifies us and according to Galatians 3 is our "disciplinarian to Christ (*Zuchtmeister zu*

97. Rhegius, F.i.r°: ". . . man guts gepeut vnd böses verpeut."
98. Rhegius, F.i.r°: "Man kömpt mit dem gesetz nicht weiter denn ynn erschrecken vnd erkentnis seiner sunde vnd verdamnis."
99. Rhegius, F.i.r°: "Das Euangelion tröst den menschen/ vnd zeigt yhm den artzt."
100. Rhegius, H.vi.v°.
101. Rhegius, H.vii.r°: "Das ist nicht recht/ man sol der büberey damit kein deckmantel machen."
102. *Disputation* (Nuremberg, 1525), C.iv.v°: "Lieber bruder sag mir wie geschicht die tödtung des alten menschen vnd das leben des newen?"

Christo)." Whatever the reasons for these omissions may have been, the end result abbreviated discussion of law and curtailed its function. Nevertheless, what remained still linked the law to mortification and, like Rhegius, stressed its terrifying nature.

Other Wittenberg Catechisms

George Rauth, silent about confession, described the law as a clear mirror which serves human beings in that it enables them to recognize their sins. When the law comes with its eternal curse and one cannot fulfill the least of it, "what can otherwise follow from that except that I have to despair of my own powers?" The law does all this through its strict righteousness "as its own work prior to the coming of grace."[103] Rauth went on to contrast the light burden of Christ with the heavy and bitter one of Moses. The work of the law in our hearts comes from God alone and is a matter of killing and making alive, which is then "the proper *Buße* for sin" preached by John the Baptist and given alone by God.[104] Rauth then described the good preacher who terrifies the people through preaching the law, so that "the whole world becomes too small for them,"[105] after which the gospel must be preached. As he expounded on the movement from law to gospel and on the terrifying nature of the law, Rauth linked the law directly to *Buße* and preaching.

Toltz explained the issue in much the same way. He defined the law in terms of recognizing both sin and God's judgment. He followed with a discussion of the gospel.[106] Hegendorfer, on the contrary, gave a completely moralistic view of the Ten Commandments. Children are to learn what they owe God and their neighbor. The notion of the law's revealing sin, terrifying sinners, or driving to Christ was not discussed at all.[107]

Agricola and Melanchthon on *Poenitentia* and the Law

Given this background, we can better understand the contributions of Agricola and Melanchthon in the mid-1520s and their developing disagreement on *poenitentia* and the law. We can discern, in at least one instance, Melanchthon's moralizing approach to the law. More importantly, we discover Agricola's distinctly different approach to both

---

103. Rauth, C.ij.rº: "Was sol denn anders draus folgen/ denn das ich an allen meinen eignen krefften mus verzagen . . . vnd das ist vor der gnad sein eigen werck."
104. Rauth, C.ij.vº: "die rechte puß der sunden."
105. Rauth, C.iij.rº: "die welt wil yhm zu eng werden."
106. Cohrs 1:247.
107. Cohrs 3:369.

topics. When Melanchthon in his own catechetical contributions began to counter this new theological option, the stage was set for controversy.

In 1525 Melanchthon's scholia to Exodus 20, first published in Latin by Setzer in 1523, was translated and published in Wittenberg. His approach to the law mirrored his earlier comments in the *Loci*. Speaking of the power of the law, Melanchthon raised the stakes above anything heretofore noted in other similar works. The knowledge of the law is absolutely necessary because we cannot discover nor experience the gospel in our hearts without it! The law must first, like the thunder at Sinai, "frighten and terrify" the consciences.[108] In his summary Melanchthon noted that in Exodus 20 we have first the recitation of the law, then the revelation of its power, and finally instruction that the law is not fulfilled through our "diligence, effort, work, or thought, and that we should not trust in our works."[109]

This straightforward distinction between law and gospel is missing from Melanchthon's other early work, the "Enchiridion elementorum puerilium." In his preface to this collection of quotations from the Bible and classical sources, Melanchthon argued that Christ's command to "let the children come to me" implied that it is necessary to learn to read. Christ has given us a gift in the Scriptures that we need to hold as religiously as we would any other gift. Those who refuse to learn to read reject Christ's command.[110]

The structure of the "Enchiridion" also set a moralizing tone. It used the traditional medieval division of the catechism, beginning with the Lord's Prayer, moving to the Creed, and ending with, not just the Ten Commandments, but also the Sermon on the Mount, Romans 12, and John 13. After a collection of wise, moralistic sayings, the "Enchiridion" concluded with a variety of prayers for schoolchildren to use as they perform their various tasks. If Cohrs is right, the "Enchiridion" reflects daily life in Melanchthon's own *schola privata*.

Certainly we find nothing in these small contributions of Melanchthon that could, in the context of the other catechetical materials under investigation, be called provocative. In Agricola's "Elementa," however, we encounter just such a work. In his introduction to the Ten Commandments, Agricola took an approach already encountered in other

---

108. *SM* 5.1:16.22 ("entsetzen und erschrecken"). This was repeated at 17.1–5.

109. *SM* 5.1:19.12–15: ". . . fleiß, müe, arbait oder gedancken, und das wir nit sollen vertrauen in unsere werck."

110. *SM* 5.1:20f. (=*MBW* 153 [*T*1:153]). It can be argued that Melanchthon understood instruction to fall under what he later called the first (i.e., civil) use of the law and not the second, a fact that could explain the moralizing tone. However, the "Enchiridion" is simply too brief to determine this with certainty.

contemporary catechisms. He too spoke about the thunder, and he maintained that the law shows us our sins for the purpose of driving every soul that recognizes the greatness of its sins to give up on itself and its own counsels.[111] But then Agricola added this characteristic twist: "[Human] nature, flesh and blood, nevertheless searches for and loves that which does it good and, again, is hostile to and hates all that does it harm and opposes it. Thus, the law is, as the Germans say, 'a cudgel by the dog,' so that it does not become too excited but rather, against its own ideas, remains a little tame."[112]

No other catechism had made such a statement. Others, as we have seen, described the law's effect in terms of terror, mortification, contrition, or *poenitentia*. They began with the human predicament and estrangement from God, but only to set the stage for the law's effect. According to Agricola, however, the law remains ineffective. It discloses sin; the human flesh is kept in check. Our lusts are tamed or restrained by the law's threats, not killed. The explanation of the commandments themselves, like Agricola's discussion in the introduction to the annotations on Luke, served to heighten the guilt of the students. It concluded: "Thus all of us, who are born of Adam, become guilty of the laws and all commandments of God our Lord."[113]

In Agricola's discussion of the Creed we do not find, as in the other catechisms, that the law drives to faith. Instead, he begins by discussing in nearly ontological terms the exclusion of knowledge from matters of faith: "The word *faith* [in the Creed] proves that these articles are all foreign to nature, strange, and impossible to understand. For what must be believed is above all sense, human reason, knowledge, and understanding. One sees nothing, grasps nothing; one only believes it."[114] This division between knowledge and faith, coupled with Agricola's negative assessment of the law, left him next to no room to move from law to gospel. Whereas Luther and most other catechists took for granted that the Ten Commandments, Creed, and Lord's Prayer impart

111. Cohrs 2:20.
112. Cohrs 2:21: "Natur, fleisch vnd blut sucht doch das vnd liebet es das yhm wol thut, herwidderumb, so ist es alle dem feind vnd hasset es, das yhm wehe thut vnd zuwidder ist. Also ist das gesetze, wie wir Deudschen sagen, ein knöttel bey dem hunde, das er nicht allzu geyl werde, sondern ein wenig zam, widder seinen danck." For the saying "to lay the cudgel by the dog," see Jacob and Wilhelm Grimm, *Deutsches Wörterbuch* (Leipzig, 1873), 5:1532. It meant "to keep one from becoming proud."
113. Cohrs 2:35: "Derhalben werden wir hie alle schüldig am gesetze vnd an allen gepotten Gottes vnsers Herrn, die von Adam geborn seyn."
114. Cohrs 2:45: "Das wörtlin glaub schleusset, das diese Artickel alle der Natur frembde, seltzam vnd vnmüglich seyn zu begreiffen. Denn was man gleuben mus, das ist vber alle synne, alle menschen vernunfft, witz vnd verstand, man sihet nichts, man greiffet nichts, man gleubt es nür."

some knowledge, Agricola began with the total impossibility of knowing matters of faith. For him faith preceded knowledge of sin.

This bifurcation makes the next move in Agricola's catechism completely understandable. In the context of the Creed he discussed the forgiveness of sins, a central category in his thought, describing it as the "military drums with which one calls the faithful to arms and defense, to the holy community."[115] In the description of the way one comes to experience forgiveness, Agricola excluded the law completely. "In matters pertaining to our Lord God, whether large or small, one must pay attention to two things: the word and faith."[116] But by the term *word* Agricola meant exclusively the gospel. Thus he continued, "Therefore, when one speaks in the gospel about the forgiveness of sins . . . let yourself be content with the words and believe them."[117]

This de facto exclusion of the law before the gospel did not mean that Agricola did not try to structure the life of the believer. He began a lengthy discussion of marriage by calling upon a distinction in Ephesians 1:8 between wisdom (*weisheit, sapientia*) and prudence (*klugheit, prudentia*). The word *wisdom* has to do with faith and doctrine, the word *prudence* with the "external way of life of those who among the people on earth are believers."[118] Just as a good soul wants a beautiful body, so the one who has the Holy Spirit (wisdom) must relate to others in a Christian and friendly manner (prudence). Agricola then divided his comments on marriage between wisdom (marriage is a blessing from God, a "hospice and house of service [*Spital vnd diensthaus*]," a secret depiction of the church and Christ) and prudence (here he described the relations between men and women in terms of Eph. 5).

Agricola concluded his catechism with a discussion of *poenitentia*. Even more than in the discussion of the law, we discover here how different his approach was from that found in contemporaneous catechisms. There is no discussion of confession or contrition, to say nothing of the law. Instead, we have here a simplified version of the ideas expounded in his exegetical works (see ch. 1):

115. Cohrs 2:64: "heertrumme, damit man berüfft zu rüstung vnd gegenwere, zu der heiligen gemeynschafft die gleubigen."
116. Cohrs 2:66: "Yn vnsers Herr Gotts sachen, sie seyn gros oder kleine, so mus man auf zwey ding acht haben. Auf das wort, vnd auf den Glauben."
117. Cohrs 2:66: "Also, wenn man saget ym Euangelio von vergebung der sunden . . . , so las dir schlecht an den worten genügen, vnd gleube yhnen."
118. Cohrs 2:75: "eusserlichen wandel der, die da gleuben vnter den leuten auf erden." It is no wonder that ten years later, during the antinomian controversy involving Luther and Agricola, the cry was heard that the law belonged in city hall ("Das Gesetz auf dem Rathaus").

On Buße

1. The person who is sorry for something is already free of sin. *Buße* is
a new heart and a different way of thinking, as when the person who previously desired to be unchaste now hates it. Ephesians 5 [4:28]: "Let the
one who previously stole steal no longer." In sum, "the highest *Buße* is
never to do it again."
2. Neither alms, works, fasts, nor our satisfaction bestows this new
heart and different way of thinking. Instead, the Holy Spirit, whom Christ
has given to us out of pure grace after he ascended into heaven, creates
them.[119]

Agricola completely severed *poenitentia* from the sacramental system
of the church. He described only an inner transformation of the mind
in which the believer has exchanged old desires for new thoughts. The
goal of the Christian life, the highest *poenitentia*, becomes the exclusion
of bad behavior. Unlike the "Artisans' Disputation," which understood
"Nymmer thun" (Christ's words to the woman taken in adultery) as excluding works of satisfaction, Agricola construed Ephesians 4:28 to
eliminate the entire sacramental movement from contrition to absolution to works. Moreover, he eliminated works of satisfaction not so
much because Christ had satisfied the just demands of the law for our
sins,[120] but because the Holy Spirit transforms our minds and does
these works.[121]

Agricola's understanding of law and *poenitentia* had moved beyond
obscure references in his commentaries and sermons into booklets intended for both the young people of Saxony and Thuringia and their
teachers. For those who had presented a more positive assessment of
law and especially of *poenitentia*, this pair of catechisms in Latin and
German could well have come as something of a surprise. As we shall
soon discover, their appearance in January 1527, along with Agricola's

119. Cohrs 2:83: "Von der Busse 1. Wem ein ding leyd ist, der ist schön der sunden
los. Busse ist ein newes hertz vnd andere gedancken, als, Wer vorhyn hat lust gehabt zu
vnkeuscheit, vnd wird yhr ytzund feind, Ephe. 5. Wer vorhyn gestolen hat, der steele ytzund nymmer, Yn Summa, Nymmer thun ist die höchste busse. 2. Dis newe herze vnd
andere gedancken gibt widder almussen, nach wercke, nach fasten, nach vnser genugthuung, sondern der heilige geist machet sie, den vns Christus geschencket hat aus laut-
ern gnaden, da er gen hymel gefaren ist." The last phrase in the Latin reads, "but the Holy
Spirit, imparted by the blood of Christ, supplies and effects them (sed spiritus sanctus,
partus Christi sanguine, suppeditat atque efficit)."
120. To be sure, in the Latin version the Holy Spirit was said to be imparted "sanguine
Christi," but this was a far cry from the discussions of Melanchthon and others on the
satisfaction of Christ.
121. Uncertainty about the gift of the Holy Spirit seems implied here. Elsewhere Agricola wrote that through the firmness of our faith we know we have the Holy Spirit.

sermons on Colossians and his new translation of Melanchthon's commentary on Romans and 1–2 Corinthians, sparked Melanchthon's two-pronged response. The exegetical response is to be found in Melanchthon's *Scholia*. The catechetical response is found in Melanchthon's "Etliche Sprüche" and especially in the Visitation Articles. As in his contemporaneous attack on Erasmus's position on free will, Melanchthon's offensive took place under cover of darkness: no names were named, and every conceivable indirect method was utilized. When, with the appearance of the Visitation Articles, Agricola found himself outflanked, he went public and created the most important early challenge from a student of Luther to Melanchthon's theology and mode of operating at Wittenberg.

3

Melanchthon's First Attacks on Agricola (1527)

Melanchthon's understanding of *poenitentia* and law constituted a crucial part of his approach to justification by faith. Thus it should come as no surprise that he began to correct and argue against the law-free system being developed at the same time by his friend in Eisleben. However, Melanchthon did not take the role of a teacher correcting a student, nor an opponent disproving an enemy. Rather, he was simply expressing his informed opinion in what we saw in the previous chapter to be an extremely fluid situation. There was no supreme court for pure doctrine in Wittenberg in 1527, neither in Luther's garden nor in Melanchthon's house. The debate in which Melanchthon and Agricola became involved could have happened only where issues had not been decided and various interpretations were still being experimented with. Nevertheless, Melanchthon clearly rejected the position argued by Agricola and, given the opportunity to regulate doctrine on the point, excluded it expressly from the teaching and preaching in electoral Saxony.

"Etliche Sprüche"

Melanchthon's third contribution to catechetical instruction appeared early in 1527 at the very time Agricola's catechism was rolling off Wittenberg's presses. The "Etliche Sprüche" presented biblical texts with brief introductions as reading material for the young. It represented a deliberate effort by an expert in the *loci* method to realize Luther's call to divide the Scripture into the topics of faith (with its subdivisions of *Buße* and forgiveness) and love (with its subdivisions of love for neighbor and the cross). Melanchthon specifically dealt with the topics of *poenitentia*, faith, and the cross.

Melanchthon's discussion of *poenitentia* delineated the split that was opening between Agricola and himself. The title of the section on *poenitentia* is itself illuminating: "On *Buße* and Fear of the Terrifying Wrath of God and the Beginning of the Christian Life."[1] Over these very words Melanchthon and Agricola debated. Melanchthon's introduction to the Bible verses on the subject sounds like a response to Agricola's "Elementa": "The beginning of the Christian life is hearty and earnest terror of God's wrath for our sins. For this reason Christ began his sermon on this topic. Therefore we should always keep in mind how severely God threatens the despisers of his wrath and how he takes pleasure in fear."[2]

Melanchthon connected the law's function to *poenitentia*, leaving no doubt that God's wrath, revealed in the law, is a crucial first step in the life of faith. In a discussion of Psalm 51:19 Melanchthon insisted that God does not look for any external offering, but only for recognition of sin and dread before his judgment. So that the children would not draw the false conclusion that this dread has no connection to the faith that follows, Melanchthon added that this same psalm contains the inexpressible comfort that God is pleased with such an offering (of dread) and will not abandon us in our anxiety.[3]

As in his 1523 comments on the Ten Commandments, Melanchthon began his discussion of faith by declaring: "Where there is no fear, there can be no faith. For faith should comfort the terrified heart, so that it firmly holds that God has forgiven sin for the sake of Christ."[4] What followed touched directly on the brewing controversy. Melanchthon went out of his way to define faith not as fleshly security and despising of the wrath of God, "but instead a true comfort in such anxiety as arises from a knowledge of sins."[5] He attacked as only a "pretend faith (*gemalter glaub*)" that other kind of faith which imagines that we can live a wild life without fear of God. At the same time, Melanchthon showed the connection between the fear of judgment and faith: the frightened heart recognizes that all our merit is too small to reconcile us to God, and thus it must trust Christ for forgiveness.[6]

---

1. *SM* 5.1:61: "Von Busse und furcht des erschreklichen zorns gottes und dem anfang Christlichs lebens."

2. *SM* 5.1:61: "Anfang des christlichen lebens ist hertzlich und ernstlich erschrecken vor dem zorn gottes uber unser sunde, Darumb hat auch Christus sein predig daran angefangen. Darumb sollen wir allweg fur augen haben, wie hart gott treuet den verechtern seines zorns, und wie ehr an forcht gefallen tregt."

3. *SM* 5.1:63f.

4. *SM* 5.1:64: "Wo nicht forcht ist, kann auch nicht glaub sein, denn der glaub soll das erschroken hertz trosten, das es gewislich halte, got hab die sunde umb Christus willen verzigen."

5. Ibid.: "sonder ein warhafftiger trost in solcher angst, die da kompt aus erkantnus der sunden."

6. The third section of the booklet, "Vom Creutz" (*SM* 5.1:66), began by describing the cross as "ubung des glaubens in anfechtung." Prayer, care for one's body, good works, obedience to the authorities, love of neighbor, and chastity are also included in the "practice of faith."

With this brief catechetical instruction, Melanchthon set the stage for conflict with any opinion that downplayed *poenitentia*, excluded contrition over sin out of fear of God's wrath, or insisted that the law has no direct, positive role in the justification of the sinner. But the tension here was hardly greater than that between Agricola and the other Wittenberg catechisms. It would take two more important challenges before Agricola was willing to pick up the gauntlet and strike back publicly.

Melanchthon's *Scholia* of 1527

Our discussion of Agricola's theology and Wittenberg's catechisms demonstrated that important differences in the understanding of *poenitentia* and law existed between him and Melanchthon. These differences first became matters of explicit debate in Melanchthon's commentary on Colossians. There are three external pieces of information in the *Scholia* of 1527 that support this contention. First, Melanchthon addressed the dedicatory epistle to one of Agricola's supporters and relatives by marriage, Alexander Drachstedt. Second, he referred in that letter to other commentaries on Colossians, most likely Agricola's sermons, that could have kept him from publishing his own. Third, he made a passing reference in the preface to "many" who teach forgiveness and faith without *poenitentia*. Directly echoing his recently completed catechism, he added, "But faith without *poenitentia* is nothing except a foolish dream."[7] With this remark Melanchthon set the stage for his careful correction of what he perceived to be a false view of *poenitentia*.

Before we consider the specifics of the debate, however, we must examine whether and to what extent Agricola's sermons on Colossians served as a source for the *Scholia*. This question has no easy answer. For one thing, we encounter immediately the problem of timing. Agricola preached on Colossians during August of 1526, and Melanchthon lectured on the same epistle in 1526 and 1527. The chances of Melanchthon's having obtained a copy of Agricola's sermons for his own lectures appear slim. Nevertheless, we know that the printer boasted on the title page that these sermons had been gone over by Luther himself, which at least increases the possibility that Melanchthon could have seen them at some point before he completed his own commentary.

A second problem in comparing the two commentaries is that their authors studied at the same institution under the same teacher, used similar methods, and employed some of the same sources. Thus, paral-

---

7. *MSA* 4:212.30f.: "At nihil est fides sine poenitentia nisi inane somnium."

lel exegetical results do not necessarily mean dependence, and an attack by Melanchthon on a particular position held by Agricola may signify only that he disagreed with one of the sources for Agricola's thought, such as Erasmus.

Comments on Colossians 1:15–20 serve as a good example. Both exegetes recognized Paul's statement here as a digression from his main argument. Agricola stated, "Here St. Paul takes some time and makes an excursus."[8] Melanchthon said, "However, a description of the person of Christ is inserted in passing."[9] This view of these verses, not found in the broader exegetical tradition, falls far short of demonstrating dependence, in this particular case because two years earlier another Wittenberg exegete, Johann Bugenhagen, had made a similar observation: "At this point he digresses with an amplification."[10] It is far more likely that at least Agricola, but possibly Melanchthon too, used the insights of their colleague to describe the verses in question. Certainly their acquaintance with rhetoric would have suggested to all three exegetes the excursive nature of the passage.

Comments on Colossians 2:8, on the other hand, demonstrate that a close relation existed between the work of Melanchthon and Agricola. Agricola interpreted this verse along much the same lines as did Melanchthon, or rather the other way around.[11] Like Melanchthon, Agricola defined philosophy in this text as "everything that comes from human reason: namely, good order and government, rule and construction of castles, cities, territories, the establishment of civil discipline, the education of the youth in all honesty and discipline, the search for peace and unity, and whatever else may be good on earth."[12] He then tied all this to the temporal sword, ordained by God to keep peace in the world. As long as philosophy remains in external "do's and don'ts (*gebot vnd verbot*)," and the conscience is not trapped, philosophy does not stand against God and in fact pleases him.

---

8. *Colosser*, E.vi.v°: "Hie nimpt yhm S. Pauel/ raum vnd macht ein ausflucht."

9. *MSA* 4:220.22f. (cf. 221.12–14): "Est autem obiter inserta personae Christi descriptio."

10. Johann Bugenhagen, *Annotationes . . . in Epistolas Pauli, ad Galatas, Ephesios, Philippenses, Colossenses, Thessalonicenses primam & secundam, Timotheum primam & secundam, Titum, Philemonem, Hebraeos*, 2d ed. (Basel: Adam Petri, 1525), 118: "Amplificatione adhuc latius excurrit."

11. For a more detailed look at Melanchthon's position see Timothy J. Wengert, *Human Freedom, Christian Righteousness: Philip Melanchthon's Exegetical Dispute with Erasmus of Rotterdam* (New York: Oxford University Press, 1998), ch. 6.

12. *Colosser*, J.ii.v°: "alles was aus menschlicher vernunfft kompt/ nemlich guete ordnung vnd politey machen/ schlosser/ stedte/ lender regieren vnd bawen/ burgerliche zucht auffrichten/ die iugent ynn aller erberkeit/ vnd disciplin auffziehen/ nach fride vnd einickeit trachten/ vnd alles was gutes ymmer mehr mag auff erden sein."

As an example of God's gift of order, Agricola cited Pliny the Elder's description of the behavior of bees:

> The bees possess many good kinds of behavior and virtues. Prudence: for they build and practice good civil order and government. They have great respect for their king, following him wherever he leads. Great courage in fighting against their enemies, the wild bees—they even die from the sting. Moderation: for they save up honey and wax. Furthermore, there is no unchastity among them.[13]

Melanchthon's comments on the same text also described the virtues of the bees, mentioning, in the same order and with nearly the same words, their prudence ("because they construct dwellings and set up government"), justice ("because they diligently obey their kings"), fortitude ("because they bitterly fight with the drones"), and temperance ("because they do not know sexual love and they make honey for our use").[14]

The virtues of the bees was an ancient topos that doubtless appeared in collections of sayings and stories from that period.[15] That two exegetes should independently of one another bring the same example to bear on the same text, and that they should make the same distinction between civil and Christian righteousness, is most unlikely. Here is what may have happened.[16]

In the winter semester of 1526, officially starting on 18 October, Melanchthon began his lectures on Colossians.[17] He completed them

---

13. *Colosser*, J.iii.r°–v°: "Die bienen haben vierley guter art vnd tugent/ Fürsichtickeit/ denn sie bawen/ vnd furen gute burgerliche ordnung vnd politey/ sie haben gros act auff yhren König/ wo yhn der hinfurgehet/ da volgen sie yhm/ Grossen mut ym streit widder ihre feinde die wilden bienen/ vnd sterben ym stiche/ Messickeit/ denn sie ersparen das honig vnd wachs/ dazu ist kein vnkeuscheit vnter yhnen." Cf. Pliny *Natural History* 8.1.1 and 11.4.11–13. Unlike Agricola and Melanchthon, Pliny did not mention the four virtues. (Ancient and Renaissance science thought that bees were headed by kings, not queens.)

14. *MSA* 4:239.14–21: "quia tecta construunt et constituunt rem publicam . . . quia suis regibus diligentissime obtemperant . . . quia acerrime dimicant cum fucis . . . quia et venerem nesciunt et mella ad usus nostros conficiunt."

15. A search of Erasmus's *Adagia* and *Parabolae*, however, as well as Luther's works, turned up no exact parallel.

16. Because we have no external references dating Melanchthon's lectures on Colossians exactly, this reconstruction should be considered simply a plausible explanation.

17. Since Melanchthon was in Eisleben at the end of October, the lectures could not have begun before November. Since he did not meet Agricola during his stay, it is impossible to say whether he saw Agricola's sermons at that time. For the timing of the lectures, see Peter F. Barton, "Die exegetische Arbeit des jungen Melanchthon 1518/19 bis 1528/29: Probleme und Ansätze," *ARG* 54 (1963): 52–89, especially 82–84; and, more recently, Timothy J. Wengert, "Melanchthon's Biblical Commentaries," in *Philip Melanchthon (1497–1560) and the Commentary*, ed. M. Patrick Graham and Timothy J. Wengert (Sheffield: Sheffield Academic Press, 1997).

by 1 May 1527, which gave him some time to edit the manuscript before John Setzer's departure on 20 May. Given the time frame, Melanchthon would probably have reached Colossians 2:8 sometime in late December or January, perhaps even February.[18] If we assume the earliest possible printing date for Agricola's sermons—his translation of Melanchthon's Pauline lectures was out by 5 January[19]—Melanchthon, who undoubtedly would have read the work of his friend, was lecturing on this text at almost exactly the time the sermons appeared.

This possibility has important ramifications for our understanding of Melanchthon's developing theology. Various scholars have argued that the distinction between the two righteousnesses (civil and Christian) became a more and more important hallmark of Melanchthon's theology during this time.[20] Yet here we have a distinction that came not simply from Melanchthon himself, but also from another within the Wittenberg circle. Add to that Luther's frequent expositions of the same distinction,[21] and it becomes clear that many changes one may wish to attribute to Melanchthon at this point in his career had a much wider currency among Wittenberg's theologians. Against the twin attacks by people like François Lambert and Andreas Karlstadt on the left (who advocated abandoning the arts) and Desiderius Erasmus on the right (who accused Wittenberg's theologians of the same), both Agricola and Melanchthon appropriated this distinction from Luther's theology.

Now that we have taken due note of the influence of Agricola, a closer investigation of the way Melanchthon appropriated Agricola's exegesis will reveal both similarities and important differences between the two thinkers. First, Agricola linked philosophy to external things, especially to political order. Melanchthon carefully broadened the term to include three areas of human endeavor: the arts and humanities, science and medicine, law and statecraft. This is typical of the way he used and improved his sources.[22]

---

18. Problematic here is that the *Scholia* contains many additions, making it hard to judge when Melanchthon's original lectures reached a particular verse. Given the additions to Colossians 2:8 and 2:23, it is possible that he lectured on this material as late as February.

19. Roth, 55, no. 103 (Gregory Borner to Stephen Roth; 5 January 1527).

20. Wilhelm Maurer, *Der junge Melanchthon zwischen Humanismus und Reformation*, 2 vols. (Göttingen: Vandenhoeck and Ruprecht, 1967, 1969); Barton, "Die exegetische Arbeit," 52–89; Paul Schwarzenau, *Der Wandel im theologischen Ansatz bei Melanchthon von 1525–1535* (Gütersloh: C. Bertelsmann, 1956).

21. See *WA* 11:245–80 ("Uon welltlicher uberkeytt"), *WA* 15:9–53 ("An die Radherren"), and *WA* 19:623–62 ("Ob Kriegesleute auch in seligen Stande sein können").

22. Regarding Melanchthon's use of Luther see Timothy J. Wengert, *Philip Melanchthon's "Annotationes in Johannem" in Relation to Its Predecessors and Contemporaries* (Geneva: Librairie Droz, 1987), 147–66.

Second, where Agricola employed the example of the bees to demonstrate that political order is a gift from God, Melanchthon used it to prove that human virtues do not justify, since the bees, though virtuous, were clearly not justified through their virtue. Even here, however, Melanchthon was building upon a small suggestion of Agricola, who, near the end of his discussion of Colossians 2:8, reminded his audience that, among other reasons, he had discussed this text at length "so that one can clearly see how civic virtues, which in part even the animals possess from nature, make no one righteous and Christian."[23]

There were other important differences. Agricola turned a portion of his sermon into an appeal to the authorities at Speyer to support good schools. For philosophy is not against the Scripture or the gospel:

> For when the gospel comes, it improves this civic discipline and makes it honest. Therefore one should allow the young children to learn pagan and world history in their youth, as well as the gospel according to the letter, in case God would want to come and improve these very *naturalia* and use them in his service. To learn languages is *Philosophia*, but nevertheless God sent the languages here long ago in the service of his gospel, which was to be preached in these last days in German lands. The same is true of the printing presses, which had never existed since the world came into being.[24]

Agricola made two important points here. First, the gospel improves "bürgerliche zucht," and God improves "naturalia" by using them for his own purposes. Second, children should learn both profane history and the gospel, according to the letter. In this connection he mentioned the importance of learning languages and of the printing press for the spread of the gospel. He concluded with a plea to the princes to support the schools, reminding his listeners what happened to education when it was in the hands of the priests and monks.

23. *Colosser*, J.iiii.r°: ". . . das man fur augen sehe/ wie die bürgerlichen tugende/ die auch die thier eins teils von natur haben/ niemands frum vnd zum Christen machen." Cf. *MSA* 4:239.21–23: "Et sicut ob has virtutes non dicuntur [apes] Christianae, ita neque homines sunt Christiani propter solos civiles mores."

24. *Colosser*, J.iii.v°: "Denn das Euangelion wenn es kompt/ so bessert es dieses bürgerliche zucht/ vnd macht sie rechtschaffen/ Darumb sol man die iunge kinder ynn der iugent/ der heiden vnd welt historien lernen lassen/ auch das Euangelion nach dem buchstaben/ ab Gott wolte kommen vnd die selben Naturalia besseren vnd zu seinem dienst brauchen/ Zungen lernen ist Philosophia/ vnd dennoch hat Gott die zungen zum dienst seins Euangelii/ das zu diesen letsten zeiten solt ynn Deudschen landen gepredigt werden/ lang zuuor her geschickt/ also auch mit der druckereien/ wilche nie gewesen ist/ sieder das die welt gestanden ist." Many of these themes came from Luther's *An die Radherren*.

Melanchthon's comments on Colossians 2:8 were both dependent upon and independent of Agricola's sermon. First, in an excerpt published in 1527 just before the *Scholia* came out, he did not mention languages. However, in the *Scholia* of 1527 he did.[25] Moreover, not until the second edition of 1528 did he make any reference to the printing press and the extraordinary nature of the times. More importantly, Melanchthon did not speak of God's or the gospel's *enhancing* philosophy's effectiveness. God uses law, reason, and philosophy in the world quite apart from the gospel, although God can also use them for the benefit of the gospel. For Melanchthon, no one use was better than the others. Moreover, when Melanchthon talked about philosophy in the service of the gospel, he did not limit it to grammar and languages, as Agricola seemed to do, but moved immediately to rhetoric and dialectic. Finally, he made no direct call for the establishment of schools.

When Agricola turned to the areas where philosophy has no place, other differences appeared. From philosophy we cannot learn about God, faith, and hope, but only an external civic virtue, which will not make a person righteous, he wrote. Melanchthon agreed, and pointed to the linking of civil righteousness and justification as one example of philosophy's errors. Agricola, however, took the discussion in a different direction. Imitating Luther's arguments in "Uon welltlicher uberkeytt," Agricola contended that Colossians 2:8 means that when princes attack the conscience, they must be told that they have no jurisdiction.

Agricola then discussed the meaning of the term "Welt satzung (human tradition)" in the text. The use of Plato in earlier times and of Aristotle in Agricola's day had ruined the interpretation of Scripture. To this were added the decrees, decretals, "extravagantes," and "extravagatorum extravagantes."[26] The only thing that saved the church was the coming of the gospel. Agricola even mentioned Jean Gerson's complaint that many people committed suicide because they could not receive good counsel for their consciences. The only sure ground we have comes not from philosophy, but from God's Word alone. Agricola then traced the loss of the gospel through the Scholastic theologians and ended with an attack on that "lying spirit" that departs from the clear meaning of the words "This is my body," and then divides itself "over

25. *MSA* 4:236.28–31. For a complete description of the excerpt, the "Dissertatio" on Colossians 2:8, see Wengert, *Human Freedom*, ch. 6.

26. *Colosser,* J.iiii.v°. "Extravagantes" were later portions of canon law not found in all collections; "extravagatorum extravagantes" was Agricola's derisive name for them.

the *'tuto,'* over the 'this,' over 'body,' and does not know where to get out—that is how crazy philosophy makes people."[27]

Melanchthon offered an entirely different set of arguments. He said nothing about the limits of civil authority. Moreover, his worry about the mixture of Plato or Aristotle in theology was not connected directly to the interpretation of the Scripture. His attack on the Scholastics was much more muted in this section of his commentary. He merely provided examples of incorrect metaphysical and theological speculation by the philosophers. In 1528 he would attack not the Scholastic exegetes' use of Aristotle in interpreting the Scripture, but their inept use of the rhetorical and dialectical tools that Aristotle provided.

Most importantly, Melanchthon targeted not the sacramentarians, but Erasmus and the debate over free will.[28] If one assumes that Agricola's attack on linking civic virtue and justification lay before Melanchthon in 1527 as he was preparing his lectures, then it becomes even more impressive that the two areas Melanchthon added to the discussion (God's *gubernatio* and *sanctificatio*) directly supported his attack on free will. It was as if he wanted to say that not only in matters directly related to justification, but also in the defense of free will philosophy errs.

There remains one more point at which Agricola's interpretation of Colossians 2:8 diverged sharply from Melanchthon's, and that is on the question of the role of the law and good works in the life of a Christian. For Agricola philosophy had no place in the interpretation of the Bible. He divided his comments on this subject into two major sections. First, he argued that the importation of first Plato and then Aristotle into the interpretation of Scripture had resulted in uncertainty and the multiplication of commentaries on commentaries; although Augustine had tried to bring people back to the Scripture, later theologians simply wrote commentaries first on Augustine and later on Thomas and others.

Second, Agricola described several instances where the importation of philosophy had occurred. Much more important for Agricola than the Lord's Supper controversy described briefly above was the failure to understand 1 Timothy 1:8–9: the law was not given for the just. That is, only apart from philosophy do Christians know that their holiness comes from Christ alone, that it has nothing to do with their works:

> If they sin, they run to Christ and shake their sins on him. If they do something good, then it is not theirs but his. They need no law. 1 Timothy 1[:8–

---

27. *Colosser,* J.v.v°: ". . . ynn das Tuto/ ynn das Das/ ym Leib/ vnd weis nicht wo er hynaus sol/ so yrre macht die Philosophey."

28. See Wengert, *Human Freedom,* ch. 6.

9]: "No law is given to the righteous." They take the middle road and are free from good and evil works in this way: that no sin harms their salvation, and no good work makes them righteous. Grace, grace it is that does not pay attention to sin nor regard good works.[29]

How serious was Agricola about the exclusion of the demand for good works from the Christian life? He pitted Christian freedom against *all* statutes and ceremonies. They are all excluded. No one rules the Word of God except God's Son:

> When they see that the people live in such disorderly ways, along come the saintliest people and want to help the situation with commands, rules, statutes, and other ceremonies. And as soon as the gospel and Christian life are comprehended in rules, then it is no longer the gospel, and God is denied, who wants his word comprehended voluntarily. Moreover, no one is to rule except his Son.[30]

With one sweeping statement Agricola had eliminated all rules from the gospel. Moreover, in very pointed terms he criticized even the holiest of people who imagine that rules and regulation will help when people live disorderly lives. He included in his attack Francis, Dominic, Basil, Bernard, "and all of the Fathers who made rules, all councils in which something was decreed concerning the external life, as in all of them, even the Council of Nicea."[31] He compared those who try enforcing ceremonies to the Jews who asked Jesus for a sign. We must have patience with the simple and must simply respect the truth.

Agricola categorically denied any role for works, good or bad, in the life of the believer. He excluded any common ordering of the Christian life. Christians live by grace alone:

> When we spend an entire day with good thoughts, service to the neighbor, preaching, working, writing, reading, we are pleased with ourselves and say, "Ach, if only I did this every day, it would be really fine and would please God." Contrariwise, when we spend a day evilly, we are so fright-

---

29. *Colosser,* J.vi.r°: "Sundigen sie so/ lauffen sie zu Christo vnd schutten sie auff yhn/ thun sie etwas gutes/ so ist es nicht ihr sondern sein/ Sie bedurffen kein gesetzs Timoth 1. Den gerechten ist kein gesetze geben/ Sie geben die mittelstrassen vnd von guten wercken vnd bösen frey/ also/ das yhn kein sunde zur selickeit schadet/ nach kein gut werck fromet/ Gnade/ gnade/ ist es/ die die sunde nicht achtet/ noch guete werck ansihet."

30. *Colosser,* J.vi.r°: "Do faren denn zu/ die allerheiligsten leute/ wenn sie sehen/ das die leute so vnordenlich leben/ vnd wollen der sachen mit geboten/ regeln/ statuten vnd anderen Ceremonien helffen/ vnd als bald wenn das Euangelion vnd Christen leben/ ynn regel gefasset wird/ so ist es nymmer Euangelion/ vnd Gott wird verleugnet/ der sein wort wil freiwillig gefasset haben/ Daruber niemand rigieren sol denn sein Son."

31. *Colosser,* J.vi.r°: "vnd alle veter die regeln gemacht haben/ alle Concilien/ darinne etwas beschlossen ist worden/ wie denn ynn allen auch ynn Nicena Synodo/ von eusserlichem leben."

ened and cry and complain, "Wrong has been done; we will only be damned." Both of these things mock Christ and his grace.[32]

In order to keep the focus solely on Christ and his grace, Agricola was determined to eliminate all externals from faith. Only faith, not works, saves; only unbelief, not works, condemns. "If you believe, you will be holy even in sin."[33]

In his summary of Colossians 2:8 Agricola focused exclusively on his final arguments. Philosophy says that when we do good works, we can be sure that we please God. But God's Word says that if we do good works, we should fear (*furchte*), because we become righteous by faith and are only unworthy servants. Philosophy says that when we sin, we are damned and should be afraid. God's Word says, "If you sin, be happy; it should have no consequence."[34] Here Agricola substituted the effect of human philosophy for the effect of the law that the other catechetical interpretations of Wittenberg's theology described. Fear and judgment connected with the revelation of sin were totally excluded from Agricola's understanding of the Christian life. Rather, he said that we should fear when we do good works; on the other hand, "when you sin, then be happy." Statements like these were on a collision course with Melanchthon's theology.

Did Melanchthon respond in his *Scholia*? Without a doubt, but not in his discussion of Colossians 2:8. There the chief opponent remained Erasmus. Instead, he returned to Agricola's theology in comments on Colossians 2:23, where he discussed human traditions.[35] His first point established what might be called the first use of the law within the churches. Traditions that do not conflict with the divine command have been created not to justify us or to placate God, but to prevent confusion in the churches. As proof he cited 1 Corinthians 14:40, a text to which Luther also often referred in this context. Examples of traditions that prevented confusion included the setting of rules for singing, Sunday services, and fasting. Melanchthon's summary took on Agricola's blanket rejection of human regulations in the church: "And exactly in this manner and for this reason the old ordinances were made, which

---

32. *Colosser*, J.vii.r°: "Wenn wir einen tage mit guten gedancken/ des nehisten dinst/ predigen/ erbieten/ schreiben/ lesen/ zubracht haben/ so gefalle/ wir vns wol vnd sagen/ Ach wenn ich alle tage also thete/ so were es yhe fein vnd wurde Gotte wolgefallen/ Herwidderumb/ wenn wir einen tag vbel zubringen/ so furchten wir vns sere/ schreien vnd klagen/ Es sey vnrecht gethan/ wir werden nur verdampt werden/ vnd das alles beides ist Christi vnd seiner gnaden gespottet."

33. *Colosser*, J.vii.r°: "Gleubstu/ so wirstu auch ynn der sunde selig."

34. *Colosser*, J.vii.v°: "Wenn du sundigest/ so sey frölich/ Es sol nicht not haben."

35. Portions of his exegesis of this text were also aimed at Erasmus. See Wengert, *Human Freedom*, ch. 7.

were preserved not as necessary for justification but for the sake of peace and to avoid confusion."[36]

Having positively defined the role of ordinances in the church, Melanchthon then took on those who would abolish them. Attacking such people as individuals who "gravely damage charity,"[37] he linked them to Jesus' strictures in Matthew 18:6 against those who scandalize the "weak (*pusilli*)." And who are the "pusilli"? Those "who when old ordinances are changed take opportunity for license and become worse."[38] Melanchthon feared that changing human ordinances led to license, not to evangelical freedom. Moreover, some people, seeing that scandal arose from the changing of unnecessary practices, came to hate the gospel itself. He included the example of the prohibition of eating food once sacrificed to idols (1 Cor. 8) and Paul's command to avoid offense. Melanchthon added two examples from the history of the church, including a positive interpretation of the canons of Nicea: "The Council of Nicea set things up this way, that when there were deliberations concerning church ordinances, the council did not want to hand down some new form for all churches, but instead commanded that in each and every place the old customs be preserved."[39] Not only did Melanchthon praise the council in general, but he specifically mentioned the decree that allowed churches to regulate themselves.

After an examination of other kinds of human ordinances in the church (including those that are harmful because they are thought to lead to salvation), Melanchthon concluded with a summary. First, he issued an explicit admonition: "I wanted to add these things at the end, so that I might urge the preservation of old ordinances, as far as it can be done without sin."[40] Melanchthon condemned people who had eliminated some old rites only to institute their own; guilty of instituting a new form of circumcision in the church (Gal. 5:2), such people are "authors of the greatest scandals, namely of dissension in the churches and license among the common folk."[41] Then, in some of the strongest lan-

36. *MSA* 4:272.33–273.2: "Et huiusmodi fere sunt veteres ordinationes et hoc consilio factae, quas servandas esse, non tamquam necessarias ad iustificationem, sed pacis causa, et ne qua confusio fiat." First Corinthians 7:18 was cited as proof.

37. *MSA* 4:273.4: "graviter laedunt caritatem."

38. *MSA* 4:273.10f.: "qui veteribus ordinationibus mutatis accipiunt occasionem licentiae et fiunt deteriores."

39. *MSA* 4:273.18–23: "Sic Nicena Synodus constituit, cum de ordinationibus ecclesiarum deliberaretur, nec novam aliquam formam omnibus ecclesiis tradi voluit, sed iussit singulis locis veteres consuetudines servare."

40. *MSA* 4:276.26–28: "Haec volui ad finem adicere, ut monerem, quantum fieri sine peccato possit, veteres ordinationes servandas esse."

41. *MSA* 4:276.32f.: "maximorum scandalorum auctores, videlicet dissensionis in ecclesiis, licentiae vulgi."

guage in the *Scholia*, he added that this was the work of the devil. While earlier the devil had sent pseudoapostles in the form of "teachers of human traditions (*doctores traditionum humanarum*)," now people needed to fear "lest the devil deceive us somewhere with a false teaching of liberty."[42] Peter predicted as much (2 Peter 2:19), and Paul admonished people not to use freedom as an opportunity for the flesh (Gal. 5:13).

The battle lines were clearly drawn. When in the Visitation Articles Melanchthon attempted to preserve a tradition of the old church, namely the threefold division of *poenitentia*, criticism would inevitably come from John Agricola, who portrayed Christian life as free from such burdens and who criticized those well-intentioned people who reintroduced them for the sake of order.

Among the other differences between the two exegetes is that they divided the Book of Colossians differently. Whereas Melanchthon, in agreement with Bugenhagen and some of the medieval tradition, divided the book in half, with the first two chapters pertaining to the definition of the gospel and the last two describing moral precepts, Agricola on the contrary separated the first two chapters. In the first Paul tells about "the goodness of our Lord God" and "in what way, how, where, when, through whom, why, and to whom" that goodness occurs. In the second Paul insists that his readers come to a full understanding of the "riches in the knowledge of the secret of God" (Col. 2:2) and not be seduced by the face of an angel, pretty words, philosophy, or God's laws. To comfort and strengthen the Colossians, Paul describes the victory of Christ over his enemies.[43]

Melanchthon found precepts in Colossians, while Agricola completely ignored them in his introduction. For Melanchthon the issue was defining the gospel. For Agricola it was the goodness of God and its recognition, that is, faith. Even their descriptions of Christ's death differed, with Agricola using the motif of Christ's victory over evil and Melanchthon maintaining a more judicial model that emphasized how Christ's death on the cross satisfies God's wrath.[44]

---

42. *MSA* 4:277.5f.: ". . . ne nunc diabolus alicubi vitiata doctrina libertatis nos decipiat."

43. *Colosser*, A.iii.r°–v°: "Sum ersten erzelet er die güte vnsers herngots/ die er vns erzeiget hat vnd sagt auff was weyse/ wie/ wo/ wenn/ durch wen/ warumb/ vnd wem das alles zu gut geschehen sey/ . . . Zum andern dringt er mit gewalt auff die Colosser den volligen verstand/ des reichtumbs ym erkentnus des geheimnis gotes/ das sie darynne bleiben vnd mutig mit freuden beharren sollen/ vnd sich durch kein engel gesicht noch hubsche rede/ noch philosophei/ noch gottes gesetze selbs nicht binden noch verfüren lassen/ noch von dieser fulle der schatzkamer gottes/ von Jhesu Christo/ abwenden lassen/ Vnd ynn dem zu yrhem trost vnd störcke/ beschreibt vnd malet er/ den triumph vnd herlichen sieg Christi Jesu/ mit seinen feinden."

44. *MSA* 4:211–12.

Melanchthon's and Agricola's introductions to the Book of Colossians foreshadowed other disagreements between these two interpreters of Paul. We have already mentioned Melanchthon's warning in the preface against those who preach forgiveness without *poenitentia*. In his sermon on Colossians 1:3–8, Agricola spent a great deal of time proving that the connection between works of love and hope did not indicate that we merit eternal life.[45] Melanchthon said simply, "Concerning this text I know that others have debated many things subtly, but I think that this kind of question does not benefit the common folk."[46] In one sentence Melanchthon dismissed over twenty pages of Agricola's argument as being unfit for the common folk. In the edition of 1528 Melanchthon rewrote his comment to read, "Concerning this text I know it is usual that it be debated subtly. But we will explain it as best we can, most crudely."[47]

In 1527 Melanchthon cited Paul's advice that the common people need to be fed with milk; that way they can understand "what it means to serve God freely with no thought of reward."[48] But even more pointedly he added, "Indeed it is useful to incite them to godliness by mention of rewards and punishments, just as by preaching of the law."[49] This final comment revealed the gulf between Melanchthon and Agricola over the preaching of the law. For Agricola, the law had no place in the life of the Christian. Thus pages of his sermon on Colossians 1:3–8 had to be spent explaining away Paul's apparent reference to reward. Melanchthon pointed out that punishments and rewards can move a person to do good rather than ill, because the former are witnesses to the divine will and the latter are signs of divine favor. The saints at Colossae were moved to do good by the magnitude of the reward, not that their doing good increased the reward, but that, having been accepted by God, they wished to show him their gratitude. This shows that hope and the expectation of heavenly blessings do not rest on our merit but on the divine promise.[50] With talk like this, it is no wonder that Agricola could accuse Melanchthon of reverting to papal practices. Merit, reward, punishment, preaching

---

45. *Colosser*, B.iii.r°–C.vii.r°.

46. *MSA* 4:215.29–31: "De hoc loco scio alios multa subtiliter disputasse sed ego hoc genus quaestionis nihil existimo prodesse ad vulgus."

47. *Scholia* 1528, 5v°: "De hoc loco scio subtiliter disputari solere. Nos vero explicabimus eum, quam poterimus, crassissime." For a detailed look at the changes in 1528 see pp. 156–69. Melanchthon rewrote this entire section.

48. *MSA* 4:215.32f.: "quid sit gratis nec praemii respectu Deo servire."

49. *MSA* 4:215.33–216.1: "Immo prodest illos tamquam legis praedicatione ad pietatem excitare poenarum et praemiorum mentione."

50. *MSA* 4:216.

the law—the very things Agricola's gospel excluded—Melanchthon's commentary welcomed.

Before examining the arguments concerning *poenitentia* in the *Scholia*, we must look at Melanchthon's interpretation of Galatians 3:24. This became one of the points of contention between the two exegetes at the Torgau conference in November 1527. Whereas Luther had in Agricola's opinion consistently applied this verse to the second use of the law—the law is the disciplinarian (*Zuchtmeister*) that drives to Christ—Melanchthon in the commentary on Colossians applied it to the first use of the law—an exegetical move Agricola rejected. As part of his discussion of free will in comments on Colossians 1:15, Melanchthon stated that the law "not only teaches those who do not yet have the Holy Spirit, but also drives them away from manifest and shameful acts or from transgressions; as [Paul] says, 'the law is given on account of the transgression,' that is, for coercing the flesh."[51] So while allowing this verse to apply to those who do not yet but will have the Holy Spirit, Melanchthon insisted that it also implies the coercion of sinners.

Melanchthon expressed himself even more clearly in comments on Colossians 2:17 ("These [regulations concerning food, drink, festivals, etc.] are only a shadow of what is to come").[52] He wanted to expand this text beyond simply a typological interpretation of the law. He did this by defining two uses for the law. For the first use ("to coerce the carnal human creature"—the second use is to drive us to Christ) he adduced two texts, Galatians 3:24 and 1 Timothy 1:9. Not only is Israel coerced, but God wants all people to be coerced by the law, which is why he also gives magistrates and laws to the Gentiles. Agricola had used 1 Timothy 1:9 to exclude the law from the gospel and had argued that Galatians 3:24 applied only to believers waiting for salvation; Melanchthon assigned the coercive function of the law to all peoples and all laws.

These opposing views of the law had direct consequences in two areas: *poenitentia* and Christian freedom. Both topics underwent some sharpening and changes by Melanchthon for the *Scholia* of 1528, but even in their earliest form they showed an understanding completely different from Agricola's. Melanchthon discussed *poenitentia* in his introduction to comments on Colossians 2:11f.[53] He pointed out that starting with Colossians 2:4[54] Paul had introduced a "collatio" between human and divine righteousness, which he finished in 2:11f. by teach-

---

51. *MSA* 4:224.11–15: ". . . non docere tantum eos, qui nondum habent Spiritum sanctum, sed etiam coercere a manifestis flagitiis seu a transgressionibus, sicut ait legem propter transgressionem, id est: ad coercendam carnem esse positam."
52. *MSA* 4:253.
53. *MSA* 4:246–47.
54. *MSA* 4:229.31–33.

ing that within Christian righteousness itself there are two parts: *mortificatio* and *vivificatio*. This is what Christ himself teaches in Luke 24:47. But whereas this verse was one of Agricola's favorites to prove that *poenitentia* arises from faith in the gospel, Melanchthon argued that it proves that *poenitentia* precedes faith and forgiveness.

"Mortification" or *poenitentia* Melanchthon defined as "to know sin and to be truly terrified by God's judgment. . . . Nor can faith exist without such fear and terror."[55] In his application of this definition to the verses in question Melanchthon emphasized again and again the necessity of our fearing divine judgment ("you may be truly terrified by fear of divine judgment"; "as David . . . was terrified"; "this terror is *poenitentia* itself").[56] This terror prepares one for true confession, in which the heart not only acknowledges its sin and condemns itself, but sees the impending judgment. Other words for this *mortificatio* in Paul's vocabulary include circumcision, burial, baptism, and even the hiddenness of our life in Christ.

Faith and consolation first appeared in Melanchthon's discussion of *vivificatio*, which he defined as the consummation of Christian righteousness, "to comprehend consolation through faith."[57] Such faith acknowledges and trusts that satisfaction is made to God not through our merits but through Christ's death. In this way Melanchthon drew the line between his understanding of *poenitentia* and Agricola's. The battle continued a year later when Melanchthon reworked the material into a much more careful rebuttal of Agricola's position.[58]

In his comments on Colossians 3:11 Melanchthon discussed Christian freedom.[59] He defined Christian freedom in several different ways. Most importantly, through forgiveness and the gift of the Holy Spirit God frees Christians from sin and the devil's power. Another kind of freedom involves freedom from the political and ceremonial law of Moses. Here Melanchthon rejected calls to reintroduce Mosaic laws, supporting instead the local laws and customs as well as the daily human activities they regulate.

A final level of freedom comes from the understanding that human traditions neither save nor damn us. Although Melanchthon referred

---

55. *MSA* 4:247.1–5: "Mortificatio seu poenitentia est cognoscere peccatum et vere terreri iudicio Dei. . . . Nec potest esse fides sine tali timore vel terrore." He offered a nearly identical definition in *MSA* 4:247.19–29, adding many more proof texts.

56. *MSA* 4:247: "vere perterrefias metu divini iudicii"; "sicut David . . . perterritus est"; "hic terror est ipsa poenitentia."

57. *MSA* 4:248.30: "consolationem concipere per fidem."

58. See pp. 158–64. In explaining this text Agricola, *Colosser*, K.i.v°, referred the audience to his earlier discussion of Peter and Judas (see pp. 36–37).

59. *MSA* 4:287–91.

his readers to his earlier discussion of this issue,[60] he nevertheless took this opportunity to investigate what Paul meant by saying that the law had been abrogated. Harking back to a medieval definition discussed in the *Loci communes theologici* of 1521, Melanchthon divided the law into ceremonial, judicial, and moral. Since neither ceremonies nor legal judgments justify before God, the first two kinds of law have been suspended. There follows one of the *Scholia's* most important statements in relation to the coming controversy: "However, because the gospel, as we said above, contains the preaching of *poenitentia*, it is necessary that the part of the law that teaches righteousness be retained. This is the Decalog. It condemns us and calls us to *poenitentia*."[61]

Melanchthon and Agricola agreed that the gospel contains the preaching of *poenitentia*. They also agreed that the movement from *mortificatio* to *vivificatio* is crucial for the life of a Christian. Where they disagreed was precisely what role the law plays in this scheme of things. For Melanchthon, fresh from a reading of Agricola's sermons on Colossians and reacting to what he found there, the preaching of *poenitentia* implies an important role for that part of the law that "teaches the righteousness of the heart." Melanchthon added to this comment a description of the first through fourth commandments, closing with the note that the next three commandments were interpreted by Christ in Matthew 5. To make sure his point was not lost on his readers, Melanchthon declared that Christ in Matthew 5 repeated the Decalog "lest we imagine that that part of the law has been abrogated."[62]

The moral law is written not only on Moses' tablets, but also on human hearts as natural law. It is taught for two reasons: to coerce the flesh by the fear of punishment, and to humble and fill sinners with fear by the preaching of *poenitentia*. "For remission of sins cannot be taught without the preaching of *poenitentia*."[63] Here Melanchthon echoed the preface of the *Scholia*.

With the *Scholia* Melanchthon's disagreements with Agricola reached a new stage. The *Scholia* indicates that Melanchthon was familiar with Agricola's sermons on Colossians. This means that in all probability the differences between their interpretations were not simply random divergences but, as we saw in Agricola's translation of

60. *MSA* 4:259–77, which contains Melanchthon's response to Agricola's discussion of freedom (see pp. 87–89).

61. *MSA* 4:289.15–19: "Quia vero evangelium, sicut supra diximus, continet praedicationem poenitentiae, necesse est legis partem, quae cordis iustitiam docet, retineri. Ea est decalogus, is nos condemnat et ad poenitentiam vocat."

62. *MSA* 4:289.34–290.1: "ne putaremus eam legis partem abrogatam esse."

63. *MSA* 4:290.32–33: "Neque enim potest remissio peccatorum sine poenitentiae praedicatione doceri."

Melanchthon's annotations on Romans and 1–2 Corinthians, well-thought-out rebuttals of the other's theology. Melanchthon rejected the subtleties of Agricola's interpretation of Colossians 1:5–8. His comments on Colossians 2:8 expanded the positive role of philosophy. He corrected statements that would eliminate all human traditions from the church. He dismissed any definition of *poenitentia* that excluded the law and its terrors. Having clearly spelled out his positions, Melanchthon now brought them to bear in the Visitation Articles, the third front from which he initiated the earliest intra-Lutheran battle.

The Visitation Articles

In the middle of the controversy with Agricola, Melanchthon wrote a note to his friend in Nuremberg, Joachim Camerarius, in which he complained about the attacks. Speaking of the Visitation Articles he said, "They contain nothing except some children's catechesis, as I call it, of the Christian religion."[64] He concluded with the same description: "And in that catechesis itself, what else did I strive for except that the necessary things be taught in the churches while omitting many controversies?"[65] Thus Melanchthon viewed the Visitation Articles as a children's catechism intended for the simple pastors whom he had encountered in his work as a visitor in the churches of electoral Saxony. What Melanchthon wrote in that piece, however, served as the last crucial salvo in his ever sharper correction of and controversy with Agricola's theology. Here he wrote not only as exegete or catechist, but as visitor and, if one takes seriously the definition of the episcopal office in Luther's preface to the German version of the Articles, bishop.[66]

Pressure for a visitation of the churches came originally from several sides. As we have already seen, Nicholas Hausmann of Zwickau was one of the first to call for and then to execute a visitation in his immediate area. Luther also joined in the chorus, especially once the reform of the University of Wittenberg was well in hand. After an exchange of legal opinions between him and the court, the university elected two representatives to serve on the visitation team. (The elector also named

---

64. *MBW* 610 (*CR* 1:919–21, here 919), dated 23 October 1527: "Nihil habet, nisi quandam puerilem κατήχησιν, ut ita dicam, Christianae religionis."

65. *CR* 1:920: "Et in illa ipsa κατηχήσει quid aliud secutus sum, nisi, ut necessaria in Ecclesiis docerentur, omissis controversiis plerisque."

66. For the most recent literature, see Günther Wartenberg, *MLStA* 3:402–5. Most important is the material edited by Emil Sehling in *Die evangelischen Kirchenordnungen des XVI. Jahrhunderts* (Aalen: Scientia, 1979 reprint), I.1:31–41 and 142–49; and Hans-Walter Krumwiede's excellent work *Zur Entstehung des landesherrlichen Kirchenregiments in Kursachsen und in Braunschweig-Wolfenbüttel* (Göttingen: Vandenhoeck and Ruprecht, 1967), 48–145.

two representatives from the court.) On 6 December 1526 the faculty chose Jerome Schurff from the law faculty and Melanchthon to represent the theologians.[67] Although others had nominated Benedict Pauli the rector, Johann Bugenhagen the pastor, and Justus Jonas the provost, Luther's insistence on Melanchthon carried the day.[68]

On 16 June 1527 the elector sent the visitors his instructions defining their responsibilities.[69] They were given carte blanche by the elector, who wanted to insure that within the existing church structures, especially the financial ones, the gospel would be preached.[70] While the elector's instructions concerned themselves with the external problems of the churches and their pastors and with the relation of the elector to the visitation, it seems that Melanchthon, as the sole theologian among the visitors, was then designated to come up with a proposal that would serve as the theological basis of instruction for the pastors and their people. From the beginning this proposal was intended to be worked over by the entire theological faculty at Wittenberg and, if the elector agreed, published.

During the summer, sometime after 1 July, the visitors worked their way through the region of the Saale. We have their reports from Neustadt (Orla), Kahla, Eisenberg, and, later, Altenburg.[71] Among the towns visited was Saalfeld, where the visitors reported that the pastor, John Plack, and the preacher, Caspar Aquila, were capable but unpaid. By 15 August 1527 Melanchthon had come to Jena, where the university had moved because of the plague in Wittenberg.[72] Sometime before

67. Krumwiede, *Zur Entstehung*, 70, errs when he describes Melanchthon as a member of the arts faculty alone. His comments reflect the scholarly opinion of his time.

68. Ibid., n. 83a, citing a letter to the elector which reads in part, "Darinnen sich zugetragen, das vast einmutiglich Doctor Hieronimus Schurpf und Magister Philippus Melancton fursgeslagen und genent seind. . . . Und ob wohl ethlich wenig stymmen auch auf andere neben Magister Philipp gefallen, als nehmlich uf den itzigen unser universitet Rector Licentiat Benedict Pauli, Pomeranus hye den pfarrer, den Propst Doctor Jonas, ßo ist doch aus dem, das derselb von itztlichen und disser aus bessern bedenken von Doctor Martino und den meysten stymmen angeben auf die beide eintrechtiglich beslossen worden."

69. For the text see Sehling, *Die evangelischen Kirchenordnungen*, 142–48. For the most recent analysis, see Krumwiede, *Zur Entstehung*, 71–91.

70. Sehling, *Die evangelischen Kirchenordnungen*, 142: "Und sol anfenglich diss das furhalten ungeferlich sein, das wir bevelen, inen und andern den unsern anzuzaigen. Wie wol got der almechtige sein ewiges gotlichs wort der welt reichlich und gnediglich in diesen letzten tagen widerumb hat erscheinen lassen und unser lande fur andern mit solcher heilwertigen gnaden aus uberschwenglicher guthe und barmherzigkeit gnediglich vorsehen. . . ."

71. See *MBW* 563, 565, 567, 574, 594, and the sources listed there.

72. *MBW* 575 (*CR* 1:883f.), a letter to Camerarius dated 15 August 1527. In *MBW* 589 (Bindseil, 30), a letter dated 10 September to the electoral counselors at the Torgau, Melanchthon and Schurff asked to be excused from doing any further visitations since they alone were teaching law and theology in Jena.

this Melanchthon must have begun work on a Latin version of the Visitation Articles, which in translation became the subject of discussion between the court and the theologians, who because of the plague were residing in both Wittenberg and Jena.[73] On 26–27 September a conference over the visitation and its articles took place at the Torgau with Melanchthon, Schurff, Luther, and Bugenhagen in attendance.[74]

By mid-October, much to Melanchthon's dismay, the original Latin version of the articles was published by Nicholas Schirlentz in Wittenberg.[75] By that time the debate over catechesis between Agricola and Melanchthon had broken out into the open. Before we investigate this controversy, we need both to understand how these articles contributed to that dispute and to show the intimate connection between the Latin articles and the works of Melanchthon we have already discussed.

As Erasmus commented wryly in a letter to Melanchthon in 1528, the opening table of contents did not match what was in the book.[76] In fact, it was not a table of contents at all but, as stated in Schirlentz's edition, a list of twenty articles on which the curates had to be examined. Next to that list, which may not even have come from Melanchthon, was a description of some, though not all of the articles, placed in a completely different order. Where the list began with the Decalog and moved to faith and then the sacraments, the Articles themselves began with an untitled section on *poenitentia* and forgiveness of sins, saving a discussion of the law until the end and omitting altogether such topics as schools, foundations, sacristans, and the punishment of adulterers.[77]

---

73. See, for example, *WABr* 4:229–31 (a letter dated 16 August 1527): sending Luther an early edition of the Articles in German, Elector John asked him to avoid division and work on them with Bugenhagen. Luther's response to George Spalatin (*WABr* 4:232–33, dated 19 August) included the compliment "omnia pulchra sunt," and scorned the lies of Wittenberg's adversaries.

74. Concerning a record of the expense payments for Spalatin and for Melanchthon and the other visitors (Asmus von Haubitz and Hans von der Planitz) as well as the sending of a messenger to fetch Luther and Bugenhagen from Wittenberg, see Georg Buchwald, "Lutherana: Notizen aus Rechnungsbüchern des Thüringischen Staatsarchivs zu Weimar," *ARG* 25 (1928): 1–98, especially 4 and 44. A stenographer was also paid for having written "die ordenung der visitacion" three separate times.

75. *MBW* 610 (*CR* 1:919–21), a letter to Camerarius dated 23 October 1527.

76. *MBW* 654 (*CR* 2:844 and Erasmus, *Opus epistolarum*, ed. P. S. Allen, 11 vols. [Oxford: Oxford University Press, 1906–47], 7:320f., no. 1944), dated 5 February 1528. Erasmus was referring to a printing by Johann Froben in 1527. See appendix 3 for a complete list of the Latin editions. The Visitation Articles was printed twice by Schirlentz and once by Froben; in two other cases, including an emended version as part of a collection of works by Melanchthon and Johannes Brenz, the printer cannot be identified. We will cite the Articles according to the edition in *CR* 26:1–28.

77. *CR* 26:7f. Also missing are articles on the form of the mass and on usury.

The Articles relentlessly attacked Agricola's understanding of *poenitentia* and law. In the context of the debate we have already described, the opening lines could hardly have been understood any other way: "Pastors ought to follow the example of Christ," Melanchthon began, implying some had not. Since Christ taught *poenitentia* and remission of sins, so should the pastors. "Now it is common to go on and on about faith, and yet what faith is cannot be understood unless *poenitentia* is preached." Preaching faith without *poenitentia*, that is, "without teaching the fear of God, without teaching the law," was like pouring new wine into old wineskins and simply led to a carnal security among the common people. "This security is worse than all the previous errors under the pope." Against the guilty preachers Melanchthon cited the testimony of Jeremiah, Ezekiel, and Paul. "And now those who neglect to teach *poenitentia* take away one of the principal parts from the gospel."[78]

Following this attack Melanchthon stepped back and gave positive instruction. *Poenitentia* must be taught to exhort the hearers to contrition, which is the principal part of *poenitentia* and which is called in the Scripture *mortificatio*. Here he quoted Ezekiel and Joel 2:13.[79] The preaching of the law—the first question of the visitors to the local clergy—was to be understood in this context: "The preaching of the law rouses [a person] to *poenitentia*."[80] But this preaching was to be more than simply a recitation of the commandments; it had to include the penalty for breaking them, both temporal and eternal. Melanchthon offered examples from Genesis 18 and Exodus, reminding the reader that, as Paul says, such punishments were written for our sakes, "that we may learn the fear of God."[81] Moreover, the preacher ought to explain

---

78. *CR* 26:9: "Pastores debent exemplum Christi sequi, qui quoniam poenitentiam et remissionem peccatorum docuit, debent et ista pastores tradere ecclesiis. Nunc vulgare est vociferare de fide, et tamen intelligi quid sit fides, non potest, nisi praedicata poenitentia. Plane vinum novum in utres veteres infundunt, qui fidem sine poenitentia, sine doctrina timoris Dei, sine doctrina legis praedicant, et ad carnalem quandam securitatem adsuefaciunt vulgus. Ea securitas est deterior, quam omnes errores antea sub papa fuerunt. Hoc genus Concionatorum describit Hieremias et vituperat eos, qui dicant: Pax, pax, et non est pax. Quam graviter minatur concionatoribus, apud Ezech. 3., Dominus praetermittentibus hanc partem? Si dicente me ad impium, morte morieris, non adnunciaveris ei, sanguinem eius de manu tua requiram. Itaque Paulus ait, scripturam divinitus traditam esse ad arguendam, corripiendam etc. At nunc isti, qui poenitentiam negligunt docere, unam de principalioribus partibus Evangelio detrahunt."

79. Cf. *MSA* 4:247.23, where in a discussion of mortification Joel 2:13 is also cited.

80. *CR* 26:9: "Poenitentia vero sic docenda est, ut hortentur auditores ad contritionem, quae est praecipue pars poenitentiae, et est in scripturis vocata mortificatio. . . . Aliquando totum decalogum enarrent ordine, quia praedicatio legis ad poenitentiam provocat."

81. *CR* 26:10: "Nam haec omnia non propter ipsos, ut Paulus ait, sed propter nos scripta sunt, ut discamus timorem Dei, Est autem timor Domini initium sapientiae etc."

the state of a person abandoned by God. In addition to Paul's description in Romans 1, the examples of Saul, Cain, Absalom, and Ahab are cited. Melanchthon then added a comment possibly directed at the preaching of Caspar Aquila: "It is much better to inculcate these things into the multitudes, than to go on and on about monks, eating of meat, and similar things, which the common people can scarcely understand properly."[82]

Even when Melanchthon spoke of faith, he kept coming back to the importance of *poenitentia*. Faith, or the remission of sins, can be understood only when people have heard beforehand the teaching of fear or *poenitentia*, "because faith cannot be conceived except in a contrite heart."[83] Melanchthon expanded the notion of faith to include not only forgiveness, but also God's continual rule by the Holy Spirit who sanctifies us. This forgiveness is obtained not by our merit, but on account of Christ. According to Luke 17:10, "You say, 'We are unworthy servants'"; our merit and works do not avail.[84]

Here for the first time Melanchthon mentioned that the doctors of the church divided *poenitentia* into three parts, contrition, confession, and satisfaction. In this context he was concerned to point out only that satisfaction is not a matter of our works but of Christ's propitiation for our sins. But as soon as Melanchthon concluded this discussion, he returned to the fact that there is no faith without fear of God and a contrite heart. The one follows the other as the sunrise follows the dawn. Salvation follows a specific process: "When God is about to have mercy, the heart is frightened and filled with fear of his judgment; that is *poenitentia* or contrition. If it then hears the gospel, that is, if it hears that its sins are forgiven on account of Christ, it also believes it is certainly forgiven."[85] This then is true, not simulated, faith, which is conceived by the Spirit and bears fruit.

Melanchthon returned to the importance of contrition in the next section, entitled "De cruce."[86] The human being is justified by faith, not by

82. *CR* 26:10: "Haec inculcare multitudini multo satius est, quam vociferari de monachis, et esu carnium et similibus rebus, quas vulgus vix unquam recte intelligit."

83. *CR* 26:10: "Secunda pars doctrinae est doctrina remissionis peccatorum seu doctrina fidei. Haec intelligi ita demum potest, si ante doctrinam timoris seu poenitentiae audierint, quia fides non potest concipi, nisi in corde contrito."

84. Agricola cited this verse in a different context to exclude the law from the Christian life. Here Melanchthon corrected this approach by tying the verse to the question of merit.

85. *CR* 26:11: "Quando Deus misertus, perterrefacit cor et incutit alicui metum iudicii, ea scilicet seu poenitentia, seu contritio, si tum audiat Evangelion, hoc est, si audiat sibi condonari peccata propter Christum, et credat certo ignosci."

86. This order reflects Luther's purses and pockets from the description of catechesis in the "Deutsche Messe" (see p. 50) and Melanchthon's own catechism.

human merits or works, "but there is no faith except in the heart that is contrite, or mortified, or doing *poenitentia*."[87] It seems as if Melanchthon could not repeat it often enough. He divided the discussion of the cross into four parts. First, people must be taught that all afflictions come from God. Second, they must learn that the reason for this affliction is, as part of the law and its penalty, to call us to *poenitentia*, not to crush us. Third, affliction should teach us patience and, fourth, lead us to prayer.[88]

A few sections later Melanchthon again returned to this theme under the topic "De timore Dei."[89] He again emphasized that faith cannot exist without fear of God and insisted that this faith "must be very diligently inculcated" because Christ has warned that even when Satan is expelled from someone, he comes back with seven other demons. The gospel exposes the powers of darkness, as is clear from John 16:8–11, a text Melanchthon used to structure his comments. The Holy Spirit accuses the world of sin, which encompasses not only external things, but also hidden things in the heart, among which Melanchthon included "to lack fear of the judgment of God."[90] He distinguished two kinds of fear. Some, like Satan, believe the story of the gospel but not their own forgiveness. This is servile fear. The other, called filial fear, is akin to trust, where the heart is terrified and faith is aroused to believe that one is forgiven and God is placated: "In this way fear and faith are felt and exercise themselves. Nor are the thoughts of the soul lazy, but it is necessary for souls truly to shudder with fear and afterwards truly to receive again consolation and joy through faith."[91]

In his discussion of the sacraments Melanchthon returned to this theme. Baptism is a sign of *poenitentia*, the death of the old being.[92] The effect of baptism continues throughout one's life. When Melanchthon turned to the sacrament of penance itself, he argued that it is not a sacrament distinct from either baptism or the Lord's Supper, but that it signifies both. Here again he discussed the three traditional parts of *poenitentia*. He defined contrition as sorrow over sin or fear of punishment, the feeling "that we are condemned to eternal death."[93] While contrition varies from person to person, God must be sought in order

---

87. *CR* 26:12: "sed fides non est nisi in corde contrito, seu mortificato, seu agente poenitentiam."
88. *CR* 26:12f. The final comment introduced the section on prayer.
89. *CR* 26:17f.
90. *CR* 26:17f.: "vacare metu iudicii Dei."
91. *CR* 26:18: "Taliter sentiuntur et exercent sese timor et fides, nec otiosae sunt cogitationes animi, sed necesse est revera perhorrescere animos timore, et postea iterum revera per fidem consolationem et gaudium accipere."
92. *CR* 26:18.
93. *CR* 26:20: "sentire quod sumus rei aeternae mortis."

that it be "verissima." Melanchthon added, in words that soon became the subject of debate, "people must always be exhorted to contrition."[94]

Melanchthon then turned to the second part of *poenitentia,* confession to God that we are worthy of punishment. The other type of confession, to a priest, ought not be a matter of reciting all one's sins, for that is impossible. Nevertheless, no one ought to be admitted to the Eucharist without confession. Moreover, one ought not be asked just what one thinks of the Eucharist, but also whether one is sorry for one's sins and believes that remission of sin will follow. Individuals who are particularly anguished must be encouraged and have explained to them that God gives the keys of the kingdom to the church, so that it may take his place and they may believe the absolution. The only satisfaction that must be taught is that of Christ. This ought both to show God's hatred of sin and to increase faith. Melanchthon closed this section with a summary: "The conscience, touched by the horror of judgment, feels that it is not enough to please God. But faith is to feel certain that on account of Christ our sins are forgiven and that God now wants to rule and defend the one received in grace."[95] Horror of judgment, faith in Christ's sacrifice for sin and in God's will to rule and defend us: these sum up the Christian life. Melanchthon saw in them the move from law to gospel, from *mortificatio* to *vivificatio.*

When he came to the section entitled "De traditionibus humanis," Melanchthon again returned to the theme of the entire booklet. He criticized those preachers who were only too happy to attack human traditions, but did not inculcate in their hearers the fear of God. What they were actually doing was teaching the common people, who did not know better, contempt for all laws—human and divine. He distinguished different types of traditions: those that contradict divine precepts and must be abolished, and those that concern "mediae res" (what he later called *adiaphora*) and must be performed, not as a necessary means to justification, but only for the sake of peace and order in the community. In changing such practices one must proceed with moderation, caring for the weak and easily scandalized. To dispute with the common people about such practices is simply to become "the authors of the greatest scandals" and "the authors of greater license."[96]

The section on traditions led directly into Melanchthon's discussion of Christian freedom. Here we discover another section that matches mate-

---

94. *CR* 26:20: "Semper autem homines ad contritionem adhortandi sunt."
95. *CR* 26:21: "Conscientia enim horrore iudicii tacta, sentit ea non esse satis ad placandum Deum. Fides autem est certe sentire, quod propter Christum peccata nobis condonata sunt, et quod Deus iam receptum in gratiam velit regere et defendere."
96. *CR* 26:25: "maximorum scandalorum autores" and "autores maioris licentiae." Melanchthon's comments in the *Scholia* had made the same points.

rial in the *Scholia*, this time down to individual phrases.[97] The first level of Christian freedom is forgiveness of sins and freedom from the devil's power.[98] This level of freedom Melanchthon viewed as a great consolation for human hearts. The second level of freedom is freedom from the law of Moses. Again Melanchthon divided this law into three parts, arguing that the ceremonial and judicial laws are no longer binding on Christians. Instead, as Gentiles we have our own civil law. What remains in effect is the Decalog, written in our hearts and repeated in the gospel; this moral law is not abolished. Melanchthon contrasted this view of Christian freedom to what was preached during the Peasants' War of 1525. The least important level of Christian freedom concerns human traditions that do not justify us before God. As in the previous section, Melanchthon warned about straining at gnats and swallowing camels.

As if all this were not enough, in a section called "De lege" Melanchthon returned one last time to the question of the relation between law and *poenitentia*. Here he brought into focus the great differences between Agricola's theology and his own. To begin with, Melanchthon argued: "Law must be taught for two reasons, for it has two effects: to coerce the flesh and to terrify the conscience."[99] This meant, first, that the law must be taught to coerce "rudes homines." As proof Melanchthon offered two texts: "The law was given on account of transgressions" (Gal. 3:19) and "the law is given for the unjust" (1 Tim. 1:9). Here Melanchthon explicitly censured those who, when they hear that we are not justified by our own powers or deeds, live the most impure lives. "They will incur great punishment from God."[100]

Second, the law must be taught to terrify consciences, for, according to Romans 3:20, "through the law comes knowledge of sin." Melanchthon glossed this text, "that is, so that people may be called to *poenitentia*, and through *poenitentia* to faith and Christian righteousness."[101]

97. Cf. *MSA* 4:287–91 with *CR* 26:25f.

98. *MSA* 4:287.8–10, 11–13, 22–23: "Est autem libertas Christiana: Primum conscientiam habere liberatam a peccato; Secundo habere Spiritum sanctum et esse liberatum a potestate diaboli. . . . Sic de libertate Christus loquitur Iohan. 8[:36]: 'Si vos filius liberaverit, vere liberi eritis.' . . . Et hic gradus libertatis Christianae diligenter inculcandus erat hominibus." *CR* 26:25: "Libertas Christiana primum haec est, habere remissionem peccatorum per Christum et consequi Spiritum sanctum, per quem liberemur a potestate diaboli. Ioh. 4. [sic] Si vos filius liberavit, vere liberi estis. De hoc gradu libertatis diligenter docendum est."

99. *CR* 26:28: "Lex est docenda propter duas caussas; habet enim duos effectus, cohercere carnem et terrere conscientiam."

100. *CR* 26:28: "Hi maximas poenas dabunt Deo."

101. *CR* 26:28: "Secundo, docenda est lex, ut terreat conscientias, iuxta illud: Per legem cognitio peccati, i. e. ut homines ad poenitentiam vocentur, et per poenitentiam ad fidem et ad iustitiam Christianam."

101

Then, as if making a final plea to those who might oppose him, Melanchthon concluded the same way he began the Articles:

> May they hold these two effects of the law before their eyes and in their minds. May those who teach in the churches diligently teach the doctrine of the law. Otherwise, where the doctrine of faith is taught without the law, infinite scandals arise, the common folk become secure, and they imagine that they possess the righteousness of faith because they do not know that this faith is possible only in those who have contrite hearts through the law.[102]

Over the course of a year, with the appearance of various writings by Agricola, Melanchthon had become more and more convinced of a glaring weakness in his friend's theology. When in the course of the visitation he discovered that some preachers were attacking human traditions and that the common people were flouting the law while claiming they had faith, he used his considerable authority to attack the problem directly. Of course, he did not name names and tried instead simply to refute Agricola's arguments through his own catechetical proposal. In this one small booklet Melanchthon confronted the theological aberration he most feared (lawlessness and a faith that substituted security for trust in God's forgiveness through Christ's sacrifice). His presentation of a theological program most incompatible with that of Agricola, who feared above all a return to the rules and regulations of Rome, resulted in public dispute.

---

102. *CR* 26:28: "Hos duos effectus legis ob oculos et in conspectu habeant. Hi, qui docent in ecclesiis, diligenter tradant doctrinam legis, alioqui, ubi doctrina fidei sine lege traditur, infinita scandala oriuntur, vulgus fit securum, et somniant se habere iustitiam fidei, quia nesciunt, fidem in his tantum esse posse, qui habent contrita per legem corda."

4

Tempest in the Torgau
(August-November 1527)

The public dispute between Philip Melanchthon and John Agricola over the Visitation Articles lasted scarcely more than three months. Reaction to Melanchthon's Visitation Articles was quick in coming. Discussions between Luther and the elector had begun by the middle of August. By the end of August, both Melanchthon and Luther were defending the approach to *poenitentia* found in the Articles. After the conference at the Torgau Castle near the end of September, a second storm of protest began, sparked by the unauthorized publication of a Latin version of the Articles and the arrival in Wittenberg of Melanchthon's *Scholia* on Colossians. This resulted in a second, more widely attended conference at the Torgau near the end of November, after which peace—or at least a lasting truce—was established. On the basis of the disagreements and the resulting concord, both Melanchthon and Agricola changed their exegetical and catechetical work in the following year.

Round One: The Parts of *Poenitentia* and Creeping Back to Rome

On 29 July 1527, the visitors for electoral Saxony, Hans von der Planitz, Asmus von Haubitz, and Philip Melanchthon, sent an interim report to the elector describing their work to date.[1] Among other things, they reported having visited Saalfeld on 21 July, where the pastor, John Plack, and the preacher, Caspar Aquila, were capable enough, but unpaid, in part because of a major fire in the city. Both an accompanying letter of the visitors and the response of the elector complained that problems

---

1. *MBW* 567 (R. Hermann, *Beiträge zur thüringischen Kirchengeschichte* 1 [1929–31]: 209–24).

had arisen due to attempts by Count Albert of Mansfeld to prevent the visitation in Saalfeld.[2]

From approximately this time arose an exchange of letters between Melanchthon and Aquila. The first of these letters, from the beginning of August 1527, recounted Melanchthon's direct experience with Aquila and contained an admonition to watch out for the influence of Andreas Karlstadt and his interpretation of the Lord's Supper. Melanchthon also warned that those people who do nothing else in their sermons but complain about the monks and the pope show no more concern for the church than does Karlstadt: "For this reason I have written these things, so that I may exhort you to teach most moderately, looking to what is necessary for those whom you teach, rather than how you might wound the adversaries."[3]

Aquila had good reason to rail against pope and monk. Born in 1488 in Augsburg, he went to school in Ulm; during travels to Italy he met Erasmus and thereafter became a preacher. After a brief time at the University of Leipzig, he took a position in 1516 as field preacher for Franz von Sickingen and shortly thereafter as preacher in Jengen near Augsburg. There he came under Luther's influence and was arrested and imprisoned by his bishop. Freed in 1520, he went to Wittenberg, where in 1521 he received a master's degree and became the teacher for von Sickingen's sons. During the time that the castle Ebernburg was under siege, he (as the only cleric on the premises) refused to baptize the first cannonball fired into the fortress by the enemy and would have been shot out of a cannon by von Sickingen's soldiers had the powder not failed to ignite. Allowed to escape, he became court preacher for the elector of Saxony in 1524 and, at Luther's recommendation, preacher in Saalfeld in 1527.[4]

Aquila's now lost response to the young visitor must have been quite harsh, for it evoked a spirited defense from Melanchthon. Though Melanchthon's reply has been dated to the middle of October 1527,[5] there are several reasons for redating it to the end of August or the beginning of September 1527. First, in parallel with Melanchthon's initial letter, it dealt with the harsh preaching of Aquila. It referred directly to Melanchthon's visitation activities ("in hoc itinere"). The Visitation Ar-

---

2. *MBW* 566 (not extant) and *MBW* 570 (unpublished); the latter is dated 3 August 1527.

3. *MBW* 568 (*CR* 4:1035): "Haec ideo scripsi, ut te hortarer, ut moderatissime doceas et potius quid opus sit his, quos doces, spectes quam quomodo ulciscaris adversarios."

4. For this paragraph see *Allgemeine Deutsche Biographie*, s.v. "Aquila, Kaspar," and Georg Biundo, *Kaspar Aquila: Ein Kämpfer für das Evangelium in der Pfalz, in Sachsen und Thüringen* (Grünstadt/Pfalz: Verein für Pfälzische Kirchengeschichte, 1963).

5. *MBW* 604 (*CR* 4:959f.).

ticles, which Melanchthon would later refer to as a "libellus," are here called a "scriptum," perhaps indicating that they had not yet been printed. In addition, the letter referred to attacks by nonevangelical preachers and to the immediate troubles in Saalfeld, with which Melanchthon had just become acquainted. Another consideration is that the letter's rehearsal of Aquila's objections to the manuscript version of the Visitation Articles made no mention of Agricola's later challenges to Melanchthon, but only of the narrow question of dividing *poenitentia* into the three traditional parts. This reflected a simultaneous early challenge by Agricola, to which Luther responded on 31 August 1527.[6] Finally, the editors of Melanchthon's correspondence dated his letter of defense to mid-October because in a letter dated 27 October 1527 Luther mentioned Melanchthon's complaint that some (*quidam*) had attacked his understanding of *poenitentia;* Luther added that Agricola had also made an attack. Although the editors construed the "quidam" as referring to Aquila, Melanchthon was more likely referring indirectly to Agricola's renewed attack against him.[7] This interpretation squares with two other letters, dated in early November, in which Melanchthon informed Aquila of renewed attacks and mentioned Agricola by name.[8]

What was the nature of Aquila's attack? Melanchthon's letter gave a running account of the challenges. First, Aquila complained about Melanchthon's failure to deal with the "quorundam sacrificulorum importunitas."[9] Saalfeld's clergy was by no means completely evangelical, and these priests, probably encouraged by the count of Mansfeld, must have been attacking Aquila and the evangelicals. While admitting that these priests were the "semina discordiae," Melanchthon contrasted his own efforts to establish "concordia." Both during the visitation and in his earlier letter Melanchthon had urged moderation on those who preach the gospel.[10] Given this goal of moderation, Melanchthon continued, he had approved some teachings of the former age, in this case the threefold division of *poenitentia*, since, as long as satisfaction is attributed to Christ, this division is useful for teaching.[11]

---

6. *WABr* 4:241f.; see also *WABr* 4:265, 232, 255.
7. *MBW* 612 (*WABr* 4:271–73). Cf. Melanchthon's letter to Camerarius, 23 October 1527 (*MBW* 610 [*CR* 1:919–21]), which also discussed Agricola.
8. *MBW* 618 and 619 (*CR* 1:906f. and 4:957f.). On the basis of the above arguments Walther Thüringer of the Melanchthon-Forschungsstelle in Heidelberg has suggested a date of late August or early September for Melanchthon's reply to Aquila (*MBW* 604).
9. *CR* 4:959.
10. *CR* 4:959: "ut moderate et sine conuiciis suum officium faciant."
11. *CR* 4:959: "Si tamen tribuatur satisfactio Christi [=Christo?], eamque partitionem utilem esse existimo ad docendum." In 1537 the Visitation Articles again came under attack for misunderstanding *poenitentia* and law. See *WA* 39.1:344.

With this positive assessment of his work plainly stated, Melanchthon took up Aquila's second charge, that Melanchthon himself had now become a papist and a patron for the monks.[12] Melanchthon's first response was irony bordering on sarcasm, a characteristic which we will encounter time and time again in this dispute and which actually serves as one of the hallmarks of his intra-Lutheran polemic. He had once believed that the Saale River could more quickly return to its source than that Aquila's opinion of him could change so rapidly. Turning again to the major point at issue, he referred Aquila to "scriptum meum" which Aquila had at his house, a writing showing how Melanchthon divided *poenitentia*. This indicates that Aquila must have been familiar with some writing of Melanchthon describing the division of *poenitentia*, most likely an early copy of the Visitation Articles themselves.

Melanchthon then explained the reasons for this division. Everyone defined *poenitentia* as mortification of the flesh, self-denial, or knowledge of sin, but no one, neither the common people nor the doctors whom Melanchthon had heard on his recent visit, knew what that meant.[13] Thus, Melanchthon preferred to call the beginning of *poenitentia* contrition. The other parts, confession and satisfaction, were clear and caused no sane person any occasion to complain.

Aquila had a different idea about *poenitentia*. He would have liked to see it laughed off the stage.[14] Melanchthon's reply dripped with contempt. What do I hear? What reason is there for it to be laughed off the stage when in fact it is useful for teaching if rightly understood? This, of course, returned to his initial argument that the reason for using the threefold division, or any such division, was its usefulness in teaching. Melanchthon then added an attack against those who, in their great hatred of the pope, condemned both good and bad. From this behavior, however, came only scandal. Contrary to such behavior, Melanchthon argued for tolerance and leniency, referring Aquila to Romans 14:13 where Paul urges ἐπιείκεια. Melanchthon, turning the tables on Aquila, demanded the same virtue of Aquila himself, who had argued so sharply against this division.[15] He reminded Aquila that some (was he thinking of Karlstadt, Müntzer, or Zwingli?) had acted not to sup-

---

12. *CR* 4:959: "Nunc tu quereris 'me Papistam factum esse, me patrocinari Monachis.'"

13. *CR* 4:959: "Quorum verborum nihil neque vulgus intelligit neque doctores aliquot, quos quidem in hoc itinere audivi." "Doctores" could perhaps be taken to mean the teachers Melanchthon had encountered or, more likely, the Scholastic doctors who had been cited to him.

14. *CR* 4:959: "'Vellem,' inquis, 'haec nomina poenitentiae prorsus explosa esse.'"

15. *CR* 4:959: "Nunc ἐπιείκειαν in te desidero sic ἀποτόμως disputante de hac partitione."

port concord in the church, but to rule it. They thought they were wise if they totally condemned the teachings of the old church. Aquila knew this to be the case for many, but Melanchthon, true to the complimentary style of his age, added that he expected better of him. "I have always loved your modesty,"[16] he wrote, adding that he hoped others would not wrest it from Aquila. The flattery put Aquila in the awkward position of having to contradict both Paul's admonition and Philip's expectation.

Aquila had also feared that using the traditional terminology would mean that his opponents could now boast that they had carried the day.[17] Melanchthon repeated his arguments. The only aim of such people was to rule. Aquila, contrariwise, was to keep calm and remain patient.

With this out of the way, Melanchthon then turned to Aquila's pressing concern about some monks. Apparently the count of Mansfeld controlled some monasteries and preaching posts in the area. Melanchthon pointed out that, although those posts were under Count Albert's control, the monks were not allowed to teach in the city. Obviously they were trying to get Aquila to attack them. Melanchthon appealed to Aquila for restraint, this time placing such attacks in terms of the future of Christianity in Saalfeld itself. What will happen, he asked rhetorically, if the common folk curse the monks, if old customs are ignored, if the monks are thrown out of their homes, and "if barbaric soldiers are brought into this place, which has been designated for the study of Holy Writ"?[18]

In closing, Melanchthon reflected upon the state of the church he had encountered in the visitation. First, he insisted that many things were better taught now, thank God, than ever. Second, other things were taught better in the past than by some unlearned "Lutherani" now. Third, Aquila's task was to heal the souls both of the adversaries and of the common folk and to refuse to feed the hatred of these factions. Fourth, some papists actually had reason to rebuke the behavior of some evangelicals. In his final prayer Melanchthon revealed again his modus operandi. He asked for concord, convinced that Aquila could conquer his adversaries with patience. He closed by asking Aquila to respond.

16. *CR* 4:960: "Tuam modestiam semper amavi."

17. *CR* 4:960: "'Sed quidam' inquies 'tollunt cristas [bear feathers, lit. =are conceited], maledicunt Euangelio, quia quaedam in veteri doctrina approbamus.'"

18. *CR* 4:960: "Noli putare rem christianam ita futuram meliori loco, si vulgus vehementer maledicat Monachis, si omnes veteres mores irrideat, si Monachi e possessionibus eiiciantur, si inducantur in haec loca, destinata studiis sacrarum literarum, barbari milites."

Before examining Aquila's response, we need to examine a letter that Luther wrote to John Agricola at precisely the same time. Agricola, in Eisleben at the court of Count Albert of Mansfeld, had doubtless heard of the problems in Saalfeld. Aquila may even have turned to Agricola for support. (Three years later Agricola dedicated his commentary on Titus to Aquila, whom he addressed as catechist.)[19] From Luther's letter we can discern two questions that Agricola had raised. First, he had asked about Christian liberty, which was, as we have seen, a bone of contention between himself and Melanchthon as well as a subject emphasized in the Visitation Articles. Luther responded in general terms about the necessity of caring for the weak.[20] Second, Agricola must have complained about the Articles themselves. Luther counseled restraint and patience. For Luther would himself go over the Articles upon Melanchthon's return and before publication by the elector; in the meantime any disputes should be curtailed, lest the visitation itself be impeded.[21] What we learn about from Luther's letter is an early challenge from Agricola regarding Christian freedom and Luther's insistence on patience. Agricola's concern seemed to match Aquila's, and Luther's answer mirrored Melanchthon's.

A second reply to Aquila reflected a satisfactory resolution to his first challenge.[22] This letter, too, should be dated differently. For if the assigned date of the end of December is correct, Melanchthon accepted Aquila's apology for the later controversy twice.[23] However, at this

19. "IN EPIS= | TOLAM PAVLI | AD TITVM | Scholia. | IOAN. AGRICOLA | Islebio Autore. | PHIL. MEL. | οὐδὲκε δαιδάλεος τ[ὸν] Χριστὸν γράψαι | Ἀπελλῆς, | Ἔνθεος ὡς Παῦλος τῷ δ᾽ ἐχάραξε | λόγῳ. | I. K. | Non sic Daedaleus Christum pinxisset Apelles, | Vt sacer hunc Paulus exprimit ore pio." Woodcut, 8°. Colophon: "Vvitebergae apud Georgium | Rhau. M.D.XXX." [68] leaves. The preface, dated 15 March 1530 in "Salfeld," addressed Aquila as κατηχήστη. In 1537 Aquila was also named as one of Agricola's supporters. This early friendship contrasted sharply to Aquila's later harsh attack on Agricola for his support of the Augsburg Interim—"Wider den spöttischen | Lügner vnd vnverschempten ver= | leumbder D. Eßlebium | Agricolam. | Nötige verantwor= | tung/ vnd Ernstliche warnung/ | Wider das Interim. | APOLOGIA | M. CASPARIS A= | QVILAE | Bischoff zu Salfeldt. | M.D.XLVIII." Colophon: "Geben Freytag nach Jacobi [July 27] 1548 | Caspar Aquila subscrip." This attack arose when, typical of his approach, Agricola met with Aquila and later claimed that Aquila said he would accept the Interim. See *MBW* 5232 (*CR* 7:77–79), Aquila's letter to Melanchthon (whose attack on the Interim was published a little earlier). Aquila was so angry that he broke into a long passage of German to express his feelings, calling Agricola a "Grundschalk" and a wolf in sheep's clothing.

20. *WABr* 4:241.3–23.

21. *WABr* 4:241.24–28: "De visitatoribus nostris et eorum decretis agemus, cum aderit Philippus; nam hic excudetur, quantum intelligo ex Principe Electore. Interim patientiam habeto, et disputationes super hac re coerceto, ne opus istud necessarium visitationis ante tempus et ante causam impediatur in curso suo. Christus dabit, ut omnia recte fiant."

22. *MBW* 638.

23. Cf. *MBW* 633.

point the issue was not, as in the later controversy, the basis and cause of true *poenitentia*, but Aquila's preaching against the monks, Melanchthon's division of *poenitentia* into three parts, and the greed of some citizens who wanted to get their hands on the monks' property—all concerns in Melanchthon's defense against Aquila's early attack (*MBW* 604). A reference to Jerome Schurff's imminent departure suggests a date for this second reply of around 10 September 1527.[24]

Aquila's letter must have been quite an exercise in humility. Melanchthon was quick to proclaim himself satisfied with the response and of one mind with Aquila. But he immediately added the request that Aquila teach moderately and concentrate on those things that edify his hearers.[25] He again urged that Aquila not be provoked to attack by the curses of the monks or the calumnies of others. In a moment of honesty, Melanchthon admitted that he knew his division of *poenitentia* would offend some, but, as he was encouraging Aquila to do, he himself was not going to be affected by the attacks.[26] This was as close as Melanchthon came to admitting openly that the Visitation Articles were conceived as an attack against the likes of Agricola. He called his attackers "leves et frivolae sycophantes" who have nothing more to do with good men than with the peoples of India or Arabia.[27]

We have in these two replies, along with Luther's to Agricola, the outline of the earliest attacks against the Visitation Articles. The primary target of the attacks was the continued use of teachings and ceremonies from the old church, namely the threefold division of *poenitentia* and the relation between Christian freedom and certain human traditions. The objections seemed to include the rumor that the evangelicals' adversaries would view the Visitation Articles as a return to Rome. Aquila approached Melanchthon directly; and Agricola, as was his wont, approached Melanchthon indirectly through Luther. The replies to these challenges showed no sense of panic nor any hint that these matters had been reported formally to the court. Both Melanchthon and Luther argued in similar ways about the need for patience and moderation. By the middle of September Melanchthon was writing Aquila on the

---

24. Walther Thüringer, letter to the author, received on 10 September 1991. (Like Melanchthon's letter, Thüringer's memorandum is undated.) See *MBW* 592 and 616 for more information about Schurff's travels.

25. *CR* 1:899: "Mihi quidem, mi Caspar, facile patiar abs te satisfieri. Est enim perspecta mihi tua erga me voluntas perpetua. Verum hoc te rogo etiam atque etiam ut tuam ecclesiam moderate doceas ea, quae ad edificationem faciunt."

26. *CR* 1:899: "Non ignorabam ego, fore qui ex illa mea partitione poenitentiae offenderentur. Sed non putabam omnium calumniis nos moveri debere."

27. *CR* 1:899; see also *MBW* 625 (*CR* 4:962), dated 17 November 1527, where Melanchthon expressly used the term *sycophant* for Agricola.

friendliest terms, answering his questions about the pastoral problems of engagements and drunkenness.[28]

Another piece of correspondence from September revealed how both the court and Wittenberg's theologians handled the objections. On 13 September 1527 Luther wrote to George Spalatin that the adversaries' boast that the Visitation Articles signaled a return to Rome would not endure. He was more than pleased with the ordinances.[29] In any case, the visitors were going to have a hard time pleasing everyone. As in earlier letters,[30] Luther saw the problem primarily in terms of Roman adversaries. Having seen the Articles by this time, he had no reason to question their usefulness or orthodoxy.

At this point, apparently according to a prearranged plan, the visitors met at the Torgau with Spalatin and theologians from Wittenberg. Having finished their swing through Altenburg in less time than expected, the visitors even asked the electoral counselors for permission to meet earlier than 26 September.[31] But from the account books for the Torgau we learn that the meeting took place as planned. On the morning of 26 September a runner was sent from the Torgau to fetch Luther and Johann Bugenhagen, who arrived on the same day and stayed overnight.[32]

The order of the day was not so much Aquila and Agricola as Zwingli and the Visitation Articles themselves. As is typical for documents of this kind, they were worked over thoroughly, giving Hans the stenographer plenty to do.[33] Melanchthon's report to Justus Jonas shortly after the meeting showed that the participants discussed the Visitation Articles and the Lord's Supper controversy, but it mentioned nothing about Aquila or Agricola.[34] In fact, the correspondence before mid-October showed no hint of an open conflict. To be sure, however, the challenge from their adversaries that had so exercised Aquila (namely, that the Reformers were creeping back to Rome) must have been a topic for discussion. In this context Melanchthon probably learned from Luther of Agricola's similar challenge.

The results of this meeting were preserved in a letter from the elector to Martin Luther. By 30 September the elector had seen the work of the

---

28. *MBW* 592 (*CR* 4:957).

29. *WABr* 4:247.7–10: "Si de his statutis gloriantur aduersarii, misera est eorum gloriatio nec diu durabilis. . . . Mihi satis placet ista ordinatio."

30. *WABr* 4:232.

31. *MBW* 594 (*SM* 6.1:386f.); the letter is dated 19 September from Altenburg and requests a meeting on 23 September.

32. Georg Buchwald, "Lutherana: Notizen aus Rechnungsbüchern des Thüringischen Staatsarchivs zu Weimar," *ARG* 25 (1928): 1–98, esp. 4 and 44.

33. Ibid., 44: "iij gulden Hansen dem korales, hat die ordenung der visitacion iij mahl umbgeschrieben."

34. *MBW* 599 (*CR* 1:912f.).

counselors and the theologians and now was sending the Articles back to Luther and Bugenhagen for further editing. He gave them a free hand to change anything in order to prepare the document for publication. The elector then issued a challenge similar to those already made by Aquila and Agricola:

> We also do not want to conceal from you our gracious opinion that it concerns us should the papists gloat somewhat that this order of the visitation is to go out in this form: for example, with titles of *Buße*, confession, etc. For they will interpret such things in this manner, as if now one wanted to retreat from previous teachings into their abuses.[35]

Elector John worried about the papists and their glee at watching the Reformers fall back into the old Roman position. At issue was the continued use of the threefold division of *poenitentia*. The counselor Gregory Brück, who doubtless understood the dispute more fully, had in an original draft made the elector's point even clearer:

> [. . . that the order of the visitation is to go out in such a form that] from the understanding therein of satisfaction and *poenitentia* among other things, the papists imagine what they want and thus interpret these things in accord with their old manner and form. Therefore we hold that it will be necessary to explain and expand the same two articles with great care as to how they are to be understood. Consequently, it is our intent that you will be able to safeguard these same articles, so that they may not be justly assailed by the papists as they want.[36]

Given the suspicion of returning to Roman practices, the elector and his counselor seemed eager to change the Articles and clarify the issue of *poenitentia* by using other terms or, as the elector went on to say, providing an explanation of the differences in interpretation.[37]

Luther's response to the elector defined very clearly his position in the entire dispute.[38] First, he refused to give in to Elector John's pres-

---

35. *WABr* 4:255.14–18: "Wir wellen euch auch gnediger meynung nit bergen, das vns angelangt, als solten dy Bapisten etwas frolockung haben, das dise ordnung der visitation dergestalt als mit titelen der bus, beicht &c. ausgeben sol. Denn sy wollen solchs dohin deuten, als ob man yetzt von vorigen leren wider zuruck auff ire misbreuch fallen wolle."

36. *WABr* 4:255, footnote to line 17: ". . . aus dem, das dy Satisfacion vnd poenitentz vnter anderm dorynnen mitbegriffen, die vermeinen dy Bapisten irs gefallens vnd also auf ir alt weiß vnd form zudeuten. Darumb achten wir, es woll von nöten sein, das man dieselben zwen artikel mit gutem bedacht ercler vnd ausstreiche, wie die sollten verstanden werden. Wollen vns demnach vorsehen, ir werdet dieselben artikel, domit die durch dy Bapisten irs gefallens mit fug nit anzufechten, wol zuuerwaren wissen."

37. *WABr* 4:255.20–25.

38. *WABr* 4:265–66, dated 12 October 1527.

sure. He gave the assurance that he and Bugenhagen had read the Articles and found little to change. Second, like Melanchthon he kept the intended audience in view—the simple folk who need instructions they can understand: "For everything pleases us very much, because it is set out for the masses in the simplest way."[39] Third, Luther refused to change anything because of gainsayers. They would be silenced, he argued; their objections were only a sign that when one does a godly work, one has to put up with the devil's talking and lying.[40] Fourth, perhaps with a view to Aquila's behavior, Luther insisted that "our people" be prevented from using force against those preachers unwilling to change. He reminded the elector that not everything could be accomplished at once and that one had to live with a church composed of weeds and wheat. "For establishing an order and holding to an established order are two completely different things."[41] He advised the elector, according to Ecclesiastes 11:6, to do what he could and leave the rest to God, even in the area of worldly government.

This oft-overlooked letter not only clarifies Luther's position in this first phase of the controversy over the Articles, it also illumines his overall position on the visitation and church reform. His major concern here and later in his catechisms was the common people. He did not believe that polemic and new vocabulary served the purposes of the gospel. Nor did he imagine that church reform would occur by princely command. He was willing to leave old and new practices side by side, so convinced was he of the eventual triumph of the gospel, and so sure was he that force would not accomplish anything. In this irenic approach he agreed fully with Melanchthon's advice to Aquila. Luther also placed the rumors within an eschatological framework. When godly things happen, the devil cannot keep his mouth shut. That had been Luther's experience all along, and he expected nothing different in this particular case.

At the same time Luther was advising the elector, Melanchthon wrote a letter to his friend John Agricola.[42] He complained about Agricola's failure to write now that they were even closer to one another (Melanchthon was still in Jena), and he promised to continue to write

---

39. *WABr* 4:265.4f.: "Denn es uns alles fast wohlgefället, weil es für den Pöbel aufs einfältigst ist gestellet."

40. *WABr* 4:265.5–9: "Daß aber die Widerwärtigen möchten rühmen, wir kröchen wieder zurück, ist nicht groß zu achten; es wird wohl still werden. Wer was gottlichs furnimmt, der muß dem Teufel das Maul lassen, dawider zu plaudern vnd lügen, wie ich bisher hab tun müssen."

41. *WABr* 4:265.17f.: "Denn Ordnung stellen vnd gestellte Ordnung halten sind zwei Ding weit von einander."

42. *MBW* 598 (Bindseil, 511), dated by *MBW* to around 2 October 1527.

even if he had nothing worth writing about. He then reported his meeting at the Torgau with Luther and Bugenhagen. There he had discovered that Agricola had falsely accused him of renewing old practices as he inspected the churches.[43] At this juncture Melanchthon made no mention of the basis and cause of true *poenitentia* or the use of the law, but only the same accusations reflected in Melanchthon's earlier letters to Aquila and Luther's to Agricola as well as in the exchanges between Luther and the court. Melanchthon then referred Agricola to his explanation "in that booklet" (that is, the Visitation Articles), which he had reason to believe Agricola had seen.[44] It had satisfied Luther and many others.[45] Melanchthon then changed the topic to his dedication of his Colossians commentary to Alexander Drachstedt. Although he had recently seen a copy at a friend's, he did not as yet have any of his own, but promised to send copies to Drachstedt and Agricola as soon as he received some.

For those researchers who have not noticed the two distinct phases to the dispute, this letter seems misplaced, written almost as if Melanchthon did not realize the seriousness of Agricola's charges. In fact, in Melanchthon's mind there were no serious charges at this point. Clearly miffed that he had to hear about his friend's accusations from a third party and that the charges were false in any case, Melanchthon, in an uncharacteristic burst of forthrightness, brought the case very bluntly to Agricola's attention. That Melanchthon referred to the Visitation Articles in his defense showed that the battle had not yet turned to the theological content of that book itself. The reference to the *Scholia* and Drachstedt was Melanchthon's attempt to demonstrate his friendship. By referring to the commentary in this connection Melanchthon indicated that he associated his explanations in the Visitation Articles with the broader discussions in the *Scholia*. In this letter he also discussed Erasmus's *Hyperaspistes*, the other major opponent in the *Scholia*.

With this letter the first phase of the controversy came to an end. The charge was a return to Rome. At issue were the division of *poenitentia*

---

43. Bindseil, 511: "Erant ibi Lutherus et Pomeranus, ubi cognovi, me quoque falso delatum esse apud te, quod in inspectione ecclesiarum veteres ritus renovarem."

44. The history of reprints in 1527 seems to indicate that the Latin version may have been published right around this time. It could also be that Melanchthon imagined that Agricola had received a handwritten copy of the material from someone else, perhaps through Count Albert or Aquila, since he noted that it pleased Luther and others. What Luther and the others saw was not a printed Latin book but a handwritten German translation.

45. Bindseil, 511: "Ego quae gessi omnia, et in eo libello, quem vidisse te opinor, scripsi et satisfecit ipsi Luthero ille libellus ac plerisque aliis."

into three parts and the retention of old traditions in the church. The overarching concern was what Roman opponents, still active in churches and monasteries throughout the region, might say. Both Luther and Melanchthon responded by counseling patience, a renewed focus on the needs of the common people, and the necessity of avoiding confrontation and the use of force. Neither of them imagined that the theological content of the Articles was under suspicion. Despite challenges from Aquila and Agricola as well as a plea from the elector, the Visitation Articles remained virtually unchanged.

Round Two: The Basis and Cause of True *Poenitentia*

Sometime in September 1527 Nicholas Schirlentz came into possession of a copy of a Latin version of the Visitation Articles. Knowing a best-seller when he saw one, he immediately printed it. In a letter to Agricola from the end of October,[46] Melanchthon denied having had anything to do with its publication. He said the same in letters to Joachim Camerarius and Lazarus Spengler. It was also clear from these two letters that Spengler had just heard of the Articles, another indication that they had just been printed.[47] Melanchthon differentiated between the German version in the hands of the court and the Latin version, published without his permission.

The news of a second attack on Melanchthon took some time to sink in. For example, in a letter to Aquila shortly after mid-October, we find no mention of the problem at all.[48] In fact, the reference to the Torgau

46. *MBW* 615 (*CR* 1:904–6).

47. *MBW* 610 and 611 (*CR* 1:919–22), dated 23 October 1527. The letter to Camerarius in Nuremberg responded to Spengler's request for a copy of the Articles. The letter to Spengler questioned what the elector would do in regard to the entire visitation.

48. *MBW* 616 (*CR* 4:963f.; cf. *SM* 6.1:392, no. 590). *MBW* dates this letter to the end of October because of its connection to *MBW* 618, dated at the beginning of November. We accept instead the dating of *SM* 6.1. The fact that Schurff was known to be present in Jena on 28 October (see *MBW* 613) does not exclude his presence earlier, since he was the only jurist teaching classes there (see *MBW* 589, dated 10 September 1527). His departure for Jena had left a vacancy on the visitation team, filled by Spalatin (*MBW* 594). From the letter to Aquila (*MBW* 592) written just prior to the one under consideration, we know that in mid-September Schurff had just departed. Our letter itself rendered Melanchthon's judgment regarding the inability of the schoolmaster from Saalfeld to be chaplain. *MBW* 618 would make it clear that Melanchthon had not realized that the schoolmaster was already ordained. The other issues discussed in our letter, however, relate directly to *MBW* 592 (the marriage issue and drunkenness). The use of the word "argutissime" in this letter and in *MBW* 603 (to Spalatin, dated 15 October) to describe Erasmus's *Hyperaspistes* increases the likelihood that our letter was written in mid-October. The reference to the conference at the Torgau as having taken place "nuper (not long ago)" places it before the letter to Camerarius (*MBW* 610, dated 23 October) that described the conference as having occurred "proximo mense."

conference spoke only of a discussion on the Lord's Supper. The same silence echoed in letters to Spalatin on 15 and 19 October.[49] Sometime after that, in another letter to Spalatin, Melanchthon wondered in a postscript where Spalatin had come by his information about Agricola's complaints. Here we learn for the first time something about the nature of those complaints: "He censures some things in my booklet concerning *poenitentia*, because I do not begin to treat it from the love of righteousness."[50] The issue was no longer the threefold division of *poenitentia* or the rumors of returning to old church practices. It was clearly a serious theological matter. It was also an objection the gravity of which Melanchthon did not seem to appreciate: "I do not see that this has a great enough cause for his slanderous writing."[51] He closed by promising to stoop down in order to bear it, "although it continues to be irksome for me."[52]

In the aforementioned letter to Camerarius, Melanchthon complained that the Articles had been published without permission and that, although it was nothing more than a child's catechism, it had incited such tragedies. We hear also, he wrote, that someone "of our party" (Agricola) has composed "a very harsh censure (*peracerba censura*)." Melanchthon now expected an even more bitter attack. People were saying that Agricola would triumph over Melanchthon as if he had captured the king of France in battle.[53]

Melanchthon's response showed how he used the appearance of passivity to fight his battles: "But I will make the attempt to settle these things between us, and I will defeat his vehemence with my moderation and humanity."[54] Far from being either a virtue or a weakness, Melanchthon used moderation for a weapon, just as he had already counseled Aquila to do. In this instance his approach to the problem would triumph. In the same vein Melanchthon concluded the letter with a prayer that he would do nothing to increase discord. He summarized his "catechism" as a simple and pious attempt to teach the bare necessities in the church without controversy. By so doing he had hoped to cut short the "seeds of dissension."[55]

49. *MBW* 603 (*CR* 1:895f.), and *MBW* 606 (*CR* 1:896).

50. *MBW* 608 (*CR* 1:897), dated after 19 October 1527 by *MBW:* "Quaedam de *poenitentia* reprehendit in meo libello, quod non inchorim eam ab amore iustitiae."

51. *CR* 1:897: "Nec video illum satis magnam causam habere carpendi eius scripti."

52. *CR* 1:897: "Sed decrevi ferre, etiam si perget mihi molestus esse."

53. *CR* 1:920: "Nunc de me aiunt eum triumphare, tanquam si regem Gallorum in acie cepisset [=capisset]"—a feat recently achieved by Charles V.

54. *CR* 1:920: "Sed ego dabo operam, ut intra nos componatur haec res, et vincam mea moderatione atque humanitate istius vehementiam."

55. *CR* 1:920. Melanchthon had expressed a similar hope earlier to Aquila (*CR* 4:959).

Previous research by Joachim Rogge and Gustav Kawerau hypothesized that Agricola's "censura" was an identifiable, quasi-legal document now lost. More likely Melanchthon was referring to the one document Agricola did produce at this time: the "130 Fragestücke."[56] Here Agricola answered Melanchthon's "catechism" with an even sharper catechism of his own, rejecting Melanchthon's definitions of *poenitentia* and the law and calling for the elimination of the law from Christian teaching. (No wonder that at precisely this time Spalatin pleaded with Melanchthon to write a new catechism.)[57]

In the same letter to Camerarius, Melanchthon also outlined the charges, as he had heard them from friends. First, he had not taught that *poenitentia* stems from love of righteousness. Second, he had urged the preaching of the law to excess. Third, somewhere (in the *Scholia* it turned out) he distorted the Scripture. Fourth, in some places (probably in both the Visitation Articles and the *Scholia*) he hurt Christian liberty. He concluded, "[Agricola] makes me a double papist." Despite Luther's moderating letter, Agricola had not budged from his previous accusations against Melanchthon. Indeed, he had now added new ones.

At nearly the same time Melanchthon must have written a now lost letter explaining to Luther the new wave of attacks but not mentioning their source. Luther's response on 27 October not only gives us more information about the building controversy, but also reveals his own position in the fray.[58] He described Melanchthon's letter as having mentioned that someone (*quidam*) was castigating him for deriving *poenitentia* from the fear of God.[59] Luther mentioned that Agricola had made such a complaint about Melanchthon to him. Then, in words that have often been misconstrued, Luther called the whole thing a "war of words," important only to the common folk. Rogge and others have taken this to mean that Luther did not understand the seriousness (i.e., the antinomianism) of Agricola's challenge. Quite to the contrary. In terms of the sixteenth century's understanding, the phrase "a war of words" immediately put the challenger in a dispute at a distinct disadvantage. We already know from Melanchthon's letter to Camerarius that he did not want to contribute to the dissension, but wanted to win through moderation. Luther's letter meant that Melanchthon already was well on his way to victory. The burden of proof, as far as Luther was concerned, was not on the accused, Melanchthon, but on the accuser,

---

56. The preface was dated 18 November 1527.

57. *MBW* 620 (*CR* 1:902–4), written in the beginning of November; and *MBW* 624 (*CR* 1:907–8), dated 12 November 1527.

58. *MBW* 612 (*WABr* 4:271–73).

59. *WABr* 4:272.14.

Agricola, who now had to prove that his challenge was more serious than simply words.

With one phrase Luther had reduced the argument of Agricola to words, thereby refusing to acknowledge even the possibility of building a theology on Agricola's principles. This is clear from what follows: "How the fear of punishment and fear of God differ is said more easily with syllables and letters than is known in reality and feeling."[60] The ungodly, who fear hell and punishment, at the same time fear God, who is in those things. In this life, Luther went on to say, it is impossible not to have the two mixed, just as there is no spirit without flesh. He added that fear of punishment without fear of God would be useless. Then, in a rather complicated comparison, he balanced the two opinions against one another: "Therefore what is done to the teaching about the fear of God [Melanchthon's position], I believe, is the same as is done to the teaching about the freedom of the Spirit [Agricola's position]. As some pervert the latter into the security of the flesh [Melanchthon's worry], so others pervert the former into desperation or fear of punishment [Agricola's worry]."[61]

Luther saw to the heart of the problem. It lay with the hearers of the message and what they did with the proclamation of either the fear of God or the freedom of the Spirit. There were inevitable distortions on both sides. What Luther argued was that they belong together. In some ways, this was also Melanchthon's point. He wished to move from law to gospel. His definition of freedom in the Visitation Articles had to do with forgiveness of sins. Whatever nomism can be found here was only in the eyes of his opponents, whom he perceived as distorting the gospel.

Whether Agricola could adjust his theology to Luther's understanding remained an open question. Did Melanchthon appreciate Luther's position? To a letter to Spalatin on 12 November he attached a copy of Luther's letter, instructing him to put it with his treasures.[62]

At the same time Melanchthon received the letter from Luther, he also finally heard from Agricola, who in a now lost letter (most probably written in response to Melanchthon's own complaint [*MBW* 598]) outlined his newest challenge to Melanchthon. From Melanchthon's response we can reconstruct the gist of Agricola's arguments.[63] They

---

60. *WABr* 4:272.16f.: "Nam timor poenae et timor Dei quam differant, facilius dicitur syllabis et literis, quam re et affectu cognoscitur."
61. *WABr* 4:272.21–23: "Docendo igitur timorem Dei credo id agi, quod agitur docendo libertatem spiritus, ut hanc alii in securitatem carnis, ita illum alii in desperationem seu timorem poenae rapiant."
62. *MBW* 624 (*CR* 1:907f.): "Lutheri literas non reposco abs te. Potes eas inter alia tua κειμήλια ponere."
63. *MBW* 615 (*CR* 1:904–6), dated by *MBW* to the end of October 1527.

agreed with and expanded the rumors about himself that Melanchthon had passed on to Camerarius. The general charges focused on an error that Melanchthon sarcastically labeled a capital crime and sin. He had injured Christian liberty, contaminated the purity of evangelical doctrine, and defiled the purity of the Scriptures.

More specifically, Agricola charged first that on the question of *poenitentia* Melanchthon had mistakenly taught that the terrors of conscience over sin arise from a fear of divine judgment and eternal punishment. (One is reminded here of Agricola's description of Judas.) On the contrary, such movements of the heart must arise from the love of righteousness, which converts a person to God. God must be feared on account of himself, not on account of punishment. Second, Melanchthon had distorted a text of Paul in order to stress the law, and had done so in opposition to Luther himself. Third, he had not strongly enough repressed (in his capacity as visitor?) the sermons of some people. This corresponded to the earlier difficulties with Aquila.

Agricola attacked Melanchthon from two sides here. On the one hand, he called into question Melanchthon's theology and especially his understanding of law in the Christian life. On the other, Agricola presented a very different understanding of the church, an understanding based upon the authority of Luther and the responsibility of the visitor to purge the church of nonevangelical elements.[64]

Melanchthon's response to this letter highlighted both the method he used to defend himself and some aspects of the theological debate between the two men.[65] He began with the kind of humanist prose that could hide as much as it exposed. He was glad that Agricola had finally written—to Melanchthon himself, the discerning reader would add. He quoted Aristophanes about the need both to teach and be taught—a quote aimed both at himself in humility and at Agricola as a challenge. And he expressed his willingness to confess an error, if he had committed any—implying, as the letter showed, that he thought he had not.

Melanchthon commenced his investigation of Agricola's charges by putting Agricola on the defensive. The Articles were not intended to be published, but to indicate to those for whom they had been intended the principal topics of Christian doctrine. Was Melanchthon perhaps suggesting here that the Articles were not any of Agricola's business? He also put the Articles into a quite different light when he characterized

---

64. When in 1547 the authority became Joachim II of Brandenburg and Charles V, and the teaching became the Augsburg Interim, Agricola's approach remained the same, but the results for the evangelical churches were catastrophic.

65. Given the varied textual history of this letter, we have used *CR* 1:904–6 with *CR* 3:1283 and *SM* 6.1:399.

them as the "principal *loci* of Christian doctrine."[66] Of course, such a grandiose description served to conceal his motives: he had so focused the meaning of the Articles as to attack Agricola's position. More importantly, Melanchthon challenged Agricola's behavior, noting that he wrote "under a foreign character (*sub aliena persona*)," a sure sign of unfriendly and un-Christian behavior.

Having taken the moral high ground, Melanchthon attacked with stinging irony: "Since I see plainly that I have been charged with capital accusations, I will respond to them briefly," hoping that Agricola would judge the case most equitably.[67] He dismissed the general charges of Agricola out of hand. He had neither said nor written anything to damage Christian liberty; he had not knowingly even wanted to write anything to contaminate the purity of evangelical doctrine. In this controversy Agricola's hyperbole would put himself at a distinct disadvantage. Melanchthon would have none of it.

Turning first to the question of *poenitentia*, Melanchthon set up the argument in such a way that Agricola's challenge collapsed: "Concerning *poenitentia* I imagine you will agree with me that before vivification or consolation fright and terrors and confusion of conscience ought to exist in people's hearts."[68] Given Agricola's comparison of Peter and Judas, with which Melanchthon was familiar, this was hardly the way the rector of Eisleben would have described the situation. For him the fear and terror that arose from the law ran counter to the purpose of the gospel and true mortification.

From this basis, however, Melanchthon could easily defend his position. While Melanchthon admitted that he had called the catalyst of *poenitentia* either fear of divine judgment or a sense of divine wrath, he contended that the common people understood the former better, "and indeed in that agony one cannot deny that it is fear of eternal punishment."[69] As Luther had done in his letter to his young colleague, Melanchthon appealed to experience. This kind of argument was nearly impossible to refute. It also showed dramatically the difference in the opponents' theology: Agricola searching for the proper definition that most faithfully transmitted Luther's theology; Luther and Melanchthon

---

66. Cf. *MBW* 7559 (*CR* 8:524f.), dated 21 August 1555, where Melanchthon uses a similar description twenty-eight years after the event.

67. *CR* 1:904: "Et quoniam video, mihi plane 'capitolia crimina' obiici, respondebo ad ea breviter, quia apud te, hoc est, ut statuo, aequissimum iudicem, causam dico."

68. *CR* 1:905: "De poenitentia arbitror hoc tibi mecum convenire, in animis ante vivificationem seu consolationem oportere pavores et terrores et confusionem conscientiae exsistere."

69. *CR* 1:905: "Et quidem in eo agone esse metum aeternum poenarum negari non potest."

using the experience of the human predicament to define an issue. Of course Luther, more quickly than either Melanchthon or Agricola, discerned the paradox of the person living under fear of punishment and fear of God at the same time.

Melanchthon also realized that Agricola's attack was motivated by a fear that the doctrine of justification by faith alone was itself being undermined. Therefore he immediately added that the fear in humans is not something they create in themselves by their own power, but something that God effects in them. Of course at this point Melanchthon could have gone on to speak of the function of the law. In this case, however, he limited himself to the issue at hand. According to Melanchthon, Agricola had insisted that these motions in the heart ought (*debent*) to arise from the love of justice. Rather than arguing with him, Melanchthon accepted Luther's admonition and simply acquiesced innocently: "Who denies it?"[70] Of course by adding the word "debent," Melanchthon tactfully avoided the real issue. Agricola had insisted not only that *poenitentia* ought to, but that in true Christians like Peter it actually does arise from love and not fear.

Having appeared to accept Agricola's argument, Melanchthon now had to indicate why he did not so express himself in the Visitation Articles. Here he returned to the pedagogical argument set up in the introduction to the letter. It is easier to say that *poenitentia* arises from the love of righteousness than to understand it. It appeared to Melanchthon—and here he attempted to correct the instructional methods of his friend the school rector—that in teaching one should flee from "obscure *loci*." He quoted for a second time from Aristophanes' *Frogs* in his defense. A single sentence undermined Agricola's entire theology of *poenitentia:* "But you know that the Christian mind arrives there [at such love of righteousness] only late."[71] It was as if Melanchthon were arguing that someone with Agricola's Christian experience should be able to perceive that we fear God on his own account and that we are converted to God by the love of righteousness, but for the simple these things are too difficult.

Melanchthon continued the pedagogical attack in his examination of the phrase "timor filialis (filial fear)." Here he avoided the "old definition" because those who were little schooled in such things did not understand what it meant to love God on God's own account and not because of the fear of punishment. Melanchthon mentioned that he had the support of "some learned men," an oblique reference to the ap-

---

70. *CR* 1:905: "Quis negat?"

71. *CR* 1:905: "Sed scis, Christianam mentem sero eo pervenire, ut perspiciat, quid sit: 'Deum propter se ipsum timere' aut 'ad Deum amore iustitiae converti.'"

proval he had received from Luther and Bugenhagen. He graciously allowed that the old terminology (after all, the terms "filial" and "servile fear" were used by the Scholastics) could be used, but not with children who need milk. "Nor do I forbid you from placing solid food before the grown-ups."[72] In a battle over catechesis, this comment simply eliminated the opposition. The irony would not have been missed by Agricola, who had already in the first phase of this battle accused Melanchthon of reintroducing old terms into evangelical churches. Melanchthon had succeeded in turning the same charge back on Agricola's head.

Melanchthon now turned his attention to another of Agricola's charges, that he had distorted some Pauline text. Because Agricola did not say which one, Melanchthon guessed that it was Galatians 3:19, "The law is given on account of transgression." (As we have seen, Melanchthon also used Gal. 3:24 and 1 Tim. 1:8–9.) Here the charge was that Luther's and Melanchthon's interpretations did not agree: "For Luther understood it regarding the increase [of sin], and I regarding coercion."[73] To use later terminology, Luther referred the text to the second (theological) use of the law, that the law increases our transgressions, Melanchthon to the first (civil) use, that the law restrains our transgressions. Melanchthon's answer was quite matter-of-fact. He was not ignorant of this difference, but he preferred to follow the older interpreters (probably Jerome).[74] He could not imagine that this would anger Luther. He then proceeded to give Agricola a lesson in the two uses of the law: "For there is no doubt that Paul teaches that the law has been proposed for two reasons: first, to coerce the flesh with carnal righteousness; then to terrify the conscience. I have adapted the interpretation of this Pauline text to the former effect of the law; Luther adapts it to the latter."[75]

---

72. *CR* 1:905: "Et tamen illa vetus reprehendi non potest. Sed iudicavi parvulos lacte alendos, nec veto, te grandioribus solidos cibos proponere."

73. "Lutherus enim exposuit augendas, ego, cohercendas"—the reading of *SM* 6.1:399. *CR* 1:905 reads, "Lutherus eum exposuit angendas, ego, cohortandas." For the reading of "augendas" see *WA* 2:522. For the reading "cohercendas" see *MSA* 4:253 (referring to 1 Tim. 1:8f.) and *CR* 26:27f. (referring to Gal. 3:19).

74. Melanchthon seemed to have forgotten that in Luther's exposition of Galatians 3:24–29 in the "Epistel am Neujahrstage" (*Kirchenpostille*, 1522), which Melanchthon had seen through Wittenberg's presses, Luther himself connected the text to the first use of the law. See *WA* 10.1.1:450–66, esp. 454.8–12 and 455.5–6. To my knowledge this is the first time any Wittenberg theologian expressly defined two uses of the law.

75. *CR* 1:905f.: "Non enim dubium est, quin Paulus doceat, legem propter has causas latam esse, primum ad coercendam carnem iustitia carnali, deinde ad terrendam conscientiam. Ego interpretationem Paulini loci ad effectum priorem legis accommodavi, Lutherus accommodat ad posteriorem."

With this Melanchthon completely eliminated Agricola's arguments. By accepting the validity of Agricola's terminology on *poenitentia* (for the mature) and of Luther's interpretation of Galatians 3:19 (as one of two possibilities), he took the teeth out of Agricola's attack. It now appeared that Agricola had picked a fight, used terms from Scholastic theology, did not understand how to teach the young, and was trying to cause tension within the Wittenberg theological faculty. Without having yielded on a single point, Melanchthon had his friend on the ropes.

In his closing remarks, Melanchthon expressed the powerful anger behind his defense. Looking back at the letter of his friend, he again mentioned a willingness to yield, even recant, if only he could be shown where he had "contaminated the Scriptures" or "wounded evangelical liberty." This language signified that Agricola had not proven his case. The point of the visitation, Melanchthon added, had been to investigate everything as exactly as possible and to admonish the unlearned: "O that all who teach would accommodate themselves to the understanding of the hearers! I certainly try."[76] The implication was that Agricola had not. One parting shot, intended perhaps for the situation in Saalfeld, dealt with Agricola's final objection: that Melanchthon had not restrained the sermons of some, namely the evangelical preachers' Roman opponents.[77] Melanchthon again agreed completely, but reminded Agricola that this was none of his business. "For I do not dare to impose upon you, dear man, the burden of our defense."[78]

Having answered Agricola's challenges to his satisfaction, Melanchthon turned his attention in two other directions. First, he wanted to make sure that his version of the affair reached the court. For this he turned to George Spalatin. Second, having hinted to Agricola that he could defend himself against charges brought by others, Melanchthon turned to Aquila in an attempt to remove any resentment that he might still be harboring.

When he wrote to Spalatin at the beginning of November, Melanchthon had good reason to think that his response to Agricola would suffice to solve the problem. He told Spalatin not to worry about this "offensiuncula."[79] He assured Spalatin that his feelings toward Agricola had not changed and that Agricola would reciprocate that affection. Whatever the basis in fact, such comments were also meant for public

---

76. *CR* 1:906: "Utinam omnes, qui docent, ad captum auditorum se accommodarent. Ego id certe conor."
77. *CR* 1:906, but with the reading of *SM:* "Id quod scribis, 'me non valde repressisse [*CR:* reposcere] quorundam sermones,' facile patior."
78. *CR* 1:906: "Non enim audeo tibi, homini amico, onus nostri defendendi imponere."
79. *MBW* 620 (*CR* 1:902–4).

consumption. They again placed Agricola on the defensive, this time in the position of having broken a friendship. As if that were not enough, Melanchthon with more than a tinge of sarcasm described Agricola's character: "As you know, he is by nature clever and so is in love with his own inventiveness, which I gladly permit him."[80] Melanchthon's condescending attitude managed to dismiss any substantive attack by Agricola. He also predicted that the day would come when Agricola would tire of these arguments and discover how hard it is to teach simply.[81] Instead of sending Spalatin his own response to Agricola's arguments, Melanchthon sent Luther's letter. No wonder Melanchthon added to his description of Luther's illnesses: "May Christ preserve that man for us and for the church!"[82]

If Melanchthon played the diplomat with Spalatin, with Aquila he attempted to diffuse Agricola's criticisms. In November 1527 Melanchthon wrote five letters to Aquila in which he not only argued his case but, as the conference at the Torgau drew near, worried about the nature of Agricola's attacks. Just after he received Luther's and Agricola's letters, Melanchthon wrote his first letter to Aquila on the same day he wrote to Spalatin. Melanchthon worried that Aquila might have been moved by "calumnies and curses," and mentioned the attack of Agricola as an example.[83] He sketched the chief (new) charge, namely, that Melanchthon claimed *poenitentia* began with fear of punishment rather than love of righteousness. Melanchthon reminded Aquila that he, Melanchthon, had tried to avoid the whole dispute about the love of righteousness, not because he did not believe that God may be loved for himself, but because he believed that this kind of love occurs much later in the process of justification. He also reminded Aquila that they had discussed the difference between servile and filial fear.[84]

Melanchthon then turned to Agricola's character. As in the letter to Spalatin, he commented on his opponent's cleverness. On the basis of his letter to Agricola, Melanchthon expected to receive a rebuttal and feared that it would mean war. What followed typified Melanchthon's

---

80. *CR* 1:903: "Sed est, ut scis, arguto ingenio, itaque delectatur suis quibusdam inventis, quod ego illi facile permitto."

81. *CR* 1:903: "Scio futurum olim, ut capiat eum satietas argutiarum huiusmodi, cum videbit, quam sit utile, imo quam difficile, simplicissime docere, et attemperare se multitudinis captui."

82. *CR* 1:903f.: "Christus servet nobis et ecclesiae virum illum." Melanchthon told Spalatin on 12 November that he did not need to return Luther's letter. On Spalatin's urging Melanchthon to write a catechism see p. 146.

83. *MBW* 618 (*CR* 1:906f.): "Interea te adhortor, ut non sinas te commoveri improborum calumniis et maledictis."

84. *CR* 1:907. This discussion, which may well have taken place in July during the visitation, was reflected in the Visitation Articles; see *CR* 26:18.

technique of conflict avoidance: "I will ask that he find among those who fight against our doctrine another opponent with whom he can quarrel. For me it has been decided not to fight with him."[85] He had earlier admonished Aquila to deal in this fashion with his opponents. Here Melanchthon followed his own advice. By taking the moral high ground, he continued to put Agricola and his friends on the defensive. What more devastating advice to give someone who felt that his theology was under attack? "Pick on our real opponents; I will not fight you openly."

In a now lost response Aquila charged that Melanchthon had made disparaging remarks about him. Melanchthon in turn responded with righteous indignation in a letter dated 12 November.[86] He had never said such things about Aquila, who was given permission to show the letter to those who had lied about Melanchthon. He then related that he had been summoned to the court because of a text in Paul (Gal. 3:19). His defense in this letter added some interesting refinements to the arguments made to Agricola. First, his biblical interpretation followed the church fathers (he mentioned Jerome) and contained nothing absurd. Second, he agreed with Luther in points of dogma, so it should not have made much difference if he disagreed with Luther regarding this verse in Paul. Third, Melanchthon took Luther's notion that this was a war over words and turned it into an attack on Agricola. He worried that "sophistica theologia" would once again rule, and he threatened that if his opponents tried to upset him, they would get what they deserved. This surprising outburst led Melanchthon to say, fourthly, that these opponents would already have upset him had he not restrained himself; he wanted not to increase dissent, but instead to patch up (*sarcienda*) harmony.[87]

Without having received a reply from Aquila, Melanchthon wrote again on 17 November.[88] Much of the letter contained the same arguments as the preceding one. In his interpretation of Galatians 3:19, which would be discussed at court, he had followed nothing absurd and stuck to the exegetes of the ancient church. He was not, as Aquila had

---

85. *CR* 1:907: "Quod si videro, eum bellum parare, rogabo, ut sumat sibi alium quempiam ex his qui adversantur nostrae doctrinae, quicum litiget. Mihi decretum est, cum eo non rixari." Joachim Rogge, *Johann Agricolas Lutherverständnis: Unter besonderer Berücksichtigung des Antinomismus* (Berlin: Evangelische Verlagsanstalt, 1960), 111, argues that the court had put a gag on Melanchthon. This misconstrues Melanchthon's rhetorical point. It was not the court but moderation, Melanchthon's best weapon, that had decreed he should not fight.

86. *MBW* 623 (*CR* 4:958).

87. *CR* 4:958: "Et commovissent iam dudum, nisi ego in tam multis dissensionibus reprimerem me, cuperem studere non augendis dissidiis sed sarciendae concordiae."

88. *MBW* 625 (*CR* 4:960–62).

written, departing from Christianity.[89] On this point Melanchthon was indignant. Who says things like this? Christ will judge these things, not human beings. Still, "I have decided to suffer these calumnies and to bear them for God's sake."[90] Clearly Melanchthon's refusal to do open battle was a theological and tactical decision ("decrevi . . . propter Deum") designed to place the burden of proof on the attacker. Of course, at least three of Melanchthon's writings in 1527, especially the Visitation Articles, were probably construed as attacks on Agricola's theological position (see ch. 3).

Melanchthon closed the letter with a different approach. He expressed the wish that theologians of the age would not condemn the honest disciplines, and immediately flattered Aquila by counting him among those who did not. He begged Aquila to conserve the "former good feelings" toward him and not to let himself be alienated "by some perverse sycophants" who just want to sow dissension in the church.[91] Thus, using counterarguments, passivity, and flattery, Melanchthon attempted to woo Aquila back to his side. When he had not heard from Aquila by 21 November, Melanchthon made one last plea. He worried that he was to be called to the Torgau to face his *"censores,* who certainly will inquire severely (ἀποτόμως, as the Greeks say) into my booklet."[92]

Only this last letter made clear who was actually being attacked in this controversy: not Agricola, and certainly not Luther, but Melanchthon. Despite the fact that several scholars have turned even this controversy into a dispute between Luther and Agricola, we must remain quite clear that the person most dreading the conference at the Torgau was Melanchthon. In the month since the new controversy had arisen, however, Melanchthon had done his best to outmaneuver his opponent. Spalatin, Luther, and even Aquila were brought to Melanchthon's side. Although his theology and its alleged deviations from Luther's were supposed to be the center of attention, Melanchthon had done his best to place the burden of proof on Agricola's shoulders. Agricola was the cause of the controversy; Agricola used poor pedagogy; Agricola was fighting over words; Agricola was disturbing the peace of the church; Agricola was reintroducing sophistry into theology; Agricola had broken a friendship. Melanchthon portrayed himself as the of-

---

89. *CR* 4:961.

90. *CR* 4:961: "Decrevi has calumnias pati ac perferre propter Deum." The language is the same as in *MBW* 608 (*CR* 1:897).

91. *CR* 4:962: "per improbos quosdam sycophantas."

92. *MBW* 628 (*CR* 4:963), dated 21 November 1527: "Die Saturni [November 23] iter suscipiam versus Torgam, ubi audiendi mihi sunt censores mei, qui valde, ut Graeci dicunt, ἀποτόμως, inquirunt in meum libellum."

fended party, as the peace-lover, and thereby made room for his own attack.

Round Three: Eisleben Strikes Back

While Melanchthon was preparing for a long siege, Agricola formulated his own battle plan. We have already seen parts of it. After an initial, unsuccessful appeal to Luther, he tried to use his friendship with Aquila, his contacts at the court, and even a direct approach to Melanchthon to win his case. In the middle of this, however, Agricola was shepherding an even more devastating attack through the presses of Wittenberg: a reworking of his "Christliche Kinderzucht" into a catechism for the girls' school in Eisleben. This work was a refutation of Melanchthon's Visitation Articles.

The catechism itself, "Hundert vnd Dreissig gemeyner Frage stücke/ für die iungen kinder/ ynn der Deudschen Meydlin Schule zu Eyssleben," was published in 1528 and experienced immediate, though not lasting, success (see pp. 60–61). The prefatory letter, addressed to Agricola's brother-in-law, Bartholomew Drachstedt, Alexander's brother, was dated 18 November 1527, squarely in the middle of the fray.[93] Although in that letter Agricola claimed that he was just reworking the earlier catechism to make it simpler, in fact the revision represented an entirely new contribution to the flood of catechisms. It was the clearest exposition of Agricola's position in this controversy and could be interpreted as his censure of Melanchthon's Visitation Articles.

Melanchthon, especially in the Visitation Articles, saw the Christian life moving from *mortificatio* to *vivificatio*, from law to gospel, from terror to comfort and faith. Agricola began his catechism instead with a discussion of *Gottseligkeit*, which consists of Word and faith. The Word gives a promise, and faith trusts that God will keep it. Human nature and reason cannot comprehend God or God's Word, therefore they must believe it. God's promises are revealed through the preaching of the gospel. By listening to preachers and believing their words, we recognize God's goodness that is proclaimed to us, see at the same time our errors and transgressions, and cry to God for help.

Agricola had constructed a theological system that avoided the law. He derived everything, especially *poenitentia*, from the gospel promise alone. This promise reveals God's goodness; then (we could add here, out of love of righteousness or for God's sake alone) one recognizes one's sins and repents. In twelve simple questions—Melanchthon

---

93. A typographical error reads 1528. The preface, by stressing Agricola's foolish simplicity in teaching, answered Melanchthon's charge that Agricola's approach was too sophisticated for the common folk.

underestimated Agricola's pedagogical abilities—Agricola constructed a clear alternative to Melanchthon's law-gospel approach.[94]

Agricola then distinguished two kinds of sermons (law and grace) and two kinds of preachers (Moses and Christ). Moses together with the law "forces and pressures the people with punishment and pain, that they should love God above all things or else must die an eternal death."[95] As could be expected, Agricola had reduced preaching of the law entirely to forcing people to do things through fear of punishment. Agricola wanted to exclude this preaching completely from any discussion of *poenitentia* and the Christian life. Just to make sure the girls understood, Agricola summarized his arguments in question 18:

> The law says, "You must love God more than yourself or die."
>
> The gospel says, "I announce to you that God loved you first and beforehand and wants to bestow this love on you, because you love yourself so much. He also wants to give you the Holy Spirit, so that because of his goodness you can hate and abandon yourself, your life, property, and honor."[96]

The law has no positive function whatsoever. Only through the gospel, which proclaims God's prior love ("erst vnd zuuor"), does God love us in spite of our self-love and afterwards give us power through the Holy Spirit to hate ourselves and follow him.

This approach to the Christian life also changed Agricola's view of sin and baptism. Baptism removes original sin, but some little spark remains which the devil can fan into sin. When asked how one can be freed from this sin, Agricola responded, "My child, as often as you feel this poisonous spark, you should remember the three holy names, fall on your knees, and call to God."[97] Of course, by avoiding the law in one place, he let it in the back door without realizing what he was doing. He

---

94. Cohrs 2:274f. Terms such as "nomian" and "antinomian," as used in Gustav Hammann's "Nomismus und Antinomismus innerhalb der wittenberger Theologie von 1524–1530," Ph.D. diss., Friedrich Wilhelms Universität, 1952, do not do justice to the complexities of either thinker's ideas.

95. Cohrs 2:276: ". . . zwinget vnd nötiget die leute mit straffe vnd peen, das sie Gott fur allen dingen lieben sollen, odder müssen des ewigen todes sterben."

96. Cohrs 2:276: "Das gesetze sagt, Du must Gott mehr lieben, denn dich, odder must sterben. Das Euangelion sagt, Ich verkündige dir, das dich Gott erst vnd zuuor geliebet hat, vnd wil dirs schencken, das du dich so seere liebest, Er wil dir auch seinen heiligen geist geben, dadurch du, vmb seiner güete willen, dich, dein leben, gut vnd ehere hassen vnd verlassen kanst."

97. Cohrs 2:278: "Mein kind, so offt du diese gifftige funcken fülest, so offt soltu dich erynnern der heiligen dreyer namen, auf deine knye fallen vnd Gott anruffen." Agricola's understanding of baptism and the "gifftige funcken" mirrored the medieval theological perspective that limited baptism's effect and stressed the *fomes peccati*. See Heiko A. Oberman, *The Harvest of Medieval Theology*, 2d ed. (Durham, N.C.: Labyrinth, 1983), 126–28.

regarded the promise of baptism as the motivating factor in asking for forgiveness ("remember the Trinity"), but prescribed a series of actions, concluding with a prayer which beseeched God not to remove the gift of the Holy Spirit.

Thus Agricola had built into the framework of his catechetical and pastoral advice the same uncertainty found in his sermons on Colossians. Here, however, Agricola addressed this problem. Calling the entire struggle against the little spark of sin "Buße," he reminded the children that every time they sin, they should cry to God, who promises to hear us as often as we ask.[98]

In questions 66 and 67 Agricola reiterated the initial theme of his catechism.[99] A person becomes a believer when the Father draws the unbelieving heart to himself and lets it be sprinkled with Jesus' blood. With that the heart believes, cries over its unbelief (that is, it does *Buße*), is contrite, confesses, and tries hard to make sure that God, who has forgiven so much, does not reject it.[100] Once again, Agricola placed grace at the beginning, *Buße* thereafter, and the uncertainty of works at the end. In this process, preaching the satisfaction of Christ comes first and then we do *Buße*.[101]

Agricola then took Melanchthon on directly. What about those who say that if we preach Christian freedom we will make "brutish Christians" out of people? Agricola answered with the example of Paul himself: "Saint Paul did not avoid this, but instead preached the word of the resurrection and satisfaction of Christ among the heathen and Jews. For had he first wanted to oppress and burden the people with laws, fear and terror before God's judgment, and the awareness of their sins, then they would not have been able to say, 'Let us do evil so that good may come' [Rom. 3:8]."[102] Here the Visitation Articles were challenged as being un-Pauline. Agricola's charge concerning Melanchthon's use of Paul might have included more than just the single text of Galatians 3:19. On the basis of the reaction of Paul's audience, Agricola argued for an exclusion of the law and the notion that it preceded the gospel. The

---

98. Cohrs 2:279, questions 34–36.

99. Cohrs 2:285.

100. Cohrs 2:285: "Wenn der vater ein vngleubiges hertze zeuhet vnd leest es besprenget werden mit dem blute seines Sons Christi Jhesu, so wird es gleubig vnd schreyet vber seinen vnglauben, das ist, es büsset, rewet vnd klaget, vnd hütet sich mit vleis, das es yhe den forthyn nicht erzürne, der yhm souiel verzihen hat."

101. Cohrs 2:286.

102. Cohrs 2:287: "Sanct Paul hat das nicht geschewet, sondern das wort von der auferstehung vnd genugthuung Christi vnter die Heyden vnd Jüden gepredigt, Denn wo er die leute erstlich mit gesetzen, furcht vnd schrecken für Gottes gerichte vnd betrachtunge yhrer sünde hette drücken vnd beschweren wollen, So hetten sie nicht sagen dürffen, wir wollen böses thun, auf das gutes komme [Rom. 3:8]." Melanchthon responded in the *Scholia* of 1528 by citing Paul's own conversion (see p. 161).

presence of "brutish Christians" could even be taken to be a sign that the gospel was being properly preached!

At the same time, Agricola made it clear that the move from law to gospel, as Melanchthon had attempted it, was simply a reflection of this world's wisdom, which viewed evil things as a sign of God's disfavor. But the gospel is a foolish sermon, wherein God sees the human predicament and decides to win the world over not through force but through foolishness, love, and the gift of the Son. What people previously could not attain through punishment or fright (Melanchthon's "poenae" and "pavores"), they now set about happily attaining without necessity or force.[103] The world—one would have to include Melanchthon's theology here—thinks it foolish that a person is made righteous through goodness, but this is God's highest wisdom, to make a virtue of necessity.

In this scheme of things, God demands no good works for his own sake, but he wants us to do them for our neighbor. Does this mean that Agricola had fashioned a place for the law? Absolutely not. For according to question 85, "the law says, 'Love God above all else or die,' while the gospel says, 'I am too high for you, so my only desire is that everyone know how much I love you and how good I have been for you, and that everyone do what pleases me, namely, love the brother who with his needs can be seen.'"[104]

In question 105 Agricola once more returned to the law: "Should the law of Moses force Christians too?" Here again Agricola clearly had the theology of the Visitation Articles in his sights. Melanchthon's entire theological schema was being thrown overboard in favor of a theology purged of the law: "Christians do out of love and desire everything God demands of them. For they are sealed with the spontaneous Spirit of Christ. Therefore no law ought to force them, for no law is given to the righteous [1 Tim. 1:9]. Moreover, as soon as the gospel becomes a matter of compulsion and a rule, then it is no longer the gospel."[105]

Agricola showed that the inner motivation of the believer, which Melanchthon wanted to see grow and change from fear of punishment to love of righteousness, had to be correct from the very beginning.

---

103. Cohrs 2:288: "Vnd die man zuuor widder mit straff noch schrecken vermügen kond, die setzen ytzund, mit lust vnd freuden yhres hertzens, leib vnd leben yn die schantze, vngenötigt vnd vngezwungen."

104. Cohrs 2:289: "Das gesetze sagt, Du solt lieben Got vber alle ding, odder must sterben. Euangelion sagt, Ich bin dir zu hoh, vnd wil nur, das yederman wisse, wie lieb ich euch habe, wie günstig ich euch bin, wil aber yemandt thun, das mir gefelt, der liebe den bruder, den er sihet vnd sein bedarff."

105. Cohrs 2:293: "Christen thun aus lust vnd liebe alles, was Gott von yhn foddert, Denn sie sind durch den freywilligen geist Christi versiegelt, darumb sol sie kein gesetz zwingen, Denn dem gerechten ist kein gesetze geben, zudem, so bald das Euangelion ein zwang vnd Regel wird, so ists nymmer Euangelion."

Otherwise law overpowers gospel. What Agricola could not imagine was a complex human being in whom the old and the new still struggle. The very "simul," to which Luther in his letter to Melanchthon quite naturally reached to solve the war of words, was the very thing Agricola rejected in his attempt to make Christians whole through the gospel.

At this point, Agricola did allow for some use for the law. Christians may employ it under the same conditions they might use any of God's creatures, that is, without objections from their conscience and to God's honor and their benefit. Using the law of Moses is no different from using a Greek or Latin book. The law of Moses, and here Agricola included the Decalog, which he proceeded to explain, was given to the Jews in the same way Germans are given imperial law to follow.[106]

After the exposition of the Ten Commandments, Agricola closed with a *summa summarum*, taking dead aim at Melanchthon's Articles and leaving no doubt as to his censure:

> 130. In conclusion, for what purpose is the Holy Scripture given?
> Answer: Saint Paul says in 2 Tim. 3[:16], "All Scripture, inspired by God, is necessary for instruction, for punishment, for correction in righteousness, so that the person of God may be skillful in all good works." One must first instruct and then punish those who do not want to follow the instruction. The gospel says to all flesh, "You are free from all laws—even you Jews from the entire law of Moses. Only do not use freedom in a fleshly manner.[107]

Lere then *straffe*: this movement characterized Agricola's theology and his pedagogy for the Christian life. It made preaching of the law and its threats unnecessary and actually dangerous for the gospel. He even stressed that the Christian is freed from the entire law of Moses ("vom gantzen gesetz"), not just parts of it, as Melanchthon had insisted. In 130 questions and answers Agricola succeeded in undermining Melanchthon's entire theological program as formulated in the Visitation Articles. Instead of law and gospel, Agricola proposed gospel first and then, according to one's wishes and God's works, law or punishment.[108] The choice is between Judas and Peter, Moses and Christ.

---

106. Cohrs 2:293.

107. Cohrs 2:295: "130. Summa Summarum, Warzu ist die heilige Schrifft geben? A. Sanct Paul sagt 2. Tim. 3. Alle Schrifft von Gott eingegeben, ist nütz zur lere, zur straffe, zur besserung, zur züchtigung yn der gerechtickeit, das ein mensch Gottes sey zu allem guten werck geschickt. Man mus erst leren, vnd darnach straffen, di der lere nicht volgen wöllen. Das Euangelion sagt zu allem fleysch, Yhr seyt frey von allen gesetzen, Auch yhr Jüden vom gantzen gesetz Mose, alleine braucht der freyheit nicht fleyschlich."

108. For a modern version of this debate, see Gerhard O. Forde, *The Law-Gospel Debate* (Minneapolis: Augsburg, 1969), 137–74, where he describes the debate between Karl Barth ("Gospel and Law") and Lutheran theologians ("Law and Gospel").

Melanchthon, having in Agricola's eyes chosen Judas and Moses, threatened to bring the entire evangelical movement back in line with what Agricola perceived to be the Roman religion.

Round Four: The Torgau and Melanchthon's "Aristarchus"

In late November 1527 Spalatin convened a second conference over the Visitation Articles. This time, besides those who had served as visitors (Schurff, Melanchthon, and Asmus von Haubitz), the participants included Luther, Bugenhagen, Caspar Güttel, and John Agricola. The dates for the conference are somewhat in doubt. Gustav Kawerau contends it took place on 26–28 November; Susi Hausammann, following Joachim Rogge, on 26–29 November; and Gustav Hammann, on the morning of 29 November.[109] A notice in the account books of the Torgau concerning payment for the participants' stay is dated 30 November, but this indicates only when the entry was made, not when the expenditures were incurred.[110] We know from the first Torgau conference that Luther could reach the castle within a day. Chances are that his letters dated 29 November were written the same day he left the Torgau but upon his return to Wittenberg.[111] It seems most likely that the meeting took place on 26–28 November, with departure early the next day.[112]

What happened there? On 10 December Luther wrote a letter to Justus Jonas in response to an inquiry for news.[113] Irritated by the rumor mill and by the waste of time, Luther huffed, "Our famous dissension at the Torgau was scarcely more than nothing,"[114] adding that it was regarded with contempt. One thing (about which Jonas must have heard from Agricola) was proposed, immediately settled, and resulted in beautiful consensus: the way had been cleared for the publication of the Visitation Articles.[115] The most the participants did, Luther added, was

---

109. For details see Susi Hausammann, *Buße als Umkehr und Erneuerung von Mensch und Gesellschaft* (Zurich: Theologischer Verlag, 1974), 70 n. 143.

110. Thus Hausammann's conjecture that the Feast of Saint Andrew would have been celebrated on Sunday in Wittenberg is unnecessary.

111. *WABr* 4:287f. (to Justus Jonas, dated the Vigil of Saint Andrew [29 November], and filled with local Wittenberg gossip) and *WABr* 4:288f. (to Eberhard Brisger, dated the fourth day after St. Catherine's [29 November], and also filled with local news). The *WABr* editor suggests that the latter letter, which gives a different report of the health of two people, may have been written on 1 December.

112. This is also the argument of *MBW* 629.

113. Luther's previous letter of 29 November had contained no report at all of the just completed conference.

114. *WABr* 4:294–97, here 295.23: "Famosa dissensio nostra Torgae paene plus quam nihil fuit."

115. According to Hammann, "Nomismus," 60, the Articles were at the printer's by 5 February 1528.

131

to feast at the expense of the prince.[116] He then reconsidered his evaluation, adding that what was best about the conference was that the notoriety and suspicion that the disagreement had engendered had been buried there.[117]

The only other participant in this conference whose reports have survived was Melanchthon, certainly not an unbiased observer. His anger was scarcely hidden in a letter written at the Torgau and sent with Agricola to Veit Amerbach in Eisleben.[118] Refusing to use Agricola's name, Melanchthon wrote, "Now a satisfactory agreement has been reached between your rector and me."[119] This was hardly a ringing attestation of renewed friendship, nor did it agree with Luther's "beautiful consensus." Before stating his conclusion, Melanchthon included a thinly veiled defense of his own position. He made three bitter judgments against Agricola's behavior. First, he said, "I do not desire nor do I go around drumming up praise for [my] cleverness in the interpretation of the Holy Scriptures."[120] He had leveled such an accusation against Agricola. Second, he insisted that he had tried to show "simplicissime" those texts which needed to be taught in the churches. Here Melanchthon placed Agricola's pedagogical shortcomings under renewed suspicion. Third, he declared his willingness to be deeply criticized, as long as he was not judged ἀποτόμως, as Paul says (2 Cor. 13:10; Titus 1:13). Here he used a word already employed twice in letters to Aquila, this time in an effort to cast suspicion on Agricola's exaggerated accusations. Even after an agreement had been reached, Melanchthon insisted on drawing attention to his injuries.

Luther's disgust and other letters from Melanchthon give the impression that Agricola was much less ready to attack Melanchthon at the Torgau than Melanchthon had anticipated. Two points in a letter to Caspar Aquila, written on 20 December 1527, are worth noting.[121] First, Melanchthon accepted Aquila's second apology (the first having been received in September) very graciously. It seemed that Agricola's attempt to broaden the attack on Melanchthon had failed. Second, Melanchthon reported that at his whipping in the Torgau his Aristarchus was not as severe as some (including Melanchthon) had expected.

---

116. If the account books are complete, to the tune of about thirty gulden.

117. In a letter to Johannes Lang, dated 29 January 1528, Jonas reported Luther's judgment, indicating that the "rumor et sermo" of some evil people had blown the controversy out of proportion. See Jonas-*BW* 1:116, no. 120.

118. *MBW* 629 (*CR* 1:564).

119. Ibid.: "Nunc inter Gymnasiarcham vestram et me satis convenit."

120. Ibid.: "Ego ingenii laudem neque cupio neque ambio ex tractatione sacrarum literarum."

121. *MBW* 633 (*CR* 1:922).

On the same day Melanchthon wrote more broadly about the conference in a letter to Jonas, who, having failed to get any information from Luther, had turned to Melanchthon for news.[122] Melanchthon used the letter as one final opportunity to encircle Agricola. This time he employed the offices of a mutual friend to try to revive their old friendship. Melanchthon's sorrow and hurt, as well as his anger, sound forth on every page. He regretted that Agricola's little book (most likely the "130 Fragestücke") was being carried around by everyone. Everyone "per universam Germaniam," including Duke George, had known about the controversy before Agricola finally wrote to Melanchthon himself. Throughout the letter Melanchthon maintained his position as the injured party: he could have struck back but, for the sake of peace in the church and friendship, did not. For his "lenissime" letter to Agricola, he received in return only a summons to the court, where some were estranged from him—something that suited Melanchthon just fine.[123]

Melanchthon then recounted what had happened at the Torgau. Agricola began by attacking Melanchthon's view of *poenitentia*, a teaching with which others (Melanchthon meant Luther and Bugenhagen, of course) saw no wrong. Agricola claimed that it ran contrary to the Scriptures and to the dogmas of Luther. Luther supposedly taught that *poenitentia* began with the love of righteousness, as was proven in the case of the prophet Jonah and in Luke 24, where Jesus said that *poenitentia* was to be taught in his name, not Moses'. Melanchthon, who after all had already seen Luther's opinion in the matter, responded that there were always terrors before justification and that in the midst of such terrors Christians could not easily distinguish whether they were motivated by love of righteousness or fear of punishment. To protect himself from the charge of works-righteousness, he also stressed that he was not talking about a simulated *poenitentia*, but something divinely worked in the person's heart.

Agricola responded by agreeing to what Melanchthon said, except that he insisted that *poenitentia* began from "fides minarum."[124] Melanchthon retorted that such "fides minarum" was not without "terrores" and could even be defined as "pavor." He pointed out that this

---

122. *MBW* 634 (*CR* 1:914–18). Jonas was living in Nordhausen during the plague in Wittenberg. According to Jonas's note to Lang (see n. 117), Melanchthon's letter was being circulated to others. He regretted not being able to send it to Lang since it was in the possession of William Reiffenstein. This meant that the letter was viewed at least by Jonas, and probably by Melanchthon as well, not simply as private correspondence, but as a public record of the events.

123. *CR* 1:915.

124. This could be translated as "faith in the midst of threats" or "faith in the midst of signs of threats."

term, along with "amor iustitiae," was simply not used among the theologians with whom he was familiar.[125] He used Agricola's odd terminology to introduce another part of his defense: Agricola's pride. Eisleben's rector was guilty of ingratitude; he had insulted Melanchthon's intelligence, although Melanchthon had done nothing of the kind to him. At this juncture Agricola became more civil, and there seems to have been room for joking and an exchange of compliments.

At this point in the letter, Melanchthon introduced Luther's solution to the controversy. Given some of the stereotypes about their relationship,[126] it is important to note that Luther was the one ready to resolve the dispute by compromise and by—dare the term be used?—treading softly (*Leisetreten*, a favorite charge against Melanchthon). When we speak of faith, Luther proposed, we usually mean justifying faith. But we can also talk about a general faith that could be said to include *poenitentia*. That this in fact contained the kernel of Luther's solution to the dispute may be seen in a notice in Veit Dietrich's hand to the same effect.[127] Here the issue was clearly put in terms of what we know from the catechisms and other writings and letters, namely, that the dispute focused on how to order *poenitentia* and faith.

Luther also addressed the suspicion that their Catholic opponents would claim that the evangelicals had abandoned their previous teaching.[128] Luther's response? *Poenitentia* and law belonged to "gemeynen glauben (general or common faith)," since one must believe that there is a God who threatens. But "for common working persons (*fur den gemeynen groben man*)" it is better simply to leave these matters under the names *poenitentia*, command, law, and fear, so that they may more clearly understand what the apostles call "justifying faith," which makes a person righteous and forgives sin. It was to be taught that righteousness and forgiveness could not be achieved by obeying commands or by *poenitentia*, so that the common folk would not get confused and bring up unnecessary questions.[129]

Luther's solution was a marvelous example of theological diplomacy. First, he continued to insist that the controversy was a war of words and

---

125. *CR* 1:916: "Quod si uni sibi existimet ille has disputationes de fide minarum, de amore iustitiae notas esse, ac meas aures ita peregrinari, ut tot annis versatus inter Theologos, nihil de talibus rebus audierim."

126. Many of the stereotypes are refuted in Heinz Scheible, "Luther and Melanchthon," *Lutheran Quarterly*, n.s., 4 (1990): 317–39.

127. J. K. Seidemann, "Schriftstücke zur Reformationsgeschichte," *Zeitschrift für die historische Theologie* 44 (1874): 116f. The notice bears the title "Sententia de tumultu Islebij contra Philippum, quod prius sit docenda quam fides, poenitencia."

128. Ibid., 116: ". . . auff das die widdersacher nicht sagen mugen, man widderruffe vnsere vorige leere."

129. Ibid., 117.

could thus be solved with definitions. Then, he refused to accept any of Agricola's substantive argumentation and asserted that the Christian life moved from law to gospel or, in this case, from *poenitentia* to faith. The notion of a faith prior to justification was put in terms of the creative order and law and not, as Agricola stated in his latest catechisms, in terms of the proclamation of the satisfaction and forgiveness of Christ. Finally, Luther did not paper over the differences. He had read and approved the Visitation Articles. He had a clear idea of his own position in this matter, and he brooked no exception that would confuse law and gospel. In 1529 he also added a closing word to this controversy when his own catechisms replaced Agricola's in the bookstalls of Germany (see pp. 148–53).

While this was the end of public dispute, Melanchthon also reported to Jonas that the differences were discussed over breakfast on the next day.[130] At that time Agricola argued, in line with his catechism, that there is no place for the preaching of the law, since we are free from it, but only for preaching the "praecepta Pauli."[131] Melanchthon responded by pointing out that Paul's paraenesis and Christ's sermons were expositions of the Decalog. Agricola objected that Christ was speaking only to the Jews. Melanchthon here broke off his report and, using Aristophanes and bitter sarcasm to make his point, derided Agricola's position as that of a "homo subtilis."[132] He then took the opportunity to call attention to Agricola's guilt and his own innocence in the matter. Three times Melanchthon asked that their friendship be restored, but Agricola stood there like a statue.[133] Returning to the breakfast conversation, Melanchthon reminded Jonas of his attempts to accommodate his teaching to the capacities of the reader, especially in the Visitation Articles. Again he was echoing Luther's expressed concerns and portraying the rector of Eisleben as an inept teacher.

At the same time an older charge came to mind: that Melanchthon was soft on the papists. Here it can be seen how the fear of mob violence played into Melanchthon's understanding of preaching's moral function. Preaching that attacked infested pontifical doctrine resulted only in rocks being thrown at monks.[134] Melanchthon preferred to reprimand rather than to incite the mob. Here echoed again the advice to

130. Which day is difficult to tell, and does not really make much difference.

131. *CR* 1:916.

132. *CR* 1:917: "Si enim videtur tibi iustam habuisse causam, sic me arripiendi mordicus, nullam recuso poenam."

133. *CR* 1:917. Melanchthon also intimated that, unlike Agricola, he was concerned about Luther's health.

134. This medieval, unevangelical mode of church reform was seen in student riots at Erfurt in 1520.

Aquila, whose objections to Melanchthon's methods had caused the furor in the first place.

Melanchthon closed his letter in a huff of righteous indignation. Recalling to mind his abhorrence of this kind of church fight, he begged Jonas to approach Agricola on his behalf. If Agricola refused to answer, what would that be but a declaration of war? Would that not show he considered Melanchthon to be more a tree or rock than a human being? Melanchthon urged that the old relationship be restored, according to the requirements of Christian love, and he turned to Jonas to try to erase the memory of this little dissension by his intervention.[135]

The letter had one clear effect. When Jonas wrote to Luther at the beginning of January, he was squarely on Melanchthon's side. Using much of the same language to describe the dispute, he even intimated that he had requested Agricola to show first to Luther anything further he might write in relation to this controversy. He also blamed the dispute on the workings of Satan.[136]

The heated charges against Melanchthon did not die completely. In May 1528 he wrote to George Spalatin concerning a rumor that his theology was not in agreement with Luther's and that Luther had rejected the Visitation Articles.[137] Melanchthon responded to the rumor in no uncertain terms: "No word between us concerning this thing has been exchanged; nor could it have been, since I always would contend that those things that are in the commentary on the churches' inspection [the Visitation Articles] converge in all things with Luther's teaching."[138] To avoid the impression that the evangelicals dealt only in contentions, Melanchthon refused to use harsh words. He realized that some would not approve of this approach, but insisted that he would rather please God than sycophants. He invited Spalatin to show the letter to anyone he wanted, and added, "Whoever judges that Luther rejects something in my work is insane many times over."[139] If his teaching seemed to conflict with Luther's, then people should take up the matter with him, not Luther, so that he could respond. He concluded with the justified claim that Luther would vouch for his approach: "And Luther is my best witness; I had always desired in this entire dispute

135. *CR* 1:918. At the end of the letter Melanchthon announced the birth of his son George.

136. *WABr* 4:321–25.

137. *MBW* 689 (*CR* 1:898f.). The culprit was one Alexius Crosser.

138. *CR* 1:898: "Nullum inter nos verbum ea de re commutatum est; neque sane potuit, cum ego semper contenderim ea, quae sunt in commentario inspectionis ecclesiarum, convenire per omnia cum Lutheri doctrina."

139. *CR* 1:898: "Si quis Lutherum recantare aliquid in meo opere iudicat, is multipliciter insanit."

that all our own people would have used the highest degree of consideration and equanimity."[140]

This was not Melanchthon's last word on the subject. One year after the event he spoke with complete candor in a letter to Joachim Camerarius. It seemed that John Fabri, coadjutor of Constance, had written to Melanchthon in an attempt, based on what he had heard of the Visitation Articles and the surrounding controversy, to get him to defect to Catholicism by offering him various inducements. Fabri undertook this effort despite the fact that, true to his method, Melanchthon saw himself as having done nothing more than excerpt and systematize Luther's thought without resorting to sharp language.[141] An ironic reference to "homines acuti" (specifically Count Albert of Mansfeld) led to a description of a dinner at which Count Albert and Prince Philip of Hesse in the presence of some θεολογοῦσι discussed the Visitation Articles. In satirical style Melanchthon related that someone threw in a comment about confession, about which there was disapproval. Apparently the count said that they would have to guard their freedom (not to confess), lest they be returned to servitude by the evangelicals.[142] The charge was again made that Melanchthon simply wanted to renew old traditions: "So you see what they think about us—not only our enemies, but also those who want to seem to be on our side."[143]

The letter to Camerarius epitomized Melanchthon's position at this time. On the one hand, he placed himself squarely on Luther's side, using his dialectical skills to cull from Luther's thought and systematize what the older man had said. He also adopted a nonpolemical approach as the best way to deal with his enemies and as a teaching tool. On the other hand, he was misunderstood by friend and foe alike. Against these charges Melanchthon used irony, satire, and scorn, holding firm to his theological position without necessarily having to defend it directly.

Melanchthon's parting shots might have ended the dispute were it not for the fact that after the dust had settled, both Melanchthon and Agricola, as well as Luther, continued to work out their differences in print. In particular the 1528 *Scholia* testify that Melanchthon's position in fact remained very much the same, with some small, almost cos-

---

140. *CR* 1:899: "Et Lutherus mihi optimus testis est, me semper optasse in hac tota dissensione, ut summa lenitate καὶ ἐπιεικείᾳ nostri omnes uterentur."

141. *MBW* 710 (*MSA* 7.2:64–67, here 66), dated 15 September 1528: "Et interpretatur me labascere, quia in libello Inspectionis Ecclesiarum fuerim ἐπιεικέστερος, in quo tu vides nihil aliud me scripsisse, quam quod passim tradidit Lutherus. Et tamen, quia sine verborum asperitate scripsi, iudicant isti, scilicet homines acuti, me dissentire a Luthero."

142. *MSA* 7.2:66.

143. *MSA* 7.2:66: "Ita vides, quid de nobis senciant non solum inimici, sed hi, qui harum partium voluerunt videri."

metic, changes to reflect the agreement worked out at the Torgau. For Melanchthon the *Scholia* functioned as his last word in the dispute, determining the outline of his thought on the subject at least until the publication of the second edition of the *Loci communes* in 1535. Agricola, too, made changes in his commentaries to reflect the new consensus, while still maintaining his basic position. A decade later those opinions would run afoul of Luther's theology in the more famous antinomian controversy.

5

The Aftermath (1527–53)

The controversy over *poenitentia* between Melanchthon and Agricola erupted when catechetical material and theological concerns mixed with exegetical disputes. The richness of the nonexegetical sources underscores the fact that during the Reformation the interpretation of Scripture belonged as well within this world of polemic and practical problems. As important as it may be to notice the commentaries on an exegete's writing desk, it is equally crucial to pay attention to the controversies raging outside the study door. In the days before it became stylish to pretend that exegesis was pure science or simple description of a long-dead world, the interpreter of Scripture, especially evangelical theologians like Melanchthon and Agricola, thought their task incomplete until they brought the Word of God to bear on the issues that confronted them on every side. What makes Melanchthon's commentary on Colossians so noteworthy in this regard is that his dialectical method encouraged and even demanded discussion of the theological issues of the day as they arose in connection with the biblical text.

The controversy with Agricola had resulted in an accommodation of sorts. Some researchers who have dealt with the controversy have disparaged that agreement, even to the point of wondering whether Luther understood the consequences of Agricola's theology, or of Melanchthon's for that matter.[1] We must point out, however, that all of the researchers (with the exception of Steffen Kjeldgaard-Pedersen, who stops his analysis with Agricola's move to Eisleben in 1525) are actually more interested in the first antinomian controversy of the late

---

1. Gustav Kawerau, *Johann Agricola von Eisleben: Ein Beitrag zur Reformationsgeschichte* (Berlin: Wilhelm Hertz, 1881), 151f.; and Joachim Rogge, *Johann Agricolas Lutherverständnis: Unter besonderer Berücksichtigung des Antinomismus* (Berlin: Evangelische Verlagsanstalt, 1960), 117. Susi Hausammann, *Buße als Umkehr und Erneuerung von Mensch und Gesellschaft* (Zurich: Theologischer Verlag, 1974), simply skips from Agricola's writings in 1527 (*Colosser* and "130 Fragestücke") to the later controversy with Luther.

1530s than in this prelude, and as a result have ignored almost all of the sources produced immediately after the controversy. Yet these publications reveal more clearly than any other the limits of the agreement, but also the extremely wide latitude of theological opinions that were allowed to coexist in Wittenberg and its environs in the late 1520s.

Once again, to limit our attention simply to the exegetical materials in this phase of the discussion would leave the mistaken impression that the battle, having begun in the lecture halls and pulpits as a struggle over catechetical instruction in Saxony, ended in the print shops and Latin technical manuals intended for the few scholars who cared to read such esoterica. Instead, this controversy requires casting the nets widely enough to examine what happened both on the catechetical front, where the controversy began, and on the exegetical front, where each theologian changed his discussion of *poenitentia* and the law to accommodate the other and also to defend his own position more completely.

Conclusion of the Catechetical Controversy

How does one bring the gospel—Wittenberg style—to the common people? This question consumed the time of many of Wittenberg's best thinkers and finest printers. Throughout 1528 catechisms for the laity spewed from Wittenberg's presses; by 1529 the number of editions of catechisms brought to market by the booksellers totaled over sixty. At the same time, catechisms for pastors also appeared in German.

The Visitation Articles Revised

Melanchthon regarded the Latin version of the Visitation Articles as a kind of catechesis. Luther expressed a slightly different view in the preface of the German version. After describing the biblical and traditional roots of the present visitation and explaining the particular role played by the Elector John, which arose from Christian love and not from his authority as a secular ruler, Luther depicted the Articles from two sides. On the one hand, they were being published in order to do battle with the devil, embodied in Luther's enemies who had charged the Wittenbergers with having gone back on and recanted their previous teaching. The Visitation Articles proved that the evangelicals were not operating in the dark, but gladly searched out the light.[2] On the

---

2. Instead of WA 26:175–240, our references to the German version of the Visitation Articles are drawn from the excellent edition of Günther Wartenberg in *MLStA* 3:402–62, here 413. The Articles were entitled "Unterricht der Visitatoren."

other hand, distinguishing the Articles from canon law, Luther insisted that the Reformers could not allow them to be promulgated "as a strict command." Instead, they represented a history of the faith and a confession of faith. Luther hoped that this document would please pious, peace-loving pastors who would join the cause and submit to the visitation "without compulsion, following the lead of love."[3] Thus Luther retained some notion of the educational, even catechetical nature of the Articles, but completely within the framework of the visitation itself and its confessional nature.[4]

Most important for our study are the changes to the Visitation Articles that resulted from the dispute with Agricola. For one thing, Agricola's formal complaint held up publication until the Articles were gone over at the Torgau (without noticeable dissension on his part). Most of the changes were made in the first phase of the controversy, at which time the Articles were already being revised in the light of suggestions from Elector John himself.

There were three specific charges in the first phase: the general charge of returning to Rome, the specific complaint regarding the division of *poenitentia*, and the dispute over the content of preaching and its relation to Christian freedom. Luther dealt with the first charge in the preface itself. His letter to the elector also indicated that he thought this issue was more a trick of the devil than a matter for debate. After the Visitation Articles were published, both John Fabri and John Cochlaeus attacked them on just these grounds. Both attempted to show that the Articles contradicted Luther's earlier teaching. (It was for Cochlaeus's attack that the famous woodcut of Luther with seven heads was designed.)[5]

The other two charges were dealt with, among other places, in the first section, "Von der Lere." Most strikingly, the division of the Chris-

---

3. *MLStA* 3:414 (*WA* 26:200).

4. For the role of confession in the Lutheran church, see Robert Kolb, *Confessing the Faith: Reformers Define the Church, 1530–1580* (St. Louis: Concordia, 1991), 34–42.

5. By John Cochlaeus we have "Septiceps Lutherus, vbiq[ue] sibi, suis I scriptis, co[n]trarius, in Visitatione[m] Saxonica[m], p[er] D. D. Ioa[n]. Cocl[a]eu[m], [a]editus I [Woodcut of Luther with seven heads]." 4°. Colophon: "Lypsiae Impressit Valentinus Schuman[n], I Anno post Christum natum, I M.D.XXIX. I X. Maias Calendas." [64] leaves. An excerpt in German is entitled "Siebenköpffe Martini Luthers I Vom Hochwirdigen Sacrament des Altars/ Durch I Doctor Jo. Cocleus. I [Same woodcut as above]." 4°. Colophon: "Gedruckt zu Leypsig durch Valten I Schuman im XXIX. Jhar." [27] (+ 1 blank) leaves. The work by John Fabri is entitled "Christenliche vnder= I richtung Doctor Johann Fabri/ vber I ettliche Puncten der Visitation/ ßo im Churfürstenthumb Sachs= I sen gehalten/ vnd durch Luther beschriben/ Welch antzunehmen I vnd zuuerwerffen seyend. I … " No woodcut, 4°. Colophon: "Gedruckt zu Dreßden durch Wolffgang Stöckel I 24. Septemb. Anno 1528." [72] leaves.

tian life into *poenitentia* and faith was not only accepted, but strengthened. Teaching faith without *poenitentia* was called an error. Both versions categorized it as worse than "all errors before this time."[6] And the German version, while admitting some truth in the charges that the pope had made additions to the Scripture, did not excuse clerics from preaching *poenitentia*, since such an omission undercut the basic message of the Bible. Here Melanchthon's experience with Aquila fit precisely.[7] Although there was a time to speak against the tyranny of the pope for the sake of Christian freedom, what was this other than to strain at a gnat and swallow a camel?[8]

The German version completely accepted the threefold division of *poenitentia:* "People previously taught that there were three parts to *Buße*, namely, contrition, confession, and satisfaction."[9] After defining contrition as recognition of sin and mortification and repeating many of the warnings about teaching faith without mortification, the German version added, "It is also good that one use these words 'contrition' and 'sorrow.' For these words are easy to understand and clear."[10] Here the pedagogical concerns of Melanchthon found full expression, and the opposition of Aquila and Agricola was not accepted at all. To be sure, the Visitation Articles rejected papistic confession and turned confession into preparation for the Lord's Supper. Nevertheless, the German version still held confession in high esteem. As expected, satisfaction in the medieval Scholastic sense was completely discarded in favor of the satisfaction wrought through Christ's death.

In the second phase of the dispute, four interconnected issues were discussed: the role of fear in contrition, the relation of faith and *poenitentia*, the preaching of the law, and the interpretation of Galatians 3:19. In the German version the section on doctrine defined *poenitentia* as contrition and sorrow over sin and "fear before God's judgment."[11] There was no hint of compromise here. After stressing that clerics were to preach not only against gross sins but also against hypocrisy (which was a much more serious sin and demanded harder *poenitentia*), the German version reproduced word for word the agreement reached at

6. *MLStA* 3:416.12f. (*WA* 26:202).
7. *MLStA* 3:416 n. 74 points erroneously to Agricola, probably on the basis of the description in Rogge, *Johann Agricolas Lutherverständnis*, 104.
8. This phrase, which comes up repeatedly in the controversy, is one of Melanchthon's favorite metaphors.
9. *MLStA* 3:437.10f. (*WA* 26:219): "Man hat zuuor geleret/ es seyen drey teil der Busse/ Als nemlich/ Rew/ Beicht/ vnd Genugthuung."
10. *MLStA* 3:437.13f. (*WA* 26:219): "Ist auch gut/ das man diese wort/ Rew vnd leid brauche/ Denn diese wort sind liecht vnd klar zuuerstehen."
11. *MLStA* 3:417.4f. (*WA* 26:202).

the Torgau between Melanchthon and Agricola as it had been proposed by Luther.[12]

However, the very next line, in the section entitled "On the Ten Commandments," made clear that Agricola's low estimation of the Ten Commandments had no place in the teaching of Saxony: "Therefore they [the preachers] ought to preach the Ten Commandments often and diligently."[13] As in the Latin original, the German version entreated preachers to stress punishment for sin, so that the people would learn to fear God. All this indicated that Agricola's position found no ready hearing among Wittenberg's theologians or Saxony's visitors. When he accepted Luther's compromise formula and did not object to other phrasings in the document, Luther and the others had every reason to believe that the case was closed. Thus, the agreement at the Torgau reflected more Agricola's duplicity or his theological unclarity than Luther's gullibility.

The rest of the section on the Ten Commandments discussed the role of faith after the hearers have been made contrite through the preaching of the law. This section completely overturned the contentions of Agricola in his "130 Fragestücke." The people were to be warned that there can be no faith without true contrition and fear (*schrecken*) before God. This was to be emphasized so that the people did not come to the false conclusion that they had faith when in fact they did not: "Where there is no contrition, there is a pretend faith."[14]

In the midst of a discussion of contrition and satisfaction, however, the German version acquiesced to one of Agricola's objections to the original Visitation Articles. Melanchthon's version had warned only against faith without contrition. Now the document insisted that there should also be no contrition without faith. One should not only be contrite but should also know that forgiveness comes for the sake of Christ. What followed echoed the comments in Luther's letter to Melanchthon from October 1527: "For contrition without faith causes doubt, as in Judas and Saul. Likewise, one cannot have genuine faith without con-

---

12. *MLStA* 3:417.10–21 (*WA* 26:202f.); cf. J. K. Seidemann, "Schriftstücke zur Reformationsgeschichte," *Zeitschrift für die historische Theologie* 44 (1874): 116f. (see p. 134). The small changes in the text are enough to indicate that Veit Dietrich's notice was not simply copied out of the Articles themselves. For further discussion see Gustav Hammann, "Nomismus und Antinomismus innerhalb der wittenberger Theologie von 1524–1530," Ph.D. diss., Friedrich Wilhelms Universität, 1952, 57–109; and Rogge, *Johann Agricolas Lutherverständnis*, 116.

13. *MLStA* 3:417.23 (*WA* 26:203): "Darumb sollen sie [die Prediger] die zehen gebot offt vnd vleyssig predigen." This follows the Latin version (*CR* 26:9), where discussion of the issue occurs in the very first section, although Melanchthon's use of the title "Ten Commandments" comes later.

14. *MLStA* 3:418.24 (*WA* 26:203): "Wo nicht Rew ist/ ist ein gemalter Glawb."

trition."[15] The text asserted Luther's conviction that the Christian is si-
multaneously contrite and believing. It is noteworthy that the compromise even incorporated one of Agricola's favorite examples of bad
poenitentia: Judas.[16]

One final objection of Agricola found no acceptance in the German
version.[17] Agricola had challenged Melanchthon's interpretation of
Galatians 3:19 as a reference to the first use of the law; among Agricola's evidence was Luther's interpretation of the verse as a reference
to the second use of the law. Although that particular portion of the
section on the Ten Commandments that contained the citation in question did not make it from the Latin into the German version, the verse
itself did. In the section on free will, Melanchthon had originally used
only 1 Timothy 1:8–9 to prove that the law was given to limit human
freedom. In the German version Galatians 3:19 was added. Here there
was no room for compromise with Agricola. The Reformation in Wittenberg was not about lockstep biblical interpretation. A scholastic
mind-set that rejected everything not in Luther's works had yet to develop among the Lutherans—if it ever did. Within the teaching of the
gospel a wide latitude was allowed the exegete.[18] The interpretation of
Scripture was to be based on conformity to the gospel, not on conformity to a teacher.

The other area where Agricola's presence could be felt in the German
version of the Visitation Articles was its omissions. Because the German version was a complete reworking and in part restructuring of the
whole, it is difficult to determine what was left out. It would seem, however, that much of the polemical tone of the Latin version, which reflected its origins in the encounter with Aquila's preaching, was omitted. The Ten Commandments remained at the beginning, but
Melanchthon's characteristic teaching of the two uses of the law was
omitted. Nevertheless, the basic structure (*poenitentia*, faith, good
works), the movement from law to gospel, the insistence on contrition

---

15. *MLStA* 3:438.21–23 (*WA* 26:221): "Denn rew on glauben bringet verzweiuelung/
wie ym Judas vnd Saul/ So kan man auch warhafftigen glauben on rewe nicht haben."
The same point is made in the discussion of contrition, 437.6–9 (*WA* 26:219): "Aber
solcher glaube/ wie offt gesagt ist/ kan nicht sein/ wo nicht vorhin rew vnd leid ist. Denn
Rewe on glauben/ ist Judas vnd Sauls rewe/ das ist/ verzweiuelung/ Gleich wie Glaube on
rewe vermessenheit vnd fleischliche sicherheit ist."

16. Because he is less familiar with all sides of this dispute, Rogge, *Johann Agricolas
Lutherverständnis*, misses this part of the compromise.

17. This despite Rogge's claim (*Johann Agricolas Lutherverständnis*, 117) that
Melanchthon changed his opinion on the interpretation of Gal. 3:19.

18. In later works Melanchthon cited the same text as proof for the second use of the
law. This does not mean that he capitulated to Luther's authority; rather, Melanchthon
was convinced by Luther's arguments.

preceding justifying faith, and the overall tone of the work had not changed. In point of fact, none of Agricola's challenges was accepted in such a way as to change the overall tone or content of the work.

In 1528 John Setzer published a revised edition of the Latin version of the Visitation Articles.[19] For the most part the changes were minor, involving improvements in grammar or syntax, the omission of a sentence or two, or the addition of other sentences. It is not even clear whether Melanchthon himself made the changes. However, there are hints that not all the changes were simply cosmetic. Where the first edition talked about faith occurring "in the contrite heart," the second edition revised the phrase to read "in those whose hearts have been terrified or (as they say) made contrite."[20] Melanchthon maintained a discreet distance between the word "contrite" and his own theology ("as they say"). It was not his terminology but that of the "doctores." In the section "On the Fruits of the Spirit," Melanchthon originally had not clearly tied the fruits of faith to faith itself. In the second edition he stressed that any discussion of these fruits should not occur outside of a discussion of faith itself: "One must often return to this and say how [God] justifies."[21] In the section "On Human Traditions," several changes were made to lessen the criticism aimed at pastors like Aquila who railed against church practices without preaching about the fear of God.[22] The second edition also clarified the earlier comments regarding those who interpreted attacks on some traditions as attacks on all laws. Whereas in the first edition Melanchthon had simply said that a great part of the common people "do not know that the violation of traditions was made with cause, and they begin to condemn divine and human traditions,"[23] in the revised edition he stated that they do not know "for what cause it is permitted to violate traditions, nor do they differentiate between the precepts of God and human traditions. Contempt of all laws then leads them to condemn divine and human traditions."[24] Perhaps most important of all, under the discussion of the first use of the law the reference to Galatians 3:19 was deleted, again in line with Agricola's objections.

19. See appendix 3.
20. *CR* 26:11 n. 25. The change was from "in corde contrito" to "in his [hominibus], quorum corda perterrita sunt, seu (ut vocant) contrita."
21. *CR* 26:16 n. 37: "ad hanc saepe est redeundum et dicendum, quomodo iustificet."
22. *CR* 26:23 n. 74.
23. *CR* 26:24: "ex caussa traditionum violationem nesciunt fieri, incipiuntque divinas et humanas traditiones contemnere."
24. *CR* 26:24 n. 84: ". . . nesciens quam ob causam liceat violare traditiones, nec discernunt inter praecepta Dei et traditiones hominum, iuxta induit contemptum omnium legum, divinas et humanas traditiones contemnere."

Melanchthon's Catechetical Fragment

With the publication of the "130 Fragestücke" Agricola's contribution to the catechesis of Saxony came to an end. Throughout 1528, however, his catechisms were as widely distributed as any from this time. Given his sharp attack against Wittenberg's theology, it is hardly surprising that at just about the time his work was being delivered to the Wittenberg presses, George Spalatin was urging (even demanding, given the tone of Melanchthon's responses) that Melanchthon write a catechism of his own.[25] According to Ferdinand Cohrs's reconstruction, the printer George Rhau was also urging Melanchthon to write a catechism. In a letter to Stephen Roth, dated 30 October 1528, Rhau connected the revision of "Eyn buchlin fur die leyen vnd kinder," on which Roth had worked the year before,[26] with Melanchthon's renewed work on parts of the catechism.[27]

Rhau's plans and Spalatin's demands never resulted in the publication of such a book, at least not in the 1520s. All we have of the work is a single copy of the first two sheets that was once in the possession of Stephen Roth, who added to the bottom of the last page, "It was completed only to this point, and Mr. Philip does not want to work further on it."[28] Melanchthon stopped working at the time Luther began his own set of catechisms. Cohrs assumed that once Melanchthon heard that Luther was writing a catechism, he no longer saw any need to write his own.[29]

The surviving fragment reveals that for Melanchthon the debate with Agricola was still going on.[30] In the preface Melanchthon acknowl-

---

25. *MBW* 620 (*CR* 1:902–4), undated, from the beginning of November. A postscript notes that a catechism had not yet been written. *MBW* 624 (*CR* 1:907f.), dated 12 November (1527), described the vehemence with which Spalatin was making his plea and Melanchthon's unwillingness to start something new before he was done with his tract against the Anabaptists. He warned Spalatin against pushing him: "Sic flagitare est plane extorquere."

26. Roth, 66, no. 138 (dated 7 November 1527), and 70, no. 149 (dated 10 February 1528).

27. Roth, 80, no. 184 (dated 30 October 1528): "Auch so drücke ich . . . vnd hab angehaben das buchlyn, so yhr mir fur einem Jar geordnet habt, aber philippi Mel. schreibt den Decalogum selbs von newen vnd das Vater vnser vnd den glauben vnd er mach lenger denn das vorige."

28. *SM* 5.1:88 n. 3: "So ferne ists gemacht, vnd der Herr Philip. wil ferner nichts dran machen."

29. Luther's previous work on the different parts of the catechism influenced what Melanchthon had to say in his fragment.

30. We know from a letter to Agricola written shortly after 3 February 1535, *MBW* 1538 (*CR* 2:826f.), that Melanchthon was familiar with Agricola's catechisms. In sending Martin Bucer's teaching on the Lord's Supper to Agricola, Melanchthon comments, "Therefore there remains only a question about the physical conjoining of bread and

edged that the catechism had already been interpreted "by many godly people," among whom one thinks immediately of Agricola. Yet Melanchthon insisted that such interpretation should occur over and over again. There is no other sure help for the Christian surrounded by sin, the devil, and unbelief than God's Word, in which we learn about God's anger over sin and his grace for those who believe in him.

Melanchthon added, following Luther, that the Christian life is made up of two parts: faith and good works. Before anything else, however, one must come to understand what true faith is. Since the gospel is the preaching of Christ, faith in this context is the righteousness that comes not from our own works, but from trusting God's grace on account of Christ. Such faith must be, as Paul says, "without hypocrisy," that is, a matter of peace and joy in one's conscience. This implies, however, that the conscience begins its journey toward faith by recognizing its sin and being terrified (*erschrickt*) before God. Terror comes precisely when one experiences the wrath of God, which is part of God's Word. Melanchthon then declared one more time what worried him most about Agricola's theology: "It is a pretend faith when people imagine that their sin is forgiven although they are without contrition or terror. For how can faith comfort such a person who has not yet been terrified? . . . We ought to have this comfort whenever we consider God's command and await help from God."[31]

This insistence on law before gospel and *poenitentia* before faith spilled over into the interpretation of the Ten Commandments that followed. Commenting on the first commandment, Melanchthon, echoing Luther's catechetical sermons of 1528, described how both fear and faith are demanded, with fear coming first. Commenting on the second commandment, Melanchthon described Christian prayer and the cross. All afflictions in the Christian life are sent, not to condemn us, but to lead us to *poenitentia*. Melanchthon accepted one of Agricola's concerns by admitting that reason does not understand this. Only faith realizes that God does a strange work in order to do his proper work (Isa. 28:21), and that, accordingly, in the midst of afflictions the heart should cling to the promises. At the same time, faith itself breaks out in the midst of

---

body—what is the need for such a question? And certainly you handle the nature of the sacraments in a godly and serious manner in your catechism without bringing up this question (Tantum igitur reliqua est quaestio de physica coniunctione panis et corporis, qua quaestione quid opus est? Et certe Sacramentorum naturam tu sine hac quaestione tractas pie et graviter in tua catechesi)."

31. *SM* 5.1:79.31–33; 80.7–9: "Dis ist ein gemalter glaub, so einer tichtet, er glaube, die sund sei ihm vergeben, so er doch on reu und on schrecken ist, denn wie kan der glaub ein solchen trösten, der noch nie erschrocken ist? . . . Diesen trost sollen wir haben, wenn wir Gottes gepot betrachten, und hülffe von Gott warten."

such difficulties and prays to God for help.[32] We have no further indications of Melanchthon's catechetical reaction to this dispute, since he broke off his work in the middle of his explanation of the third commandment.

These arguments have been encountered in this study time and time again. This fragment, written a year after the dispute, shows how the controversy continued to weigh on Melanchthon's mind and to affect his theological formulations. When speaking of faith, he always began not with the gospel but with the law.

The Catechisms of Martin Luther

Melanchthon could break off his work precisely because another had taken up the cause and was working out his own approach to the commandments, faith, and *poenitentia*—an endeavor that was destined to have far-reaching effects for the life of the evangelical churches. The single most important correction of Agricola's catechesis came not from Melanchthon at all, but from Luther. His catechisms, viewed within the context of this dispute, arose out of and answered the challenges contained in Agricola's "130 Fragestücke." This connection has largely been ignored in the secondary literature.[33] Yet both Wittenberg's problems with Agricola's theology, sermons, and catechisms and Agricola's public dispute with Melanchthon provide essential background for understanding the timing and shape of Luther's catechisms.[34] Because they were written after the Torgau conference, there is no direct polemic against Agricola's position. At the same time, they reflect the compromise language that brought about peace between the two parties.

Participation in the visitation profoundly affected both Melanchthon and Luther. The preface to Luther's Small Catechism poignantly testi-

---

32. *SM* 5.1:86.

33. For example, Albrecht Peters, *Kommentar zu Luthers Katechismen*, vol. 1, *Die Zehn Gebote* (Göttingen: Vandenhoeck and Ruprecht, 1990), has nothing at all to say about Agricola. Johannes Meyer's exhaustive work, *Historischer Kommentar zu Luthers Kleinem Katechismus* (Gütersloh: Bertelsmann, 1929), while mentioning the visitation and the Visitation Articles, ignores Agricola's direct role. John Michael Reu's *Dr. Martin Luther's Small Catechism: A History of Its Origin, Its Distribution and Its Use* (Chicago: Wartburg, 1929) makes no reference to Agricola at all. Only Cohrs 2:262f. seems to have any idea of the connection. Kawerau, *Johann Agricola*, 151, limits Luther's problems with the "130 Fragestücke" to 1540.

34. See Timothy J. Wengert, "'Fear and Love' in the Ten Commandments," *Concordia Journal* 21 (1995): 14–27. The other influence on Luther's catechisms was the spate of catechisms being produced, some based on Luther's own work and others based on the work of Rhegius or even Agricola. See Cohrs 4:326–42 for a discussion of the influence of Luther and others on the catechisms of this early period.

fied to the "deplorable, wretched need" and the "misery" of the commoners who had no idea whatsoever of Christian doctrine and lived "like the dear cattle and irrational pigs."[35] But it also recognized that Wittenberg's gospel had led to a kind of gross antinomianism: "Now that the gospel has come, [the people] have nonetheless learned well to misuse masterfully all freedom."[36] In the new preface to the Large Catechism from 1530 Luther reiterated this complaint, speaking of "such lazy, harmful, shameful, fleshly freedom."[37]

Along with the attack on licentiousness came, in stark contrast to Agricola's catechisms, praise for the Ten Commandments. In the new preface to the Large Catechism Luther equated God's Word with the commandments.[38] He even made the startling comment that the Ten Commandments encompass all of God's Word: "For this must certainly be [the case]: all who know the Ten Commandments well and completely must know the entire Scripture, so that in all matters and cases they might counsel, help, comfort, judge both spiritual and secular issues, and might be judges of all teaching, estates, spirits, law, and whatever else may be in the world."[39] Indeed, the entire psalter was in Luther's opinion nothing less than a reflection on the first commandment, and the catechism, Ten Commandments included, was nothing other than a compendium and summary of the whole Bible.[40]

The actual comments on the Ten Commandments in the Large Catechism and the sermons from 1528 on which they were based again reflected Luther's high regard for the Decalog and contrasted with Agricola's rather ancillary handling of it in the "130 Fragestücke." The positioning of the Ten Commandments at the beginning of both the Large and Small Catechisms demonstrated Luther's conviction that law moves to gospel. Accordingly, the first commandment demands faith in the heart, and the second demands correct use of the mouth and tongue in relation to God. Only the third commandment, with its external prohibition of work on the Sabbath, is limited to the Jews: "Thus this command does not now apply in its superficial meaning to

35. SC, preface 1–3 (*BKS*, 501.11, 13; 502.6f.).

36. SC, preface 3 (*BKS*, 502.7–9): "Nu das Evangelion kommen ist, dennoch fein gelernt haben, aller Freiheit meisterlich zu missebrauchen."

37. LC, new preface 3 (*BKS*, 546.30f.): "solche faule, schädliche, schändliche, fleischliche Freiheit."

38. LC, new preface 10, 14 (*BKS*, 549.30f.; 551.1–6).

39. LC, new preface 17 (*BKS*, 552.16–24): "Denn das muß ja sein: wer die zehen Gebot wohl und gar kann, daß der muß die ganze Schrift können, daß er könne in allen Sachen und Fällen raten, helfen, trösten, urteilen, richten beide geistlich und weltlich Wesen und müge sein ein Richter über alle Lehre, Stände, Geister, Recht und was in der Welt sein mag."

40. LC, new preface 18 (*BKS*, 552.31–33).

us Christians. For it is a completely external thing, like the other regulations of the Old Testament."[41] But then Luther contrasted this crude understanding to the true intention of the commandment: to allow workers rest and to set aside a day for the hearing of God's Word. At this level the commandment still applies to the Christian. Luther refused to limit Moses to the *Rathaus* and completely reduce the Decalog to a Jewish *Sachsenspiegel*.

Luther's practical and thorough exposition of the second table of the law also revealed his conviction that all people stand under the law and that no one is exempt from its demands. A curious exception came in the introduction to the ninth and tenth commandments, where he applied them to the Jews.[42] However, Luther went on to say that the reason these commandments were added for the Jews was to make clear to them what Christians already understood about the commandments, namely, that they were not fulfilled merely through external compliance but spoke to the heart.[43]

The conclusion to the discussion of the commandments distinguished Agricola's antinomianism from Luther's theology. Luther asserted that the tenth commandment, like all the others, "accuses us without ceasing and shows how righteous we are before God."[44] More than just a threat, the commands are the font of all good works; outside of obeying them no work or being can please God.[45] Luther also tied the commandments directly to the other chief parts of the catechism. Because no one can keep even one of the Ten Commandments, everyone needs the Creed and the Lord's Prayer.[46]

The conclusion to the discussion of the Ten Commandments pointed to yet another connection with the dispute over the Visitation Articles: Luther used the compromise language he had proposed at the Torgau conference. Already in his third series of sermons on the commandments Luther had connected fear and faith as a "little wreath" that

41. LC, "Ten Commandments," 82 (*BKS*, 580.40–43): "Darumb gehet nu dies Gepot nach dem groben Verstand uns Christen nichts an; denn es ein ganz äußerlich Ding ist wie andere Satzunge des Alten Testaments."

42. LC, "Ten Commandments," 293 (*BKS*, 633.37f.): "Diese zwei Gepot sind fast [=genau genommen] den Jüden sonderlich [=ausschließlich] gegeben." Luther followed the Roman church's traditional division of the commandments.

43. LC, "Ten Commandments," 293 (*BKS*, 633.43–46). Moreover, because the commandment on covetousness described servants and wives as property—a situation that no longer was the case—it did not apply directly to Christians (293–95 [*BKS*, 634.2–21]).

44. LC, "Ten Commandments," 310 (*BKS*, 639.3–5): ". . . uns ohn Unterlaß beschüldigt und anzeigt, wie fromm [=rechtschaffen] wir fur Gott sind."

45. LC, "Ten Commandments," 311 (*BKS*, 639.11–19).

46. LC, "Ten Commandments," 315–17 (*BKS*, 640.31–49 and 641.6–23). See also LC, "Creed," 1–2 (*BKS*, 646.3–26), and LC, "Lord's Prayer," 1–2 (*BKS*, 662.17–31).

binds the first to the last.[47] In the Large Catechism he included love as well. Fear, love, and trust in God fulfill the first commandment and thereby all the others.[48] Luther repeatedly stressed this fear and love throughout his explanations of the commandments in the Small Catechism, thereby reflecting his conviction that the repentance brought about by the commandments involves both. The Ten Commandments provide the correct antidote for human works. To divide fear and love or to lessen the commandments' importance, as Agricola did in his catechisms, was unthinkable for Luther: "one should certainly hold them above all other teachings as precious and valuable, as the highest treasure given by God."[49]

Gustav Kawerau has insisted that Luther made no attacks on Agricola's catechisms between the time of Agricola's dispute with Melanchthon and the outbreak of the antinomian controversy in 1537. This contrasted, he claims, to Luther's condemnation in 1540 of a new Latin version of the "130 Fragestücke."[50] Yet even before that time, in the 1539 tract "Wider die Antinomer," Luther recalled that his exposition of the Decalog in the catechisms had always stressed the law.[51] Luther was recalling one of the original motivations for his catechisms and the reason for their heavy emphasis on the law. In fact, nearly half of the Large Catechism was devoted to the Ten Commandments!

Another evidence against Kawerau's claim is that at the very time Luther was preaching his second series on the catechism (1528), rumors reached him from the court (possibly from Spalatin) of a suspicious sermon preached by Agricola in the presence of John Frederick. Luther's subsequent letter to Agricola (11 September 1528), having expressed concern that Agricola had preached that faith could exist without works, warned him to beware of the devil's tricks.[52] Agricola's response, written in unusually clear, Lutheresque language, affirmed his commitment to justification by faith alone.[53] Luther's belated reply (1 February 1529)

47. WA 30.1:85.5–12, 20–32.
48. LC, "Ten Commandments," 326 (*BKS*, 643.24–41). This *Furcht* includes fear of punishment; see LC, "Ten Commandments," 330–31 (*BKS*, 644.36–645.20).
49. LC, "Ten Commandments," 333 (*BKS*, 645.41–43): "Darümb soll man sie je fur allen andern Lehren teur und wert halten als den hohisten Schatz, von Gott gegeben."
50. See Kawerau, *Johann Agricola*, 151f., citing Karl Eduard Förstemann, ed., *Neues Urkundenbuch zur Geschichte der evangelischen Kirchen-Reformation* (Hamburg, 1842), 223 [*sic;* =322?]. In a letter to Elector John Frederick on 1 March 1540 Agricola complained that Luther had prevented the catechism's publication (see Förstemann, *Neues Urkundenbuch*, 319). A printing of the new version of the catechism did appear in Berlin in 1541.
51. WA 50:468–77.
52. WABr 4:557f.
53. WABr 4:562–65; Rogge, *Johann Agricolas Lutherverständnis*, 118–22, details the unusual language employed by Agricola.

gave lukewarm approval to Agricola's explanation.[54] All the while, in catechetical sermons and in the catechisms themselves, Luther defended the role of law and works in the Christian life, nowhere more clearly than in his sermon on the fourth commandment, delivered on 17 September 1528: "Here good work and a holy life are commanded for children, what people unfortunately despise and do not consider to be a precept of God."[55]

There is additional evidence that Luther's catechisms were a response to Agricola's. We saw earlier (p. 49) that Luther had called for new evangelical catechisms in 1525, giving the task to Justus Jonas and Agricola. When that team broke apart in mid-year, Luther intimated to Nicholas Hausmann that he would take on the job himself. The intervening hiatus of four years has been difficult for modern scholarship to explain. Perhaps "Eyn buchlin fur die leyen vnd kinder" and Agricola's catechisms seemed sufficient to Luther, burdened as he was by the growing controversy over the Lord's Supper and the establishment of evangelical churches throughout the empire. By his own testimony, what moved him to action was the Saxon visitation itself, coupled with both the misery it revealed and the controversy it engendered. Spalatin demanded action. Melanchthon tried to respond. But Luther, thrust into the middle of the catechization of his own parish by the absence of Johann Bugenhagen and confronted with mistaken understandings of the law and *poenitentia*, finally had to provide evangelical resources faithful to Wittenberg's theology and practice.

This chain of events may also explain the peculiar place confession held in both catechisms. For one thing, the first edition of neither the Small Catechism nor the Large Catechism contained an explanation of confession. However, in both cases Luther added material. The additional material for the Large Catechism appeared already in 1529. It clearly reflected the earliest struggles over the Visitation Articles and their inclusion of contrition and confession in the definition of *poenitentia*. Luther, avoiding the traditional language, distinguished evangelical private confession from its medieval predecessor. However, he rejected the argument that evangelical freedom was an excuse not to come to confession.[56] He insisted that sorrow over sin, confession, and absolution defined the rite. Although Luther's explanation accorded with the Visitation Articles, he also insisted beyond any shadow of a

---

54. *WABr* 5:14f.

55. *WA* 30.1:33.17f.: "Ibi mandatum est bonum opus et sancta vita liberis, das man leider veracht, et non gedenckt, quod dei praeceptum sit." Luther also (44.1–6) complained about clerics who thought they could do better than the Decalog. This language also appeared in LC, "Ten Commandments," 114 (*BKS*, 589.27–36).

56. LC, "Confession," 5–7 (*BKS*, 726.26–727.19).

doubt that private confession did not simply bind consciences to the law but freed them through the gospel. Thus in the Large Catechism, unlike the Visitation Articles, absolution itself, not confession, stood at the forefront. The reason was not that Luther here was tilting toward antinomianism, but that he assumed that Christians come to confession because the law has done its work. Because they see their great need, Christians are hungry for forgiveness.[57] The whole point of Luther's lengthy exposition of the Ten Commandments was to demonstrate that need.

In his 1531 addition to the Small Catechism, Luther underscored the connection between commandment and confession. While he still emphasized absolution, a brief form of confession made reference to the Ten Commandments: the list of sins for the head of a household concluded with "and whatever else he has done against God's commandments and his own station in life."[58]

With the publication of Luther's catechisms in 1529 a turning point was reached in evangelical catechesis. Agricola's best-selling works sank into obscurity, and during the antinomian controversy the Latin translation of the "130 Fragestücke" even ended up under Luther's ban. After 1529, Luther's catechisms ruled the marketplace, finally becoming in 1580 a part of the confessions of the Lutheran church.[59] They arose in the aftermath of a conflict over the law, a conflict that had a profound bearing on their form, content, and perhaps their very existence. As a contrast to Agricola's catechisms, they defined, perhaps more clearly than has heretofore been noticed, the contours of the later conflict between the two men. At least by 1540 both realized this fact and allowed it, too, to become a part of their struggle.

The Battle of the Commentaries

If the Visitation Articles and even more so Martin Luther's catechisms decisively shaped the struggle over catechetical instruction, a similar statement cannot be made for the exegetical contributions of the combatants. In fact, completely unnoticed by previous scholarship is the

57. LC, "Confession," 23–24 (*BKS*, 730.42–731.21), esp. 23 (*BKS*, 731.1–6): "Sein eigen Gewissen würde ein iglichen wohl treiben und so bange machen, daß er sein froh würde und täte wie ein armer elender Bettler, so er höret, daß man an einem Ort ein reiche Spende, Geld oder Kleider austeilet."

58. SC, "Confession," 23 (*BKS*, 518.40f.): "Und was er mehr wider die Gebot Gottes und seinen Stand getan etc." The Latin version translated by George Major in 1531 (*BKS*, 518.44f.) reads "contra decem praecepta."

59. For a systematic examination of later catechisms, see John Michael Reu's encyclopedic *Quellen zur Geschichte des kirchlichen Unterrichts in der evangelischen Kirche Deutschlands zwischen 1530 und 1600*, 4 vols. in 9 (Gütersloh: C. Bertelsmann, 1904–35).

fact that in the commentaries, especially in Melanchthon's *Scholia* of 1528, the dispute continued to simmer. (That in 1536 another phase of this same disagreement became public in the Cordatus controversy is, in light of this fact, hardly surprising.)[60]

Agricola's Annotations on the Gospel of Luke

In May 1529 John Setzer once again published Agricola's commentary on Luke. It contained a new dedicatory epistle to George Alemann of Magdeburg, dated 29 March 1529. In it Agricola mentioned that he had made only small changes in the commentary. Most reflected responses to current theological questions. For example, into his discussion of Luke 18:15–17 he inserted a defense of infant baptism against the Anabaptists. He expanded other sections with the additions of German sayings or scriptural examples. The only other substantive changes came in the area of *poenitentia*.

In 1525 and 1526, as part of his discussion of John the Baptist's preaching of repentance, Agricola had written: "Without a doubt you may understand that 'to do *poenitentia*,' 'to be justified,' 'to have a change of heart,' is solely a work of God, not of human powers, and that as many as divide the reckoning of *poenitentia* most ineptly into attrition, confession, and satisfaction err to the highest heaven."[61] In 1529 Agricola struck out the last part of this sentence.[62] There is no doubt that, although he did not use the threefold division of *poenitentia* himself, Agricola was now willing to allow some to use it without "erring to the highest heaven." This indicates that Agricola accepted some sort of compromise at least on the first phase of the dispute.

A less clear indication of compromise came in Agricola's discussion of the story of Zacchaeus (Luke 19). Here the reference to Ephesians 4 ("Let the one who stole no longer steal") remained, as did the German saying. One word changed, however. Whereas in 1525 and 1526 Agricola stated, "Nimmer thun ist die hochste buß (No longer to do a thing is the highest *Buße*)," in 1529 he changed it to read, "Nimmer thun ist die hertest buß (No longer to do a thing is the hardest *Buße*)."[63] The two words are very closely related in German. Nevertheless, it would seem that Agricola was willing here to admit that his favorite way to understand *poenitentia*, namely, as a changed life that needs no repentance,

---

60. See pp. 206–10 and Timothy J. Wengert, "Caspar Cruciger (1504–1548): The Case of the Disappearing Reformer," *Sixteenth Century Journal* 20 (1989): 431–37.

61. *Luke* 1525, 23v°: "Procul dubio intelliges poenitere, iustificari, mutare cor, solius dei opus esse, non uirium humanarum, errareque toto caelo, quotquot poenitentiae rationem, in attritionem, confessionem & satisfactionem ineptissime partiti sunt."

62. *Luke* 1529, 32r°, omitting "errareque . . . sunt."

63. *Luke* 1525, 144v°; *Luke* 1529, 173r°.

was not simply the highest or best way, but rather the hardest way, a path that beginners would not easily be able to follow. Melanchthon's criticism, with its insistence on feeding beginners milk, not meat, had had some effect.

By far the largest and most important addition came in a section entitled "De poenitentiae ratione." In addition to the small excision we have already noted, Agricola tacked on to the end of his discussion eight numbered statements explaining his position. This description was his last word on the subject until the antinomian controversy of 1537.

More clearly than heretofore, Agricola defined *poenitentia* in terms of justification by grace alone. His first point, that *poenitentia* is not some sort of external work prepared by the free will, revealed his underlying opposition to those who tried to smuggle in works in order to justify themselves. Contrary to this misconception, Agricola argued, secondly, that *poenitentia* is a gift of God. To emphasize this point, Agricola excluded both the preaching of the law *and of the gospel*, if it occurred without the Holy Spirit. But the way in which he excluded such preaching shows that he was still adamant about his position on the law:

> For it cannot occur that the mind of a person is moved in such a way that he changes his own skin—neither by the preaching of threats (which God did not intend for the *poenitentes*) nor by the preaching of the mercy of God (by which he promises life and remission of sins to those who are truly *poenitentes*)—unless the Holy Spirit imbues the human heart with heavenly inspiration and power, so that it agrees to be pure and holy.[64]

Here Agricola excluded the preaching of threats from the process completely. His caveat concerning the preaching of the gospel was that it would not function properly without the Spirit.

In the next three points, Agricola explored the nature of the preaching of *poenitentia*. He began with a definition of *poenitentia* clearly different from Melanchthon's. The right name for *poenitentia* was *resipiscentia*, a coming to one's senses, which occurs precisely as John the Baptist described it, namely wherever the kingdom of heaven draws near. This meant for Agricola that the preaching of *poenitentia*—really for him the heart of the controversy—was nothing other than "a word that teaches why a life must be changed."[65] Now in his view this word

---

64. *Luke* 1529, 32vᵒ: "Fieri enim non potest ut commouetur animus hominis, ut mutet pellem suam, neque praedicatione minarum, quas intentat Deus non poenitentibus, neque praedicatione misericordiae Dei, qua promittit uitam et remißionem peccatorum uere poenitentibus, nisi Spiritus sanctus imbuat coelesti adflatu & numine cor hominis ut placeat illi puro esse & sancto."

65. *Luke* 1529, 32vᵒ: "uerbum quod docet, cur sit mutanda uita."

was precisely that of the benefits of God, healing the sick, raising the dead, and driving out the demons. He summarized in German the gist of such preaching: "Let yourselves be moved by this goodness and renounce your previous life."[66] Agricola's conviction that only the gospel ("dise gute") brought about *poenitentia* remained unaffected by the dispute. It also remained bound to a command ("Last! . . . stehet!") and hence was perhaps even more nomistic than Melanchthon's law-based system of thought.

The last three points demonstrate that Agricola still viewed the preaching of *poenitentia* within the context of polemic against late medieval piety. That is, precisely the factor that had motivated Melanchthon to write the Visitation Articles the way he did, namely preaching by the likes of Caspar Aquila against the old church, remained crucial to Agricola's understanding of *poenitentia*. He divided the gospel, which is light, from the world, which is darkness. In this darkness the human heart had imagined that practices like invocation of the saints, distinction between foods, observance of certain days, and the wearing of certain clothes were sacred means of pleasing God.[67] But, he continued, now that the gospel has appeared in our age and we have discovered that there is only one mediator between us and God, namely Christ, we have to beware of making distinctions between foods and the like, which are in reality the doctrine of demons. Once we have seen the light, we begin to loathe the darkness of past practices. *Poenitentia*, which Agricola defined as a change of heart, counsels, and actions, arises from the light, but teaches us at the same time ("simul") knowledge of our infirmities, so that we long for God to complete in us what he has begun.[68] With this single "simul" Agricola came as close as he could to accepting Melanchthon and Luther's understanding of law and gospel. However, here he was talking of what the human being experiences in hearing the gospel and not a movement from law to gospel. At least he admitted that seeing the light and seeing one's infirmities take place at the same time.

Melanchthon's *Scholia of 1528*

After the confrontation with Agricola, Melanchthon also returned to his writing desk to edit for a second time his *Scholia* on Colossians. He brought with him the memories of the four-month-long public struggle over the meaning of *poenitentia* and the law. He also brought with him

---

66. *Luke* 1529, 32v°: "Last euch dise gute bewegen/ vnd stehet vom vörigen leben abe."
67. Agricola included the examples of praying to Margaret, Barbara, or Catherine, of abstaining from certain foods on Friday, of wearing black or white habits.
68. *Luke* 1529, 33v°.

the outline of the agreement worked out at the Torgau for dealing with the differences and the personal hurt inflicted by a former friend who had refused to shake his hand. All these experiences played themselves out in the *Scholia* in a much fuller way than in any other writing of Melanchthon from this time. We have here Melanchthon's last and most complete word on the subject.[69]

There are several small signs that Melanchthon tried to lessen the sharpness of his differences with Agricola. One such sign came outside the major area of dispute. It will be remembered that Melanchthon wrote the *Scholia* in part as a reaction to Agricola's sermons on Colossians, published at the very beginning of 1527. One of their early disagreements involved the interpretation of Colossians 1:3–9. In 1527 Melanchthon was not afraid to say, "Concerning this text I know that others have debated many things subtly."[70] In 1528, with the omission and addition of just a few words he revised the sentence to read, "Concerning this text I know it is usual that it be debated subtly."[71] Then, taking the edge off his typical "I will keep things simple for the common people,"[72] Melanchthon added, "But we will explain it as best we can, most crudely."[73]

Melanchthon's actual interpretation of Colossians 1 (in which Paul seems to imply that the Colossians will be rewarded by God with eternal life for their good works) varied little in content from the previous year, except that he clearly granted the law a positive role in all aspects of the Christian life. Of course, Melanchthon began, we are to do good works without thought of reward. But because of the flesh, whose love for reward we cannot purge during this life, the teaching of the law is like a guide (*paedagogia*) inviting with rewards and deterring through punishments.[74] For the saints rewards and punishments function as signs for discerning God's will. Punishments signify wrath; rewards, mercy and grace. The saints avoid punishments and thus God's wrath, of which they are signs. At the same time faith is aroused by rewards,

---

69. Hans-Georg Geyer's discussion of Melanchthon's understanding of *poenitentia*— *Von der Geburt des wahren Menschen* (Neukirchen-Vluyn: Neukirchener Verlag des Erziehungsvereins, 1965)—is completely unusable because he fails to place the *Scholia* of 1528 in any meaningful historical context. Changes he thought took place over twenty years in fact took place in one.

70. *MSA* 4:215.29: "De hoc loco scio alios multa subtiliter disputasse."

71. *Scholia* 1528, 5v°: "De hoc loco scio subtiliter disputari solere." The peculiar passive grammar heightened the change.

72. *MSA* 4:215.30f.: "Sed ego hoc genus quaestioni nihil existimo prodesse ad vulgus."

73. *Scholia* 1528, 5v°: "Nos vero explicabimus eum, quam poterimus, crassissime."

74. *Scholia* 1528, 5v°: "Nam caro ita est mercenaria, ut etiam sancti non possint abijcere amore mercedis. Itaque doctrina legis est ac paedagogia, inuitare premiis, ac poenis deterrere."

which the saints view not just as signs of grace, but signs of the magnitude of God's goodness and of God's promises.[75] God makes promises so that the saints know from whom to expect blessings and to ask for all things. The hope spoken of in this text is, then, the expectation of good from God not because of our merits but because of God's promise.

What had changed? By stating that "it is usual that [Col. 1] be debated subtly" (instead of that "others" have debated it subtly), Melanchthon gave the impression that he himself could have argued in a more complicated manner. Accordingly, he excused himself for speaking in a very crass manner. Already in the *Scholia* of 1527 Melanchthon had argued that rewards are signs of the divine will, of God's magnanimity, and of God's promise. However, in 1528 for the first time he connected such rewards to the law. Through punishments and rewards the law guides the believer. In 1534 this understanding of the law's function would become a central part of Melanchthon's interpretation of Colossians (see pp. 195–96). In 1528 the law was already viewed as a guide for the *carnal* believer. Of course, this resulted in Melanchthon's further distancing himself from Agricola's position. The law now gained a positive function in the life of the believer—not just terrifying the conscience, but also guiding the believer further in mortification and faith.

Disagreements with Agricola, however, did not occur only over peripheral matters. They also touched the heart of the controversy. On the one hand, Melanchthon took the opportunity, much as Agricola had in his annotations on Luke, to define more precisely his understanding of *poenitentia*. On the other, he also went out of his way to define the correct preaching of the law in the context of Christian freedom.

Melanchthon discussed *poenitentia* in the context of remarks on Colossians 2:11–12. He completely reworked his original comments of 1527, expanding them from three pages to eight.[76] From the very first words there is little doubt who the opponent was: "This text gives the order and form of our justification; for it describes mortification, or *poenitentia*, and vivification or remission of sins."[77] Working with dialectical precision, Melanchthon first defined righteousness as properly and truly *fides qua*, the faith by which we believe that we are received in grace by the Father on account of Christ. This was crucial for his argument. He wanted to avoid any criticism that he had abandoned the evangelical faith. He also explained away the agreement worked out at the Torgau which had allowed that in some sense faith was already

---

75. *Scholia* 1528, 6r°. Melanchthon added to the examples of Job and Jacob (*MSA* 4:216.4, 13f.) that of Paul; the reference to David was omitted.

76. *Scholia* 1528, 40r°–43 v°; cf. *MSA* 4:247.19–249.10.

77. *Scholia* 1528, 40r°.

present in contrition.[78] Here Melanchthon stressed justifying faith and refused to use language that both he and Luther considered confusing for the common folk.

Having made this beginning, Melanchthon added, "People must be taught how they receive faith."[79] The issue, even here, was a catechetical one. After all, Melanchthon conceived the commentary in just this light. He included a description of the danger that had remained constant throughout the dispute. Many imagine that they believe, when in fact they depart from faith "longissime (by a long shot)." Such faith as they think they have leads to hypocrisy and "most harmful security (*nocentissima securitas*)." In a direct reflection of the Visitation Articles he referred to John 16:8 ("The Holy Spirit convicts [*arguet*] the world of sin, righteousness, and judgment") and stressed that the verb "arguere" means "condemnare ac perterrefacere (to condemn or terrify)." He concluded, "Therefore this is *poenitentia*, so to acknowledge sins that we truly sense the wrath and judgment of God against sin and are truly terrified."[80] Melanchthon was arguing here in his best syllogistic style. The major came from the Scripture. The minor was based upon a definition ("arguere" means "perterrefacere"). The conclusion provided the central definition for Melanchthon's entire argument.

In the next paragraph, Melanchthon discussed, as he had the year before, the various words for mortification. This time, however, he reflected upon what this variety meant for the exegete. First, it caused trouble for the unskilled (such as Agricola?). Because of this, Melanchthon painstakingly explained what the various words meant. Second, Melanchthon argued that Paul used so many different words in order that "we may more correctly understand the power of *poenitentia*." Each word helped fill out the meaning of *poenitentia*. Precisely this kind of *collatio* stood at the heart of his *loci* method. Each of the words revealed a different part of the definition that made up the commonplace *poenitentia*, a commonplace that excluded Agricola's theology by definition.

Melanchthon then discussed the first phase of the controversy over the Visitation Articles. On his own terms he criticized the way in which the Scholastics had divided up *poenitentia*! "The Schools made three parts out of *poenitentia*: contrition, confession, and satisfaction. They took this division more from the rites of the church than from Scrip-

---

78. Among the medieval Scholastic definitions of faith was faith such as the devils have. See Heiko A. Oberman, *The Harvest of Medieval Theology: Gabriel Biel and Late Medieval Nominalism* (Durham, N.C.: Labyrinth, 1983 reprint), 468f.

79. *Scholia* 1528, 40r°–v°: "Sed hic docendi sunt homines, quomodo fidem concipiant."

80. *Scholia* 1528, 40v°: "Est itaque poenitentia, ita agnoscere peccata, ut uere sentiamus iram ac iudicium Dei aduersus peccatum, ac uere terreamur."

ture."[81] After censuring the Scholastic theologians' neglect of the Scripture, he attacked their misunderstanding of satisfaction. According to Melanchthon, satisfaction had originally been instituted by bishops not as a way of making atonement for sins or meriting grace, but as a way of either readmitting lapsed sinners into the church as an example of God's grace or discovering whether they had undergone a change of heart. This was not understood by the Scholastic theologians, who used an old name for a new idea, namely that we make satisfaction for sin through our own merits. But there is no satisfaction for sin other than Christ.

Of course, these were criticisms found in the Visitation Articles themselves. New, however, were the specific reference to the practice in the ancient church and the complaint that Scholastic theologians had misused the word. Given the attack on the threefold division of *poenitentia*, Melanchthon felt compelled to agree with the attackers, but on his own terms.

Turning to the second part of *poenitentia*, confession, Melanchthon assumed that his audience knew the ecclesial origins of the word and proceeded immediately to a scriptural definition. Confession occurs when the conscience, terrified before God, acknowledges its sin and admits that it is justly condemned. It does not accuse God's judgment but only asks for grace and mercy and praises the God who justifies sinners. Melanchthon, stung by the charge that his understanding of *poenitentia* led to a simulated sorrow for sin, added that this kind of confession occurs only "amid true terrors and the most bitter afflictions."[82] The word "true" protected Melanchthon from the charge, and the whole phrase set up his argument that contrition arises from fear.

At this juncture Melanchthon referred to the results of the Torgau conference: "Regarding these affections, reference must be made that some taught a *poenitentia* coming from a love of righteousness."[83] In this one sentence lurked the entire year-long debate. This was not a chance reference to an intriguing point of view. It was much more the one place that, for the peace of the church, Melanchthon was willing to allow Agricola's position. He did not defend it; he may not even have understood it. He simply allowed for it under the terms of the agreement worked out. Along with Agricola's excision of the attack on the threefold form of *poenitentia* from his 1529 commentary on Luke,

---

81. *Scholia* 1528, 40v°: "Scholae fecerunt partes poenitentiae tres contritionem, confessionem, & satisfactionem, quam partitionem magis ab Ecclesiae ritibus sumpserunt, quam ex scriptura."
82. *Scholia* 1528, 41r°: "in veris pauoribus & adflictionibus acerbissimis."
83. *Scholia* 1528, 41v°: "Ad hos adfectus referendum est, quod quidam docuerunt poenitentiam ex amore iusticiae."

this one sentence reflected the truce to which both men were willing to adhere.

Having made that statement, Melanchthon then proceeded to defend his own approach and to attack Agricola's. To answer those who defined *poenitentia* in terms of no longer committing sin, Melanchthon turned to the remaining part of *poenitentia*,[84] contrition, which, in his opinion, more properly corresponded to the name *poenitentia*. Immediately he defended himself against Agricola's charges by making clear that by contrition "you may understand not a simulated sorrow by human exertion, but true terrors that God brings about when he shows us our sin."[85] The passing reference to John 16:8 and the definition of *poenitentia* that Melanchthon had gained from it now took full effect. He cited the examples of David before Nathan and Paul on the road to Damascus, what Paul had called in Romans 1 "shame or confusion."[86] He then discussed the possible parts of contrition: "true, not simulated, fear of divine judgment, acknowledgment of sin, and shame before God."[87] Again, in reaction to Agricola, he stressed that this was true, not simulated fear. His insistence that it was fear of divine judgment was enhanced by the two other parts of contrition.

Next came the heart of Melanchthon's attack on Agricola's position: "It is not necessary to separate these affections more subtly. Nor is it necessary to debate more subtly what is the difference between the contrition of Judas and the contrition of Peter."[88] The initial dismissal of this dispute by Luther—that Agricola was prosecuting a war of words—Melanchthon echoed here by the word "subtiliter." This condemnation linked Luther's charge (that it was impossible to separate out one's affections in this matter) to Melanchthon's criticism of Agricola's sermons on Colossians. Dividing up penitents into Judases and Peters was too subtle.

Having said that, however, Melanchthon also gave his own interpretation of the *poenitentia* of these two disciples of Jesus. It is enough (*satis est!*) to hold that those who in their terrors receive consolation from the gospel imitate Peter's *poenitentia*. Those who do not want to believe

---

84. The very fact that he reversed the order of the three parts shows the cleverness of Melanchthon's argument.

85. *Scholia* 1528, 41v°: "intelligas non humana diligentia simulatum dolorem, sed ueros terrores quos Deus incutit, cum ostendit nobis peccata nostra."

86. Latin: "pudor seu confusio"; in contrast, Agricola relied on Romans 6 to define *poenitentia* in terms of faith and gospel alone.

87. *Scholia* 1528, 41v°: "metus iudicii diuini uerus, non simulatus, agnitio peccati, & pudor coram Deo."

88. *Scholia* 1528, 41v°: "Nec opus est hos adfectus subtiliter discernere, Nec est opus subtiliter disputare, quid inter contritionem Iudae & contritionem Petri intersit."

the gospel of forgiveness follow the *poenitentia* of Judas. Here Melanchthon stood Agricola's argument on its head. For Agricola the prior promise of Christ worked repentance and sorrow for sin in Peter. Peter had a word; Judas did not. For Melanchthon those in the midst of terror grasped the promise. Peter had faith, Judas did not. The order of terror to consolation, law to gospel, was thus preserved. Melanchthon had completely revoked his lip service to Agricola's position.

But Melanchthon's attack was not complete. He returned to the various Pauline terms for *poenitentia*, beginning with *mortificatio*. He rejected the interpretation of this word as regarding merely external things. Of course, this could have been understood in part as polemic against monastic mortifications of the flesh. However, Agricola's sermons on Colossians also defined mortification in terms of the external: Peter and Judas underwent the same mortification. Thus Melanchthon suggested that Agricola's position fostered hypocritical, or at least superficial, *poenitentia*. Over against Agricola's (Platonic) division of soul and body, Melanchthon argued that mortification involved not just the external misdeeds, but "the entire carnal nature corrupted by original sin."[89]

After a brief examination of the words *circumcision* and *baptism*, Melanchthon revisited the question of the order of *poenitentia* and faith. Faith arises when the terrified heart hears the promise of forgiveness. "Therefore faith cannot be experienced without *poenitentia* or contrition."[90] This was the heart of Melanchthon's understanding of *poenitentia*. He tied his analysis of the Pauline vocabulary to his conclusion by adding that first ("primum") there are circumcision, mortification, and baptism, then ("postea") follows being revived with Christ through faith. As protection against any charge of works-righteousness, he used capital letters for the phrase PER FIDEM to stress that faith excludes merits and satisfactions. "It is faith alone that rescues us in those terrors and justifies us before God."[91]

Melanchthon concluded this complicated argument by returning to the question of the division of *poenitentia*. He penned an appeal to Agricola: "Let us therefore understand there to be two perfect parts to *poenitentia*: contrition or mortification, and vivification or justification, when through faith the terrified minds receive remission of sin and peace."[92]

---

89. *Scholia* 1528, 42r°: ". . . sed significat totam carnalem naturam corruptam esse peccato originis."

90. *Scholia* 1528, 42v°: "Non igitur sine poenitentia, seu contritione fides sentiri potest."

91. *Scholia* 1528, 42v°: "Sola fides est, quae in illis terroribus erigit nos, & coram Deo iustificat."

92. *Scholia* 1528, 42v°: "Duas igitur perfectae poenitentiae partes esse intelligamus, contritionem seu mortificationem, & uiuificationem, seu iustificationem, cum per fidem consequuntur remissionem peccatorum, & pacem mentes territae."

To this argument Melanchthon appended a section that may well be seen as an early attempt to develop the concept of a third use of the law. In the light of the battle with Agricola the reasons seem clear. Agricola, after all, had a place to discuss the new life because of his movement from gospel to *poenitentia*. Melanchthon, having placed gospel at the end of the movement in the Christian life, now felt compelled to discuss what happens after justification. He argued that because new life arises in the heart as a result of *poenitentia*, it follows that the external members must be restrained lest they do something against the will of God. Human nature is then renewed through the Holy Spirit, who acts to perfect the Christian throughout life. Thus one experiences a growth in faith and its fruits.

This discussion allowed Melanchthon to return to his defense that *poenitentia* as he defined it is not simulated. When Paul talks of circumcision, he is talking of something that takes place in the heart, "not a simulation of sorrow" or some external work. Again Melanchthon built upon John 16 and pointed to the work of the Holy Spirit through the Word. He "convicts (*arguit*) concerning sin, righteousness, and judgment"[93]—sin, because reason does not see unbelief as sin and tries to justify itself by works; judgment, because we do not condemn our concupiscence but love it; righteousness, because terrified consciences are consoled by the announcement of forgiveness of sins.

Finally, Melanchthon could discuss one of Agricola's most cherished texts, Luke 24:47. Jesus' command that the disciples preach *poenitentia* and remission of sins in his name, Melanchthon argued, must be understood in the light of the two parts of Christian teaching. The first shows and accuses sin and occurs in the preaching of the law. And then Melanchthon adds, "Christ employed [such preaching] in Matthew 5,"[94] a perfectly harmless comment until connected to the breakfast debate with Agricola at the Torgau. That Christ preached the law is in line with Paul's comment in Romans 3:20 that through the law comes knowledge of sin. The second part of Christian teaching "is properly called the 'gospel,' namely, the preaching of remission of sins and the promise of the Holy Spirit."[95] This dual sermon is best shown by the prophet Nathan's preaching to David.

Thus ended Melanchthon's most extensive attack against Agricola's position on *poenitentia*. Jesus preached the law. Faith arises from the gospel; it has nothing to do with contrition. The preaching of the law is

---

93. *Scholia* 1528, 43r°.
94. *Scholia* 1528, 43v°: "Christus usus est Matth. 5."
95. *Scholia* 1528, 43v°: ". . . quae propria habet Euangelij nomen, scilicet praedicatio remissionis peccatorum, & promissio spiritus sancti."

part of the order of Christian life and doctrine. The only part of the complex of Agricola's ideas that Melanchthon did not attack here concerned the preaching of the law itself. That he left for his discussion of the meaning of Christian freedom.

Agricola's concept of Christian freedom was based upon what he deemed to be the exclusive role of the gospel. The gospel freed the Christian from the law: ceremonies, traditions, and even the Decalog. Only in external things of the flesh, including government, did the law have some provisional part to play. For Melanchthon this smacked of fleshly freedom and license. It undermined the authority of government and good order in the church. In the *Scholia* of 1528 as nowhere else at this time, Melanchthon dealt with this web of issues and defined his views on the matter over against those of Agricola.

In the context of his discussion of Colossians 3:11 (a verse to which Luther had referred in the German version of the Visitation Articles)[96] Melanchthon inserted an aside on Christian freedom. About half of the original comments from 1527 remained in 1528, but even they were thoroughly edited by Melanchthon. For example, in 1528 while arguing that Christians are free not to follow the Mosaic code in matters of public law, Melanchthon added that we ought to obey the commandments and "not set the promise against the command."[97] Such a comment, directed in the first instance against Thomas Müntzer and others, also fit Agricola's insistence in the "130 Fragestücke" that the Ten Commandments no longer applied to Christians.

This discussion led Melanchthon directly to the problem of preaching the Decalog, a major bone of contention between him and Agricola. He began by dividing the law into three parts, ceremonial, judicial, and moral. This was parallel to his discussion in 1527. Now, however, Melanchthon felt compelled to defend his use of this division. First, he pointed out that the church fathers (*veteres*) had used it. He claimed to follow it and to use it for instructional purposes "because it contributes something in teaching of the light."[98] Again, as with the use of the threefold division of *poenitentia*, Melanchthon claimed to have a pedagogical reason for his division of the law. Of course, it also helped him refute Agricola's claims.

And refute them he did. Several biblical passages stood in Agricola's way. First, already in 1527 Melanchthon had argued that the messianic prophecy in Genesis 49:10 predicts the passing away of the ceremonial

---

96. *MLStA* 3:427.16 (*WA* 26:211).

97. *Scholia* 1528, 88v° (cf. *MSA* 4:288.11): ". . . non occupare promissa contra praeceptum."

98. *Scholia* 1528, 89r° (cf. *MSA* 4:288.33): ". . . quia non nihil adfert in docendo lucis."

and judicial laws. Then he turned to the Jerusalem Council in Acts 15, to which Agricola had also appealed to show that all law no longer applies. Melanchthon, on the contrary, interpreted the passage as excluding ceremonies such as circumcision.

After rejecting the notion (proposed by radicals during the Peasants' War) that the Old Testament laws be applied in Germany, Melanchthon turned to the question of the Decalog and set his sights on Agricola. Again the subtlety of Agricola's arguments came under attack: "But perhaps someone may subtly object that the Decalog does not pertain to us, insofar as it is part of the political ordinances given to the people by Moses. I do not like this useless subtlety, but I will walk in the well-trodden way."[99] Melanchthon took a third (well-trodden) path for himself, placing Agricola, who wanted to exclude even the Decalog from the Christian life, on the one side, and radicals, who wanted to bring ceremonial and judicial practices of the Old Testament back into the common life, on the other.

Melanchthon's proofs subtly accused both sides of innovations. He began with the observation that the Decalog, unlike the ceremonial and judicial laws, does not define a people but commands purity of the heart. The Decalog has not been abrogated, for it is in fact the law of nature written in every human heart, and it always accuses and condemns the guilty. By removing our guilt the gospel takes away even this law. However, although the *accusatio* has been dropped, the *notitia* remains. Melanchthon went even further, offering this syllogism: in the gospel Christ gave the command to love; Paul said that all the precepts of the law are contained in the command to love; therefore, the Decalog is repeated in the gospel and must be retained. This was no theoretical argument! Once again Melanchthon was sitting at breakfast in the Torgau and refuting Agricola's claim that only Paul's precepts, not the Decalog, ought to be taught. Melanchthon added that faith is not lazy. The law shows us works, not so that we may be justified through them, but so that, since we cannot get through this life without works, God may reveal to us the particular works to be done.

After summarizing his arguments,[100] Melanchthon introduced the two offices of the law.[101] For the first use he cited 1 Timothy 1:8f. and

99. *Scholia* 1528, 90v°: "Fortasse autem aliquis subtiliter disputet nec Decalogum ad nos pertinere, quatenus pars sit politicarum ordinationum quae sunt traditae populo Moisi. Ego non delector illa inutili subtilitate, sed trita via ingrediar."

100. *Scholia* 1528, 91r°: the Decalog is taught not because it was handed down by Moses, but because nature teaches it; the gospel repeats it so that faith has works by which to exercise itself.

101. In 1527 (*MSA* 4:290.12f.) Melanchthon spoke of the two "causae" for preaching the law.

Galatians 3:24. The gospel teaches the righteousness of the heart; only the law teaches civil righteousness, a righteousness written on human hearts. The other function of the law is to show sin and terrify the conscience. Here Melanchthon cited Romans 3:19. This discussion of the law very closely matched other discussions of Melanchthon's from the same period. What followed reflected his answer to Agricola's exclusion of the law from the gospel. Using a broader definition of gospel (not simply the mercy and goodness of God, but the New Testament), Melanchthon proposed an enthymeme: because the gospel contains the preaching of *poenitentia*, it is necessary to accuse and show sin. Citing Romans 1:18, Melanchthon then constructed the following syllogism: The accusation of sin takes place through the law written on human hearts. This law is nothing other than the Decalog. "Therefore we use the Decalog or the law of nature for preaching *poenitentia*, that is, for the convicting [cf. John 16:8] and showing of sin."[102] Agricola's rejection of the Decalog had been overturned with the syllogistic precision of a master.

Remember that Melanchthon began with a peace gesture, the premise that the preaching of *poenitentia* is part of the gospel. He moved logically from that premise, however, to the law. Did he now mean to fight Agricola in the open? Not at this time. Immediately after his triumphant conclusion he added this conciliatory comment: "Whoever contends that convicting of sin is not part of the law but of the gospel—with him I will not fight very much."[103] He reduced even this objection of Agricola to a war of words and refused to fight. Nevertheless, he went on to insist that "I call (*voco*)" the remission of sins the gospel and "I call (*voco*)" that which accuses, condemns, and terrifies consciences the law. Thus "I want (*volo*)" the law to be understood to accuse us not just of external trespasses, but also of concupiscence. Here Melanchthon was personally arguing his case against one man, Agricola. He again pointed out that Christ preached on the law in Matthew 5 and that Paul called the law spiritual, so that it did not concern only civil discipline. Suddenly, he was back at the Torgau making the connection between the preaching of the law and *poenitentia*:

> Some teach that the principal element of *poenitentia* is knowledge of the benefits of Christ, which I grant. Nevertheless, it is necessary to convict of sin, which happens through the law, because the remission of sins cannot be understood or received without prior conviction of sins. And these

---

102. *Scholia* 1528, 91v°: "Vtimur itaque decalogo seu naturae lege ad praedicationem poenitenciae, hoc est ad arguendum & ostendendum peccatum."
103. Ibid.: "Siquis contendet non legis, sed Euangelij partem esse, arguere peccata, cum hoc non magnopere digladiabor."

are the reasons why the Decalog is retained, although other parts of the Mosaic law are no longer taught.[104]

The agreement was intact ("quod ut largiar"), but the disagreement still festered ("tamen opus est"). Returning to the language of John 16 ("arguere peccata"), Melanchthon pled again for the use of the law, without which remission of sins cannot be received. He assumed that his syllogistic best would help Agricola see the necessity of the law in this situation. Only ten years later did he and Luther discover how great the differences between them and Agricola had become.

From this basis, Melanchthon then described a third level of Christian freedom, pertaining to human traditions. Here, too, the Visitation Articles and their controversies were not far in the background, especially the preaching of Aquila. Even more strongly than in 1527, Melanchthon begged for moderation. He argued here that those who follow traditions, including the ancient canons, should not do so as if they were necessary for salvation.[105] For we have freedom in such matters. At the same time, Melanchthon counseled that we should not simply break old traditions at the expense of scandalizing the weak, who might interpret their freedom as a license to sin. Traditions were to be violated when the Pharisees implied that they were necessary for salvation, but otherwise they were to be followed for the sake of the weak multitude. Melanchthon connected this principle specifically to church practices and worship and argued that there was no need to foster unrest.[106]

In comments on Colossians 4:5 Melanchthon returned to the issue of freedom, again arguing against those who use their Christian freedom as license and speaking of an "intemperate use of Christian liberty in unnecessary things." When faith was at stake, then the *clausula Petri* (Acts 5:29) had to be invoked, but "in 'middle things,' as they are called, certainly it is beneficial to watch carefully lest we abuse lib-

---

104. *Scholia* 1528, 92r°: "Quidam docent principium esse poenitenciae, cognitionem benefictorum Christi, quod ut largiar, tamen opus est arguere peccata quod per legem fit, quia neque intelligi neque adprehendi remissio peccatorum potest, nisi prius arguantur peccata. Et hae fere caussae sunt, cur decalogus retineatur, cum aliae legis Mosaicae partes prorsus non doceantur."

105. The same argument appeared in Melanchthon's comments on Colossians 2:23, *Scholia* 1528, 77v°–78v°, where he gave a lengthy defense of the old canons and their usefulness in keeping order in the church, in remembering history, and in teaching the young. "Non uideo in ueteribus Canonibus onerari consciencias, quod peccent mortaliter, qui non obseruent eos canones" (78r°). Thus Melanchthon allowed for the use of canons. He even refuted the objection raised by Matthew 23:3. He also discussed the question of "traditiones de mediis rebus" (78v°).

106. *Scholia* 1528, 92v°–93r°.

erty."[107] Here Melanchthon invoked the concept of *adiaphora*, which he called "res mediae" (the Greek appeared first in 1534), a term he acknowledged was not of his own devising ("ut uocantur"). This concept would reappear in the later dispute with Agricola over the Augsburg Interim.

In the *Scholia* of 1528 Melanchthon attacked Agricola in one other way. He did not limit himself to exegetical and theological battles, but also raised questions of his opponent's moral behavior. Given the comments in Melanchthon's correspondence concerning this controversy, this comes as no surprise. In a discussion of the virtues listed in Colossians 3:12, Melanchthon emphasized toleration. He mentioned the dangers of intolerance in the household, where neither person is willing to yield. He discussed the need for public tranquility, reminding his readers what happened to the Roman republic when neither Pompey nor Caesar was willing to yield. He concluded with a third example that, given what has been discussed here, was probably written with Agricola and Aquila in mind:

> Furthermore, those who teach in the churches ought to be especially endowed with this virtue, so that one interprets the statements and writings of another appropriately and avoids besmirching them with some abuse. Now with such false interpretation of all sayings, writings, and deeds, teachers of Christian love exasperate one another with the most bitter hatred. And immediately other controversies are born from these.[108]

Perhaps this appeal for tolerance, coupled with the personal mediation of Justus Jonas, led to the renewal of the friendship between the two protagonists in this drama. However, the memory of the battle continued to affect Melanchthon's theology and his standing in the developing Lutheran church.

What kind of reception did Melanchthon's work on Colossians receive? When Jonas translated the 1528 *Scholia* for publication in 1529, Luther himself provided the preface. He contrasted his own woodsmanlike manner of clearing a path with Melanchthon's more agrarian approach in sowing theology. He recommended the work of his younger

---

107. *Scholia* 1528, 104r°: "intempestiuus usus libertatis Christianae in rebus non necessarijs" and "in rebus mediis, ut uocantur, certe prodest diligenter cauere, ne libertate abutamur."

108. *Scholia* 1528, 94r°: "Porro in primis hac uirtute preditos esse oportuit eos qui docent in Ecclesiis, ut alter alterius dicta & scripta commode interpretaretur, dissimularet etiam aspersus aliquo maledicto. Nunc in tam calumniosa interpretatione omnium dictorum, scriptorum, & factorum, & exasperunt inter se acerbissimis odiis doctores Christianae caritatis, & aliae lites ex aliis subinde nascuntur."

colleague as something all Christians should daily carry in their bosom. In the commentary Melanchthon had summarized Christian teaching and life. Luther worried that, despite such a gift, the times were so evil that, like the Israelites in the wilderness, people would become sick of such heavenly treasures as were contained in the *Scholia* and have the gospel taken from them. He was convinced, on the other hand, that the more people read this work, the less they would hunger after Egyptian leeks and garlic (Num. 11:4–6).[109]

But did Luther notice Melanchthon's spirited defense of *poenitentia* in the *Scholia*? At table in 1540 he made a comment about "Philip's books," recorded by John Mathesius: "Philip has written good books, and no one writes better concerning *poenitentia*. Both the [commentaries] on Romans and Colossians and the *Loci communes*—those are godly books—and the [Augsburg] Confession and Apology. Ach, how fine it is to be studying now in contrast to past times."[110] Although Luther was referring to the third edition of the *Scholia* from 1534, the material on *poenitentia* had undergone no major changes between 1528 and 1534. Placed in the context of Luther's own disputes with Agricola, this endorsement ("nemo melius scribet de poenitentia") assumes even greater importance. Melanchthon and Luther clearly agreed that the Christian life moved from death to life, from law to gospel, and from *poenitentia* to *fides*.

Melanchthon's Memory of the Battle: A Long *Iliad*

After the conflict at the Torgau, Melanchthon and Agricola quickly restored a good relationship with each other. On 14 June 1529 Agricola sent a poignant letter of comfort to Melanchthon, who, he had learned, was beset with trials.[111] In a previous letter to Justus Jonas, Melanchthon had praised Agricola's preaching at the second Diet of Speyer and dismissed rumors that Agricola was a Zwinglian.[112] In October 1529 Melanchthon sent Agricola a full report of the Marburg Colloquy, and he tried to intervene on Agricola's behalf in a dispute with Duke Ulrich of Württemberg over Agricola's recently published collection of ad-

---

109. *WA* 30.2:68–69.

110. *WATR* 4:610 (no. 5007): "Philippus scripsit bonos libros, et nemo melius scribet de poenitentia. Et epistola ad Romanos et Coloss[enses] et loci communes, das sindt göttliche bucher, vnd die confessio vnd apologia! Ach wie fein ists itzt studiren weder vor zeiten!"

111. *MBW* 794 (Bindseil, 515f.); see also *MBW* 788 (Bindseil, 514f.). Already on 23 October 1528 (*MBW* 718 [Bindseil, 512f.]) Agricola had sent a courteous letter asking Melanchthon and Luther for a tutor for the son of Count Albert of Mansfeld.

112. *MBW* 762 (*CR* 1:1040), dated 22 March 1529.

ages.[113] In 1531 Melanchthon trusted Agricola enough to ask him for advice in making corrections to the Apology of the Augsburg Confession.[114] And shortly before the storm clouds of the first antinomian controversy broke over Wittenberg, Melanchthon sent Agricola, whose family had just arrived in Wittenberg, a charming letter describing how their daughters loved to play together.[115]

This renewed friendship was severely strained by the events of the first antinomian controversy. By October 1537 Melanchthon was writing to friends that he was the real target in the controversy. He sent Joachim Camerarius his sarcastic declamation (entitled "Concerning the Cuckoo") attacking Jacob Schenck, a suspected antinomian, along with Luther's sermon against the antinomians.[116] Despite the strain in relations during this time, Melanchthon served as a witness (with Luther!) for Agricola's purchase of a house[117] and later as go-between in the dispute itself.[118] After Agricola's flight to Berlin, Melanchthon again resumed a cordial exchange of letters and was even involved in trying to sell Agricola's house in Wittenberg.[119]

The controversy over the Augsburg Interim finally destroyed the friendship between the two men and caused Melanchthon to reassess his earlier disputes with Agricola. Already shortly before the Smalcald War of 1547 Melanchthon had complained that some in Berlin did not like him or his writings.[120] During the war itself, Agricola supported the

---

113. *MBW* 829 (*CR* 1:1107f.), dated 12 October 1529. For this dispute see Rogge, *Johann Agricolas Lutherverständnis,* 84–94.

114. *MBW* 1164 (printed in Kawerau, *Johannes Agricola,* 341f.), dated June 1531. Agricola had signed several of the *Gutachten* written during the negotiations at the Diet of Augsburg in 1530; see *MBW* 929, 930, 961, and 1024. Melanchthon also provided assistance in Agricola's ongoing confrontation with George Witzel in Eisleben; see *MBW* 1370 (*CR* 2:677–80), dated 22 October 1533.

115. *MBW* 1871 (*CR* 3:328f.), dated 16 March 1537.

116. *MBW* 1952 (*CR* 3:390f.), dated 12 October 1537 to Johannes Brenz, and *MBW* 1953 (*CR* 3:419–21), the same day to Camerarius. For the declamation see *CR* 11:335–42. See also *MBW* 1971 (*CR* 3:459f.), dated 7 December 1537 to Veit Dietrich.

117. *MBW* 2013 (printed in *Martin Luther: Briefwechsel,* ed. Ernst Ludwig Enders, 19 vols. [Frankfurt and Leipzig, 1884–1932], 18:7–9), dated 30 March 1538.

118. See the report to the elector by Jonas, Melanchthon, and their colleagues, *MBW* 2409 (Förstemann, *Neues Urkundenbuch,* 325–27), dated 5 April 1540, in which Melanchthon recounted his role in the formulation of Agricola's retraction in 1538, which led eventually to the publication of Luther's "Against the Antinomians" (1539). This letter also demonstrated that Agricola's charges against Luther were unfounded. The second report, *MBW* 2446 (*CR* 3:1035–38), dated 8 June 1540, was not nearly as conciliatory and rejected Agricola's defense completely.

119. *MBW* 3133 (*CR* 4:749–51), dated 2 January 1543. This letter seemed to signal the resumption of correspondence. See also *MBW* 3158 (*CR* 4:771f.), dated 1 February 1543. For the sale of the house, see *MBW* 3461 (*CR* 6:63f.) and *MBW* 3462 (*CR* 6:63).

120. *MBW* 4362 (*CR* 6:217f.), dated 19 August 1546.

emperor.[121] However, the real rift appeared in the spring and summer of 1548 during negotiations at the Diet of Augsburg over the Augsburg Interim. After the emperor's stunning victory over the evangelical princes, the imperial diet had assembled in Augsburg, where Charles V was determined to correct the damage wrought by thirty years of evangelical reformation. Because the general council that had begun to meet in Trent had not yet progressed so far, the diet formulated an "interim agreement" (hence its nickname, Augsburg Interim) on matters of religion that, with the exceptions of communion in both kinds and the marriage of priests, reversed the practices and proclamation of the church in Germany to conform again with the Roman party's wishes.

While Agricola was one of the Interim's formulators and Joachim II of Brandenburg one of its chief defenders, Melanchthon had steadfastly counseled his new prince, the victorious Elector Maurice (an evangelical who had won the electorship of Saxony from John Frederick, his cousin, by siding with the emperor), against its acceptance, first on the grounds that it reintroduced the mass and later for its misunderstanding of justification.[122] After one of his sharpest memoranda found its way into print that same summer, Melanchthon was forced to defend himself to Maurice and stood in danger of remaining out of favor with the imperial court.[123] Agricola attacked him publicly from the pulpit.[124]

---

121. Agricola was reportedly gleeful over Wittenberg's troubles (*MBW* 4657 [*CR* 6:442f.], a letter from Melanchthon to Paul Eber that was dated 22 March 1547) and gave thanks for Elector John Frederick's capture, while praying for his conversion from the Lutheran heresy (*MBW* 4795 [*CR* 6:588–90], Melanchthon to Camerarius). For other early reports see also *MBW* 4715 and 4717.

122. See *MBW* 5040, 5096, 5110, 5117, 5121, 5130, 5137, 5139, 5170, 5182 (a memorandum published without Melanchthon's knowledge), 5208–10, 5214, and 5215. For a reconstruction of this correspondence and its relation to the famous letter to Christopher von Carlowitz (*MBW* 5139), see Heinz Scheible, "Melanchthons Brief an Carlowitz," *ARG* 57 (1966): 102–30. In a letter to Camerarius on 24/25 April 1548, *MBW* 5138 (*CR* 6:877–79), Melanchthon reported that to his astonishment Agricola and the Elector Joachim of Brandenburg imagined that the Interim supported the evangelical understanding of justification.

123. Melanchthon's attack was entitled "Bedencken auff das I INTERIM I Von einem Hochgelerten vnd I Ehrwirdigen Herrn/ ei= I nem Erbarn Radt sei= I ner Oberkeit vber= I reicht. I . . . I 1584 [*sic* =1548]." At the same time Agricola claimed that Caspar Aquila had accepted the Interim and made Aquila so angry that he published a scathing attack on the Interim himself. He recounted his encounter with "der Grundschalk Eyslebio" to Melanchthon in a letter dated 22 July 1548, *MBW* 5232 (*CR* 7:77–79); see p. 108 n. 19.

124. Agricola's attack was reported in a letter from George Buchholzer to Melanchthon that was dated 4 August 1548, *MBW* 5249 (unpublished). The correspondence between the latter two at this time depicted clearly the growing animosity. See *MBW* 4608, 4717, 4739, 4908, 5064, 5151, 5176, 5199, 5239, 5247, 5250, 5299, 5338, 5344, and 5398, spanning the period from 24 February 1547 to 6 December 1548. Other letters describing Agricola's attacks on Melanchthon include *MBW* 4657, 4715, and 4795.

Even the republication of a portion of Agricola's sermons on Colossians from 1527 in which he had attacked the mass did not weaken his support for the Interim.[125]

Throughout the fall of 1548 Wittenberg's theologians continued to reject the Augsburg Interim; at the same time they kept working with officials at the elector's court to produce a church order that could preserve evangelical preaching and teaching without enraging the imperial forces. In negotiations with the newly appointed bishops, Julius Pflug of Naumburg and Johann VIII of Meißen, an agreement was reached in the matter of justification (the so-called Pegau formula).[126] Negotiations regarding the mass dragged on through the fall, with Melanchthon and his colleagues willing to make concessions only on practices they regarded as neutral, *adiaphora*. In mid-December the electors of Brandenburg and Saxony met in Jüterbog to formulate a common church order for their two lands. That formula, based for the most part on the "Zellische Abschied" penned by Melanchthon, was to present a united front to the emperor.[127] Even here the question of the mass loomed large.[128]

Agricola seized upon this agreement and attempted to use it in an effort to bring into line the evangelical clergy of Berlin, including George Buchholzer, formulator of the original evangelical church order for Brandenburg (1540). After receiving a copy of the agreement in late December 1548, Agricola called a special worship service at which he read it aloud from the pulpit and proclaimed that it proved that Saxony's elector and theologians had finally agreed to the Augsburg (!) Interim. He took the agreement's general statement about *adiaphora* to include

---

125. Agricola's encounter with Georg von Anhalt over this matter was described by Melanchthon in a letter to Paul Eber, *MBW* 5329 (*CR* 7:249f.), dated 17/18 October 1548. The excerpt, "Von der Messe vnd | ihrem Canone Magistri Johan= | nis Agricolae Eysleben/ Lhere | vnd schrifft/ Welche er auff dem | Reichstag zu Speyer in der Epistel zu den Collossern | geprediget/ vnd folgend Anno M.D.XXVII. | zu Wittenbergk im Druck offentlich hat | ausgehen lassen/ Dem Interim so er ytzt | hat helffen stellen/ gantz entgegen/ | Daraus sein geyst zuuer= | mercken. | Psalm. cxlj. | HErr behüte meinen mund/ vnd beware meyne lip= | pen/ Neige mein hertz nicht auff etwas böses/ ein | Gottloß wesen zuführen mit den vbelthe= | tern/ Das ich nicht esse/ von dem | das ihnen geliebet. | Hiero. super Esaiam. | Non sic adulandum est Principibus, ut | Sanctarum scripturarum ueritas negligatur," was probably published in Magdeburg with the help of Matthias Flacius. In one of his marginal comments he coined a new monicker for Agricola, "Scheißleben."

126. *MBW* 5268 (*CR* 7:120 with 51–64), dated 24 August 1548.

127. For the "Zellische Abschied" of 22 November 1548 see *MBW* 5359 (*CR* 7:215–21). For Melanchthon's report see *MBW* 5385 (*Dr. Johannes Bugenhagens Briefwechsel*, ed. Otto Vogt [Hildesheim, 1966 reprint], 434f.).

128. For Melanchthon's formula on the sacrifice of the mass, see *MBW* 5384 (*CR* 4:309–16).

all practices of the old church and insisted that the church order of 1540 had been effectively overturned.[129]

Buchholzer's urgent letter to Melanchthon describing Agricola's behavior marked the earliest public questioning of *adiaphora* among the evangelicals and began the protracted controversy over the so-called Leipzig Interim, the text of which matched the agreement reached in Jüterbog.[130] This letter indicated that the final break between Melanchthon and Agricola had occurred. Their correspondence, interrupted by the war in 1546, never resumed.[131] Melanchthon had nothing more good to say about Agricola. For example, in 1549 he drew a parallel between his struggles over the Leipzig Interim and the dispute over the Visitation Articles. As Agricola once had raised a hue and cry over returning to Rome, now others were doing the same:

> For another thing, this proposed order has been proposed principally for an honorable uniformity of the teaching and ceremonies in these churches and not for strengthening the papacy. And it is true that in the first visitation, where in many places private absolution, Lent, and many other honorable ceremonies had been completely done away with, some of the same were reinstituted. And although at the time [John Agricola of] Eisleben and others cried that we were reinstituting the papacy, nonetheless that institution of ceremonies was not held to be such.[132]

But Melanchthon did more than just draw parallels to earlier times; he blamed the earlier controversies with Agricola for his present problems. Thus, in 1556, in the midst of the Majorist controversy over the necessity of good works, he blamed the antinomian controversy of some twenty years earlier for the new dispute. Agricola with his claim that "das Muß ist versalzen (the must/mash [of the law] is oversalted)"

---

129. *MBW* 5398 (*CR* 7:292–96), dated 7 January 1549, a letter from Buchholzer on behalf of the evangelical clergy in Berlin to Melanchthon, Bugenhagen, and the other theologians in Wittenberg. For Wittenberg's response see *MBW* 5401 (*CR* 7:299–301).

130. For further discussion of this dispute see Kolb, *Confessing the Faith*, 63–98; and Joachim Mehlhausen, "Der Streit um die Adiaphora," in *Bekenntnis und Einheit der Kirche: Studien zum Konkordienbuch*, ed. Martin Brecht and Reinhard Schwarz (Stuttgart: Calwer, 1980), 105–28.

131. *MBW* 4242 (*CR* 6:116f.), dated 20 April 1546.

132. *MBW* 5501 (*CR* 7:363–66, here 365): "Zum Andern, so ist dies Ordnung, die bedacht ist, fürnehmlich zu einer ehrlichen Gleichheit der Lehre und Ceremonien in dieser Kirchen bedacht, und nicht zu Stärkung des Papstthums, und ist wahr, daß in der ersten Visitation, da an vielen Orten die Privat Absolutio, sechs Wochen, und viel ehrlicher Ceremonien ganz abgethan waren, hat man derselbigen etliche wiederum aufgerichtet; und ob wohl die Zeit auch Eißleben und und [*sic*] andre schrieen, wir richteten das Papstthum wiederum auf, so ist gleichwohl solche Aufrichtung der Ceremonien nicht dafür gehalten worden."

had driven Melanchthon to take the stand he was now defending.[133] To no less an opponent than Matthias Flacius he wrote: "But concerning necessity, I confess that the furies of the antinomians attacked me twenty years ago when a court preacher, to the applause of the entire audience, said, 'Das Muß ist versalzen.' And how I say that these propositions are true and eternal, I have explained enough."[134]

In the Osiandrian controversy Melanchthon also recalled Agricola's calumnies. To Andreas Musculus, Agricola's brother-in-law, Melanchthon complained that a book presumably written by Agricola was filled with stylistic flaws and a misuse of the ancient church fathers.[135] To Eberhard Schnepf he complained, "I could write you a long *Iliad* concerning [Agricola's] calumnies."[136]

Part of that *Iliad* involved the dispute over the Visitation Articles. Writing from the Torgau almost exactly twenty-five years to the day after the 1527 conference there, a heavyhearted Melanchthon complained to George Buchholzer: "Then during the inspection of churches we discovered many kinds of ineptitudes. Doctor Jerome [Schurff], a wise man who worshiped God with true faith and prayer, remembers. When we tried to emend these things, I also got my ears boxed, so that *afterwards others often attacked me.*"[137]

"So that afterwards others often attacked me." The intervening twenty-five years with their disruptive struggles against Agricola finally brought Melanchthon to the conclusion that the controversy over the Visitation Articles served as the headwaters for the flood that followed. However Melanchthon may have fared in the later disputes, his position opposing Agricola's understanding of the law won widespread acceptance among Lutherans. Melanchthon's notions of the eternal law—always ordering, always accusing, always instructing—and of the movement in the Christian life from law to gospel carried the day.

133. See *MBW* 7054 (*CR* 8:194f.), dated 1553; *MBW* 7385 (*CR* 8:410–13), dated 12 January 1555; and *MBW* 7945 (*CR* 8:839–44), dated 4 September 1556 to Matthias Flacius. I am indebted to Heinz Scheible for explaining the wordplay to me.

134. *CR* 8:842: "Sed de Necessitate fateor, me Antinomorum furores ante viginti annos reprehendisse, cum aulicum concionator, toto theatro applaudente, diceret: das Muß ist versalzen. Et quomodo has propositiones veras et aeternas esse dicam, satis enarravi."

135. *MBW* 6798 (*CR* 8:67f.), dated 12 April 1553.

136. *MBW* 7021 (*CR* 8:171f.), dated 10 November 1553: "Possem tibi longam Iliada de his calumniis scribere."

137. *MBW* 6654 (*CR* 7:1144f.), dated 28 November 1552, italics added: "Deinde quales in inspectione Ecclesiarum ineptias invenerimus, meminit vir sapiens et Deum vera fide et invocatione colens, dominus doctor Hieronymus [Schurff]. Has cum emendare studeremus, tunc quoque colaphos accepi, ut postea saepe alii in me incurrerunt." See also *MBW* 7559 (*CR* 8:524f.), dated 21 August 1555 to A. Hardenberg, in which Melanchthon described the Visitation Articles as the means by which disputes were settled.

Nowhere is Melanchthon's victory more clearly depicted than in the church architecture of the time. In 1605 the capital city in the duchy of Braunschweig-Wolfenbüttel set about to build a new evangelical Marienkirche to replace the medieval edifice destroyed in a fire. The sculpture inside and out attest to the central tenets of orthodox Lutheranism as Melanchthon first formulated it. Guarding either side of the main entrance stand massive statues of Moses and Aaron. Above them hover heroes of the ducal family and a reigning Christ. Inside the sanctuary itself, the largest, most imposing figure in the nave is not Mary, reduced to a single portrait on the side wall, nor Christ, whose triumph is displayed in the gilded, foreign-made altar in the apse, but Moses, whose larger-than-life figure bearing the two tablets of the law forms the single pillar holding up the pulpit and represents with unmistakable clarity the centrality of the law.[138] Along the sides of the stairs up to and around the pulpit itself small panels, decipherable only by the keen-eyed observer, depict the Apostles' Creed. Thus the pulpit moves the listener visually through the catechism from commandments to creed, from law to gospel. The enthusiastic, lawless preaching of Agricola finds no expression here. The gospel and its joys rest firmly upon the unceasing demands and terrors of the law. The Christian moves from fear to faith, not the other way around. At least in Wolfenbüttel even the stones and wood declare Melanchthon's victory in this dispute.

138. Figures of Moses support the pulpits of numerous churches in Thuringia, even the small Johanneskirche built in Auguststadt, a suburb of Wolfenbüttel, during the Thirty Years' War.

6

Justifying Good Work:
The Origins of the Concept
of the Third Use of the Law (1534)

In 1534 Philip Melanchthon, perhaps in conjunction with lectures on Colossians delivered around this time, produced a third edition of the *Scholia*. In it, for the first time, he increased the number of functions, or uses, of the law from two to three. This chapter will examine the exegetical and theological causes for this shift in Melanchthon's understanding of the law.

The origins of the 1534 *Scholia* are shrouded in mystery. Sometime that year a new edition came off Joseph Klug's press in Wittenberg. Could the unauthorized reprinting of the second edition in August 1534 by John Setzer's successor in Haguenau have provoked Melanchthon into providing his own printer with a new version? Or, alternatively, could a new edition by Melanchthon have caused the Haguenau printer to try to gain a piece of the market? Perhaps Melanchthon simply lectured again on Colossians and made changes to his commentary to reflect alterations in his lectures.

The changes wrought on the 1528 edition in 1534 were small in comparison to the massive changes made in 1528 to the original edition. In only eleven places did Melanchthon greatly revise his comments, and even these revisions rarely amounted to more than a page of additional text. For the most part Melanchthon seemed content with the version from six years earlier. On the other hand, the fact that most of the alterations focused on various facets of one topic, justification, is clear indication that a dramatic shift had taken place in Melanchthon's understanding of that doctrine—dramatic enough to force revision in his old commentary along some surprising new lines.

The 1534 edition of the *Scholia* represented an important transition in Melanchthon's understanding of justification, connecting his work in the Apology of the Augsburg Confession (1531), his Romans commentary (1532), and lectures on the *Loci* (1533) on the one side, with the second edition of the *Loci* from 1535 and the contemporaneous controversy with Conrad Cordatus on the other. In addition to the first definition of the three uses of the law, it was in the *Scholia* of 1534 that Melanchthon argued most clearly for the necessity of good works in the believer's life. And here the forensic nature of justification became the bedrock for his explanation of that doctrine. Much of the doctrinal language used in many of the controversies that involved Melanchthon or his students and rocked Lutheranism after Luther's death also made its first appearance in the 1534 *Scholia*.[1] Whereas most scholars are aware of the changes to the *Loci* in 1535, and some have examined Melanchthon's commentary on Romans (1532), no one outside of Hans-Georg Geyer has thought to use the *Scholia*.[2]

By employing the *Scholia* of 1534 not only can comparisons be made to earlier and later books and lectures, but the *Scholia* of 1528 can serve as a benchmark showing exactly where Melanchthon's theology had changed in the intervening six years and where he felt the need to make corrections. In intellectual history it is tempting to place unrelated documents of a single author side by side and guess what the differences between them may mean. Here Melanchthon was changing his own text, the *Scholia* of 1528. This allows the historian a unique opportunity for tracing through a single text actual changes in a thinker's vocabulary and theology. Once these alterations have been identified, an intriguing question remains: why might Melanchthon have made such modifications? The answer to this question will arise from examination of Melanchthon's method and his earliest conversations with some moderate Roman opponents around the time the *Scholia* appeared. Our investigation will uncover both the origins of his new language on justification and works and its impact upon a thinker to whom theological definitions offered doctrinal certainty for faith. The answer to the question will also underscore the continuing importance of Agricola's theology for Melanchthon, especially in the related controversy with Conrad Cordatus over the necessity of works, a controversy that served as a prelude to the antinomian controversy between Agricola and Luther of 1537–40.

---

1. The topics of these debates included the role of the free will (the synergistic controversy), the forensic nature of justification (the Osiandrian controversy), the necessity of good works (the Majorist controversy, foreshadowed by the Cordatus controversy of 1536–37), the third use of the law (a second antinomian controversy). The resolutions of these controversies form the bulk of the Formula of Concord.

2. Geyer's use of sources makes his work *Von der Geburt des wahren Menschen* (Neukirchen-Vluyn: Neukirchener Verlag des Erziehungsvereins, 1965) less than helpful here. Even Martin Greschat's important work *Melanchthon neben Luther: Studien zur Gestalt der Rechtfertigungslehre zwischen 1528 und 1537* (Witten: Luther, 1965) fails to use this source.

Forensic Justification

By 1534 Melanchthon had narrowed the metaphors for the essence of human salvation to a single one: forensic justification. This was already spelled out in 1532, in the argumentum of his commentary on Romans:[3]

> "To be justified" properly signifies to be reputed righteous, that is, to be reputed accepted. Thus it should be understood relatively, just as in a law court, according to Hebrew custom, "to be justified" is used for "to be pronounced righteous," as when someone says, "The Roman people have justified (that is, pronounced righteous, absolved, approved) Scipio, who was accused by the people's tribunes." Although it is necessary that new motions exist in those who have been reconciled, nevertheless "to be justified" does not in a strict sense signify to have new virtues. But it should be understood relatively concerning the will of God: to be approved or accepted by God.[4]

Melanchthon here expressed all aspects of this new teaching. Justification is a matter of pronouncement, not a matter of an inner change of virtues, or, as he put it, it is to be understood not "proprie" but "relative." It is directly connected to the actions "in foro," in the court of law, as the example of Scipio indicates. It is a matter of divine acceptation.

This emphasis was not altogether lacking from earlier statements, and some would argue that forensic justification was the hallmark of Melanchthon's theology throughout his career.[5] However, there is no question that in the commentary on Romans the definition of justifica-

---

3. *MSA* 5, entitled "COM l MENTARII IN EPISTO l LAM PAVLI AD l ROMANOS, RE- l cens scripti a l PHILIPPO MELAN. l ANNO. l 1.5.3.2." Colophon: "IMPRESSVM VITE- BERGAE l IN EDIBVS IOSEPH CLVG." [264] leaves. See Greschat, *Melanchthon neben Luther*, 133–50.

4. *MSA* 5:39.7–16: "'Iustificari' proprie significat iustum reputari, h. e. acceptum reputari. Sic intelligatur relative, sicut in foro usurpatur Hebraica consuetudine iustificari pro eo, quod est iustum pronuntiari, ut si quis dicat: Populus Romanus iustificavit Scipionem accusatum a tribuno plebis, h. e. iustum pronuntiavit, absolvit, approbavit. Quamquam autem novos motus exsistere in his, qui reconciliantur, necesse est, tamen iustificari non significat proprie habere novas virtutes. Sed relative intelligatur de voluntate Dei pro eo, quod est approbari seu acceptari a Deo."

5. Karl Holl, "Die Rechtfertigungslehre in Luthers Vorlesung über den Römerbrief mit besonderer Rücksicht auf die Frage der Heilsgewißheit," in *Gesammelte Aufsätze zur Kirchengeschichte*, 3d ed., 3 vols. (Tübingen: J. C. B. Mohr/Paul Siebeck, 1923), 1:124–29, who argued that Melanchthon's forensic understanding distorted Luther's breakthrough to understanding justification as sanative; and Lowell Green, *How Melanchthon Helped Luther Discover the Gospel* (Fallbrook, Calif.: Verdict, 1980), who insists that Melanchthon helped Luther discover this very forensic notion and contributed to his breakthrough. On Luther, see Alister McGrath, *Luther's Theology of the Cross* (New York: Blackwell, 1985) and his discussion of the shift in the definition of *iustitia*.

tion was considerably narrower than in earlier works and explicitly eliminated any internal change in the person. Virtue was now completely excluded from the definition. Even the Apology lacked this clarity. There, as Melanchthon explained to the Swabian Reformer, Johannes Brenz, in a letter written at nearly the time of publication, he was inhibited by his adversaries and, perhaps, by his need in that context not to attack Augustine's notion that we are reputed righteous on account of the fulfillment of the law effected in us by the Holy Spirit.[6] Thus, in one part of the Apology he wrote that in James "to be justified does not mean to be made righteous from having been ungodly, but, as in the forensic use, to be pronounced righteous."[7] But in another passage he still held that "we are justified by faith alone, where justification must be understood as being made righteous or being regenerated."[8] Brenz's letter at the time the Apology was being published alerted Melanchthon to the danger of Augustine's (and Brenz's) misinterpretation of justification and led him to stress our acceptation by Christ: "Therefore we are righteous by faith alone, not because it is the root [of our own righteousness], as you write, but because it apprehends Christ, on account of whom we are accepted."[9] Brenz's position was rejected not only implicitly in the argumentum to the commentary on Romans, but also explicitly in comments on Romans 3:21f.: "The fancy of others, who think we are justified by faith because faith is the beginning of renovation, must be rejected."[10]

The *Scholia* of 1534 also reflected the new clarity and precision. Throughout the work Melanchthon scattered formulas similar to those in the 1532 Romans commentary. His comments on Colossians 1:23 were typical. In 1527 Melanchthon glossed the text ("You have been re-

---

6. *MBW* 1151 (*CR* 2:501–3), dated 12 May 1531. Melanchthon described Augustine's position in these terms: "Deinde imaginatur, nos iustos reputari propter hanc impletionem legis, quam efficit in nobis spiritus sanctus." Concerning the Apology he wrote, "Ego conatus sum eam in Apologia explicare, sed ibi propter adversariorum calumnias non sic loqui licet, ut nunc tecum loquor, etsi re ipsa idem dico."

7. Ap IV.252 (*BKS*, 209.32–34): "Et iustificari significat hic [in James] non ex impio iustum effici, sed usu forensi iustum pronuntiari."

8. Ap IV.78 (*BKS*, 175.37–39): "Igitur sola fide iustificamur, intelligendo iustificationem, ex iniusto iustum effici seu regenerari."

9. *CR* 2:501: "Ideo sola fide sumus iusti, non quia sit radix, ut tu scribis, sed quia apprehendit Christum, propter quem sumus accepti."

10. *MSA* 5:100.5ff.: "Repudianda est et imaginatio aliorum, qui ideo putant nos fide iustificari, quia fides sit initium renovationis." Melanchthon mentioned that this opinion was drawn from Augustine. See the footnote to this text for other references. For an analysis of the text and the development of Melanchthon's doctrine of justification during this period, see Robert Stupperich, "Die Rechtfertigungslehre bei Luther und Melanchthon 1530–1536," in *Luther and Melanchthon in the History and Theology of the Reformation*, ed. Vilmos Vajta (Philadelphia: Muhlenberg, 1961), 73–88.

deemed if you remain firm in faith") by writing simply, "You have obtained remission of sins, if you believe your sins have been forgiven because of Christ," and by referring the reader to Romans 3:28 and the *Scholia*'s later discussion of the two kinds of righteousness.[11] In 1528 an entire paragraph was added, beginning, "None of our works merit justification before God."[12] Saint Anthony and Saint Martin were not justified by their good works, but by faith. When God judges and terrifies our hearts, then we realize that we are not able to please God by our works, but depend on the grace promised through Christ. This is the chief teaching of the gospel which gives great consolation. Without it, no one can stand before God.[13]

In 1534 Melanchthon excised the paragraph from 1528, though not the original material from 1527, and replaced it with a two-page excursus on justification. The opening sentence made Melanchthon's concerns clear: "Let us talk briefly concerning justification so that it can be understood how works and how faith are required."[14] Here the balance between faith and works (also a concern in the Augsburg Confession [VI, XX]) had become the center of attention. Immediately Melanchthon worried about license: "For faith is not praised in order that the license of omitting works may be granted, since faith itself is the chief or most difficult work."[15] (Brenz, too, had made the point that according to John 6 faith is a work.)[16] The opponents here were of two kinds. On the one side, the references to works and license pointed to Melanchthon's continuing concern over antinomianism. On the other, he also had to defend himself against this very charge of license made by Roman opponents.

Agricola's position was still in the back of Melanchthon's mind when he insisted that contrition ("pavor & dolor conscientiae") is a necessary first step in conversion. Faith, defined here as trust (*fiducia*), then follows, establishing that "our sins are forgiven and we are pronounced righteous through mercy on account of Christ, not on account of the

---

11. *MSA* 4:228.2–5: "Consecuti estis remissionem peccatorum, si credideritis propter Christum remissa esse peccata."

12. *Scholia* 1528, 16v°: "Nulla nostra opera merentur iustificationem coram Deo." Melanchthon omitted the cross-reference to the later discussion in the *Scholia*.

13. *Scholia* 1528, 16(a)r°. (The number 16 is used on two consecutive leaves, B.viii and C.i. This is C.i.)

14. *Scholia* 1534, XVII.r°: "Breviter dicemus de iustificatione, ut quomodo opera, quomodo fides requiratur intelligi possit."

15. *Scholia* 1534, XVII.r°: "Non enim ideo fides laudatur, ut licentia concedatur omittendi opera, cum fides ipsa sit uel precipuum ac difficilimum opus."

16. *MBW* 1163 (*CR* 2:510–12): "Quoties enim de iustificatione cogitabam quod non esset ex operibus, illud subinde incidebat, nonne et fides ipsa opus est? Et dominus ait, hoc est opus Dei ut credatis."

worthiness of our contrition or works."[17] Were all of this to depend upon our contrition, the conscience would again become uncertain.

After discussing the necessity of good works (see p. 186) Melanchthon focused on justification by faith. It ought to be understood "relative," that is, "we are pronounced righteous by faith in the mercy promised on account of Christ." The stress on pronouncement throughout this section and the use of the code word "relative" indicated the forensic nature of his definition, as did the next sentence: "For justification is understood relatively for the remission of sins and for the reception or imputation of righteousness."[18]

Melanchthon's comments on Colossians 2:10a ("And in him you are brought to perfection [consummati]") similarly reflected the complexity of the transformation in his language on justification. In 1527 he treated this passage as a "basis and definition of Christian righteousness."[19] As grace-centered as the definition might have been, there was still no clear distinction between intrinsic and extrinsic righteousness. Christian righteousness is what pleases God. God is not pleased with human works, only with Christ. Thus, those are brought to perfection ("consummati") who believe in Christ and are sanctified by Christ through the Holy Spirit. This second phrase forced Melanchthon to discuss the role of the Holy Spirit in mortifying the flesh and making us new creatures ("perfect, renewed, made new creatures by the reception of the Holy Spirit").[20] Reason and free will cannot change the heart in this way. Melanchthon did not distinguish clearly between Christ's satisfaction of the Father and the renewal of the Holy Spirit. They were two aspects of the same thing.

In 1528 Melanchthon revised and expanded his comments.[21] He replaced the reference to free will with a reference to reason's powers. The two parts of justification remained, but he greatly expanded the first part, discussing Psalm 143:2 ("No living thing will be justified in his sight"; cf. Rom. 3:20). Even Paul's good works, which Melanchthon enumerated, did not justify him, as the apostle himself confessed in 1 Corinthians 4:4 and Philippians 3:9. Instead, what makes us "consummati" is the righteousness of faith, which believes that we are pleasing to the Father because of Christ. Here Melanchthon referred to Psalm

---

17. *Scholia* 1534, XVII.v°: "nobis remitti peccata, nosque pronunciari iustos per misericordiam propter Christum, non propter dignitatem nostrae contritionis aut operum."

18. *Scholia* 1534, XVII.v°: "Fiducia misericordiae propter Christum promissae iusti pronunciamur. Iustificatio enim relatiue intelligatur pro remissione peccatorum, & pro acceptatione seu imputatione iusticiae."

19. *MSA* 4:244.11f.: "ratio et definitio Christianae iustitiae."

20. *MSA* 4:244.30f.: "perfecti, renovati, facti nova creatura accepto Spiritu sancto."

21. *Scholia* 1528, 36r°–37v°, expanding from one page to four.

32:1. Without Christ as the mediator who satisfies God's wrath, the frightened conscience has no safe haven, must rely on its works, and is driven to despair. Since the Father pronounces us ("pronunciet nos") brought to perfection ("consummati"), it would be blasphemy to leave that perfection and to take our perfection and justification from our works. In these comments the Father's "pronouncement" defined justification, but the consequences of its forensic character had not yet been clarified.

Having made such a strong case for the Reformation's chief doctrine, Melanchthon added a paragraph in 1528 warning that such faith is not lazy or devoid of good works. Believers who understand Christ's consolation and forgiveness ask God to rule them, are transformed by the Holy Spirit, and grow to hate sin. Melanchthon was convinced that this was the teaching of John and Paul.

At the end of the entire section Melanchthon broke off his exegesis to explain to the readers why he once again had discussed this topic. The text of Paul (Col. 2:10a) drove him to it. He wished to expound on Paul's idea "simplicissime."[22] Scholastic theologians neither taught the righteousness of faith nor understood the distinction between philosophical and Christian righteousness. Thus Melanchthon was forced to refute their pernicious errors so that the "summa Christianae doctrinae" might not be obscured.

By 1534 Melanchthon's comments on this verse no longer satisfied him, and he replaced them with a completely new exposition. Now Melanchthon interpreted this text in antithesis to civil righteousness, Jewish ceremonies, and monastic traditions. Paul argues that only "on account of Christ (propter Christum)" do his readers receive the benefit of "being reputed as righteous, as if you had satisfied the law."[23] Here Melanchthon emphasized the forensic nature of justification ("reputemini") and its relation to the accusing law ("ac si satisfaceretis legi").

Melanchthon proceeded to make three points. The first and longest reiterated the forensic nature of justification.[24] "The conscience ought to stand on this, that we are pronounced righteous freely on account of Christ, although we have not yet satisfied the law."[25] As in 1528, Melanchthon referred to Psalm 32:1, but now it became the centerpiece

---

22. *Scholia* 1528, 37v°.

23. *Scholia* 1534, XXXVI.v°: "ut reputemini pro iustis, ac si satisfaceretis legi."

24. In the other two points, not discussed here, Melanchthon rejected the notion that abiding by human traditions is the basis of perfection—a view held by the Jews of Jesus' day and the monks—and he explained how Christ through the Holy Spirit effects perfection, which differs from civil and monastic righteousness.

25. *Scholia* 1534, XXXVII.r°: "Conscientia statuere debet nos gratis propter Christum pronunciari iustos, etiamsi nondum satisfaciamus legi."

of his discussion. He paraphrased it to mean that the saints have sins, but they are pronounced righteous by God's mercy. This is "the fullest consolation" for those who see their sin through the law. Despite the remnants of sin within themselves, they are commanded here to look outside themselves to Christ for their righteousness.

Although here and elsewhere Melanchthon insisted that "the renewal and righteousness of a good conscience" are also necessary, nevertheless his emphasis was on the righteousness of faith.[26] God is pleased with the obedience of faith, as if we had fulfilled the law. In defense of this statement Melanchthon misquoted Romans 10:4 ("Christ is the summation of the law for the righteousness of every believer [*Summa* legis Christus est ad iusticiam omni credenti]") and glossed it to read, "The one who trusts in Christ is already righteous and has what the law requires; the law does not accuse or condemn such a person."[27] The believer's works please God as if they satisfied the law, although in reality they do not.

Melanchthon then summarized what he characterized as a clear and very simple teaching:

> First, faith is necessary, by which is established that we are pleasing to God gratis on account of Christ. Next, we say that the righteousness of a good conscience is necessary. But this is still impure and imperfect before God, according to [Psalm 143:2], "No one living will be justified in your sight." Therefore, we return to faith and teach that it must be established that the person [not the person's works] is pleasing gratis on account of Christ. So the conscience is freed from the terrors of sin and death, and on account of this faith that renewal is pleasing. These things are not taught by the Scholastics, who dream that a human being satisfies the law; likewise they dream that a human being is pronounced righteous before God on account of one's own worth and the fulfillment of the law. These dreams obscure Christ's benefit and lead consciences into despair.[28]

---

26. *Scholia* 1534, XXXVII.r°: "Sed persona semper illum scopum teneat, placere nos propter Christum etiamsi non satisfaciamus legi."

27. *Scholia* 1534, XXXVII.v°: "Qui confidit Christo, is iam iustus est, et habet id quod Lex requirit, Lex non accusat, non condemnat eum." For "summa" the Vulgate reads "finis" and Erasmus "perfectio."

28. *Scholia* 1534, XXXVII.v°: "Primum fidem esse necessariam, qua statuendum est, quod gratis Deo placeamus propter Christum. Deinde dicimus & iusticiam bonae conscientiae necessarium esse. Sed haec coram Deo adhuc est immunda & imperfecta, iuxta illud. Non iustificabitur in conspectu tuo omnis uiuens. Ideo redimus ad fidem, et docemus statuendum esse, quod propter Christum persona gratis placeat. Ita conscientia liberatur a terroribus peccati & mortis, & propter hanc fidem placet illa nouitas. Haec non docent scholastici, qui somniant hominem legi satisfacere, item somniant hominem propter propriam dignitatem & legis impletionem, iustum coram Deo pronunciari. Haec somnia obscurant Christi beneficium, & conscientias adducunt in desperationem."

Here Melanchthon expressed his mature understanding of justification. Faith in God's being pleased "gratis propter Christum" (the first righteousness) was necessary for the righteousness of a good conscience (the second righteousness). But the impurity of this second righteousness, as described in the Bible itself, forced Melanchthon back to faith, so that even good works depended on Christ's acceptation. Melanchthon's enemy here was not so much Agricola as the Scholastics—one thinks of the authors of the *Confutatio*—who attacked the Lutherans for ignoring good works and turned justification on its head by making God's pronouncement of righteousness depend upon one's own worth and fulfillment of the law's demands. This obscures Christ's blessing and leads to despair. That is, the effect of this "gospel" proves that it is not good news at all.

Melanchthon's response to Scholastic theology, however, did not include elimination of the law as a result of justification. Because of God's forensic proclamation of righteousness, the law no longer accused; because of the remnant of sin in us, the law could not be fulfilled (no "simul" here!); but it did not disappear. The law had become the measure of righteousness in a good conscience; faith was now clinging to the only one in whom the law culminated (*summa legis!*), Jesus Christ. There was now a necessity for both faith and works, but, given human weakness, faith dominated and provided the conscience the only way out from under the law's accusation. Thus, forensic justification, far from eliminating the law from Melanchthon's theology, had actually increased its significance.[29] The purpose of emphasizing the divine decree of righteousness and even the necessity of the righteousness of a good conscience was to underscore the centrality of God's grace outside of us that works (imperfectly because of sin) inside us.[30] Later, Melanchthon's students upset this delicate balance and took individual parts of this equation separately, thereby undermining Melanchthon's stated intent and emphasizing law to the exclusion of grace.

The Necessity of Good Works

The most dramatic change in Melanchthon's 1534 *Scholia* on Colossians occurred in his understanding of the law and good works. It involved persistent emphasis on the necessity of good works. In comments on Colossians 1:23 Melanchthon insisted, "In conversion some

29. Over and over again Melanchthon stressed that we are declared righteous, *as if* we had satisfied the law.

30. Melanchthon concluded the entire section, *Scholia* 1534, XXXVIII.vº: "Fide pronunciamur iusti & perfecti propter illud extra nos, scilicet propter Christum. Et tamen nostra obedientia, quatenus in nobis est, est imperfecta & immunda."

contrition is necessary, that is, terror and sorrow of the conscience are necessary."[31] Later in the same passage he wrote, "Now the new life ought to be obedience to God, and now the righteousness of good works is necessary."[32] To underscore his point he added, "Therefore good works are not disapproved but are greatly required." In comments on Colossians 2:10a the same note was sounded: "Thereupon we say that the righteousness of a good conscience is necessary."[33]

This theme recurred in comments on Colossians 2:17. Whereas in 1527 only justification by faith was mentioned,[34] already in 1528 Melanchthon began to respond to Agricola's questioning of the necessity of the law: "Why then, you ask, is it necessary to observe the law?"[35] But Melanchthon then attacked "our theologians" (he meant his Roman opponents and Erasmus) who made both Christ and Moses lawgivers. He also pointed to the example of David, justified by faith not by works. Here he was willing to admit that "there ought to be some exercise of faith in this life."[36] He concluded from the entire disputation in Romans, however, "that moral works do not justify."[37] Were Paul wrong, Christ would have died in vain. At this juncture any discussion of necessity had to do with faith: "When the promise was made, it was necessary that faith justify, because the promises are received by faith not works."[38] Only at the close of his remarks in 1528 did Melanchthon deal with the question "why the works of the Decalog are demanded if they do not justify."[39] While referring readers to his later discussion, where he took issue with Agricola's formulations (see pp. 164–67), here Melanchthon stated that the Decalog, unlike human rites and traditions, pertained to the heart's purity. Nevertheless, he stressed that it was faith that actually purified the heart and then bore the fruit of obedience.

In 1534 Melanchthon preserved all of his 1528 comments on Colossians 2:17. However, he inserted three pages of commentary dealing with the question "whether people are pronounced righteous on ac-

31. *Scholia* 1534, XVII.r°: "In conuersione necessaria est contritio aliqua, hoc est, pauor & dolor conscientiae, necessaria est."

32. *Scholia* 1534, XVII.r°f.: "Iam noua uita debet esse obedientia erga Deum, & necessaria iam est iusticia bonorum operum. . . . Non igitur improbantur bona opera, sed maxime requiruntur."

33. *Scholia* 1534, XXXVII.v°: "Deinde dicimus & iusticiam bonae conscientiae necessarium esse."

34. *MSA* 4:253.32–254.4.

35. *Scholia* 1528, 48r°: "Quid igitur, inquies, opus erat obseruatione legis?"

36. *Scholia* 1528, 48(a)r°: "oportet aliqua fidei exercicia in hac uita."

37. *Scholia* 1528, 48(a)v°: "quod nec moralia opera iustificant."

38. *Scholia* 1528, 49r°: "Cum promissio facta est, necesse est quod fides iustificet, quia fide, non operibus promissiones accipiuntur."

39. *Scholia* 1528, 49v°: ". . . cur exiguntur opera Decalogi, siquidem non iustificant."

count of the moral code [=the Decalog]."[40] He divided his answer into two parts. First, the ungodly, who have not been reborn in Christ, cannot offer the perfect obedience demanded by the law, although they can produce some civil works from the powers of human nature. Second, those reborn ought to know that only by faith do we receive forgiveness of sins. Fulfillment of the law is not a prior condition for us, lest the conscience again become uncertain. The law demands perfect obedience, which because of the "remnants of sin" even those declared righteous cannot fulfill. Having said this, however, Melanchthon insisted that "the righteousness of a good conscience or of good works ought to accompany faith."[41] He immediately added that this righteousness of a good conscience does not satisfy the law perfectly and that the person is reconciled to God on account of Christ. Nevertheless, this second righteousness pleases God despite its imperfection precisely because the person is in Christ. Melanchthon declared this a "great and necessary consolation for the godly."[42] Once again, however, he would make it clear that faith is preeminent: "The righteousness of a good conscience is necessary, as I have said. However, faith or trust in Christ has been placed far above this righteousness of ours."[43]

Here, as in his comments on the previous two verses of Colossians, Melanchthon steered a course between the (to him unfair) charge that Lutherans neglected good works and the theology of his Roman opponents, who insisted that people are made righteous before God because of their own worth or their own fulfillment of the law. There were in Melanchthon's view two necessary kinds of righteousness for the Christian. The one arises from faith, or trust, that clings to the external pronouncement of righteousness, that is, satisfaction of the law, on account of Christ. The other arises from the good conscience (good on account of Christ through faith). Good works are pleasing to God and acceptable not because they are perfect, as the law demands, but because the person is in Christ.

The law did not disappear in Melanchthon's eyes, although for the *bona conscientia* its accusation had. The necessity of works also did not disappear, although the reason for it had changed. For Melanchthon there was no longer a necessity to satisfy the law's demands, but the necessity of faith's own internal, imperfect obedience. Realizing the im-

---

40. *Scholia* 1534, XLIX.v°–LI.r°: "An propter moralia pronuncientur homines iusti."

41. *Scholia* 1534, L.r°: "Debet autem fidem comitari iusticia bonae conscientiae seu bonorum operum." He repeated himself on the next page: "Et tamen quod necessario fidem comitari debeat iusticia bonae conscientiae, seu moralium operum."

42. *Scholia* 1534, L.v°: "magna & necessaria piis consolatio."

43. *Scholia* 1534, L.v°: "Necessaria est, ut dixi, iusticia bonae conscientiae. Sed fides seu fiducia in Christum longe collocanda est supra hanc iusticiam nostram."

perfection of works, the believer returns to faith "that on account of Christ the person freely pleases [God]," and thus the conscience remains free from the terrors of sin and death.[44] This third necessity, the "necessaria consolatio," explains the peculiar tension in Melanchthon's discussion. Melanchthon wanted desperately both to defend the Reformers from the charge that they denied the necessity of good works and at the same time to avoid robbing the conscience of the gospel's consolation. So he devised a way to speak of the necessity of works for the believer by excluding their necessity for justification.

Melanchthon returned to this dilemma in his introductory comments to Colossians 3 and 4, completely rewritten in 1534.[45] Good works, the topic of these chapters, form the second part of Christian doctrine, the first part being Christ's benefits.[46] In a curiously unbalanced structure, Melanchthon emphasized first that it is necessary to know ("necesse est scire") how we receive remission of sins (it is given on account of Christ and received by faith). Next, it is necessary to obey the law of God.[47] Because of our weakness, however, our obedience is imperfect. Thus it is necessary to know ("necesse est scire") how this obedience pleases God. It does not please God because it satisfies the law—indeed, it cannot—but because "the person has been reconciled and is just by faith."[48] This obedience now pleases God and becomes a kind of righteousness, it ought to be added, "not because it satisfies the law, but because we have been made sons."[49]

This doctrine was for Melanchthon "an enormous mercy." God approves our obedience despite its distance from the perfection of the law and views it as if it had real integrity! Melanchthon concluded with a flourish: "What human words can explain this blessing satisfactorily?"[50] Melanchthon felt he had to instruct his readers about the doctrine of good works, so that they would understand how obedience is pleasing to God in spite of weakness, and so that they would keep in mind that the person is righteous "by faith on account of Christ" and that obedience is pleasing to God "propter Christum."[51] In this way the

---

44. *Scholia* 1534, XXXVII.v°: "quod propter Christum persona gratis placeat."

45. *Scholia* 1534, LXXXII.v°–LXXXIII.v°.

46. For a discussion of the importance of this particular phrase for Melanchthon, see Ralph Quere, *Christum cognoscere: Christ's Efficacious Presence in the Eucharistic Theology of Melanchthon* (Nieuwkoop: B. De Graaf, 1977).

47. *Scholia* 1534, LXXXII.v°. Note the imbalance from "scire" to "obedire" (and later back to "scire").

48. *Scholia* 1534, LXXXII.v°: "persona est reconciliata ac iusta fide."

49. *Scholia* 1534, LXXXII.v°: ". . . non quia legi satisfacit, sed quia filij facti sumus."

50. *Scholia* 1534, LXXXII.v°: "Quae vox humana potest hoc beneficium satis explicare?"

51. *Scholia* 1534, LXXXIII. r°.

conscience would have "firma consolatio." Melanchthon referred the reader to Romans 6:14 and 8:1 and discussed briefly the meaning of being not "under law" but "under grace." He concluded that the fact that our works are accepted "propter Christum" ought to exhort us to good works. Otherwise we would be deterred from good works by despair, unsure of whether God approves of our love or not. Furthermore, the consolation that God's mercy is so powerful that it approves our imperfect obedience should arouse us to good works. We are thus filled with thanks and obey God, knowing that our pious efforts are approved by him.

Again, Melanchthon tried to ground his discussion of good works in the consolation of God's mercy. However, he wanted to do this without compromising the necessity of good works. The very order of his argument—from the necessity of knowing how we are forgiven, to the necessity of obeying the law, to the necessity of knowing how this obedience pleases God—placed the law and obedience to it squarely at the center of Melanchthon's theology. Not death and resurrection or even repentance and faith, but knowing (that we are declared righteous and that our imperfect works are accepted) and obeying (the law) had become the centerpiece of his theology. Not that Melanchthon did not speak of the necessity of good works in earlier versions of the *Scholia*. Already in the 1527 introduction to chapters 3 and 4 he wrote, "It is necessary that such actions and moral behavior as God demands follow."[52] But this was in no sense his central concern. By 1534, however, the necessity of good works had taken over and dominated his discussion of justification.

This turn in Melanchthon's theology was foreshadowed in the Augsburg Confession. Article XX, completed after his arrival in Augsburg, contained this comment in the Latin version: "For this reason our people teach that it is necessary to do good works, not that we trust that through them we merit grace, but on account of God's will."[53] In the Apology Melanchthon stated, "However, it is indeed necessary to do good works."[54] Here the attacks by the *Confutatio* and perhaps by Johannes Mensing in his "Bescheid, ob der Glaube allein, ohne alle gute Werke dem Menschen genug sei zur Seligkeit" weighed on his mind.[55] Yet here, immediately prior to his strict redefinition of justification in

---

52. *MSA* 4:278.9f. (=*Scholia* 1528, 80v°): "Necesse est sequi actiones et mores quales Deus exigit."

53. Augsburg Confession XX.27 (*BKS*, 80): "Praeterea docent nostri, quod necesse sit bona opera facere, non ut confidamus per ea gratiam mereri, sed propter voluntatem Dei."

54. Ap IV.348–55: "Imo vero necesse est bene operari."

55. See *BKS*, 227 n. 1.

forensic terms, Melanchthon still spoke only of regeneration, of growing in faith, and of the results of justification. The language of obedience to the law played no role in the discussion.

In the commentary on Romans from 1532, however, in part of an excursus on Romans 6:14 entitled "On the Abrogation of the Law," Melanchthon did use much of the same language found in the 1534 *Scholia*.[56] After first eliminating civil righteousness from the discussion (the gospel does not corrupt the good of nature, but heals it), Melanchthon defined abrogation of the law in terms of forensic justification. Remission of sin comes on account of Christ, not on account of the law, which chiefly condemns us. To be free from the law means to be free from its curse and condemnation. After being reconciled to God, "we please God on account of Christ, not on account of fulfillment of the law, because those who have been renewed do not satisfy the law."[57] This theme was sounded again and again in 1534. We are incapable, even as "renovati," of fulfilling the law. In all our prayers and deeds we have the consolation and confidence that, despite our unworthiness, we are pleasing to God on account of Christ. Melanchthon distinguished between the person accepted by mercy and the good works which we do out of obedience. We are free from the Decalog as far as justification goes, but not as far as obedience. The moral law remains written in our hearts.[58] He concluded with a description of the consolation that God's acceptance of us and our works on account of Christ brings. We avoid misery only when we learn that our persons are accepted by trust in Christ ("fiducia Christi") and that our works and afflictions please God only "after the person pleases him."[59] This acceptance actually helps us continue doing good and prevents our giving up in despair.

Clearly, much of what Melanchthon said in 1534 he had already formulated in 1532. As Melanchthon reviewed the *Scholia* in the light of his sharper understanding of justification, he now saw that his 1528 comments on the law were out-of-date. Yet even between 1532 and 1534 there was some movement. By 1534 the law itself dominated the discussion. There was consolation less from the gospel itself and more from the knowledge of doctrine. One almost detects a double imputation of righteousness here: one for the ungodly and the other for the

56. *MSA* 5:209.10–214.12.
57. *MSA* 5:210.13f.: "Placemus Deo propter Christum non propter legis impletionem, quia neque renovati satisfacimus legi."
58. *MSA* 5:211.29–32. Melanchthon also outlined another possible interpretation: the Holy Spirit through the gospel moves those who consent to do the law of God. Rolf Schäfer points out (*MSA* 5:212, note on line 5) that this represented Melanchthon's earlier position.
59. *MSA* 5:213.25–33: "postquam persona placet."

works of the good conscience. Both were accounted as righteous "propter Christum," with the startling result that the obedience of the human being (not simply the work of the Holy Spirit) and the demand of the law (not simply the declaration of the gospel) had become the foci around which the Christian life now revolved for Melanchthon.

The Third Use of the Law

Nowhere was the shift toward a law-centered theology more clearly evident than in Melanchthon's discussion of the uses of the law. The notion that the law has uses or functions is a peculiarly Protestant concept with origins deep within Martin Luther's theology. Gerhard Ebeling has demonstrated how the distinction between law and gospel and Luther's insistence that God works on human beings through the Word resulted in Luther's developing a twofold use of the law.[60] First, God uses the law in this world to restrain the wicked and maintain order in creation. This "civil use of the law" is closely connected to the "kingdom on the left" and God's governance in this world. Second, God uses the law to terrify the conscience, reveal sin, and put to death the old creature by driving it to Christ. This "theological use of the law" was associated in Luther's mind with Paul's statements about the law in Romans 3:20.

Luther did not come to this understanding of the law's twofold use overnight. In his 1520 tract "Von der Freiheit eines Christenmenschen," he focused only on what Lutherans later called the second use of the law.[61] In "De votis monasticis" (1521) Luther spoke for the first time of an "officium legis," but again only to show sin.[62] Definitions of two uses of the law first appeared in an exposition of the epistle lesson for New Year's Day; this sermon was published in 1522 as part of Luther's *Weihnachtspostil* and seen through the presses by Melanchthon.[63]

In the first edition of the *Loci communes theologici* (1521) Melanchthon connected his favorite Aristotelian dialectical categories ("quid

---

60. Gerhard Ebeling, *Luther: An Introduction to His Thought* (Philadelphia: Fortress, 1970), 125–40. Luther's insight depended upon Augustine's distinction between the letter and the spirit. See Leif Grane, *Modus loquendi theologicus: Luthers Kampf um die Erneuerung der Theologie (1515–1518)* (Leiden: E. J. Brill, 1975).

61. *WA* 7:23f. and 34f., esp. 34.12–14: "Die gepot sol man predigen, die sunder zurschreckenn und yhr sund zu offenbarnn, das sie rewe haben und sich bekehren."

62. *WA* 8:609.16–17.

63. *WA* 10.1.1:450–66 (an interpretation of the epistle for New Year's Day [Gal. 3:24–29]), esp. 454.8–12 and 455.5–6: "Alhie sihestu yhe, wotzu das gesetz nodt und gutt sey, und was gott darynnen suche. Nemlich die zwey stück: Das erst, das er uns ynn der tzucht behallte unnd uns ynn eyn erber weßen treybe eußerlich, das wyr unternander leben mugen und eyner den andern nit fresse. . . . Das ander, das der mensch sich alßo durchs gestz erkenne, wie falsch und unrecht seyn hertz sey."

sit" and "quid effectus") to Luther's insight into the working of the Word. First he defined what the law and the gospel were and then investigated their power or effect.[64] At this time, however, following Luther's direction in "Von der Freiheit eines Christenmenschen," Melanchthon described only a single use of the law: to terrify the heart by revealing its sin.[65]

From Melanchthon's 1524 tract dedicated to Philip of Hesse, "Epitome renovatae ecclesiasticae doctrinae," we can infer two uses of the law.[66] We can do so only because the tract had two main divisions: *iustitia christiana* and *iustitia humana*. Under the first he discussed repentance and faith (=[the second use of the] law and gospel). Under the second he talked of a pedagogical use of the law for the ungodly, who must be coerced into doing right. Following Luther's sermon on the epistle for New Year's Day, he used Galatians 3:24 as a proof text for the latter. As long as Melanchthon organized his thinking along the lines of human and divine righteousness, however, there was no reason to count the uses of the law. Only when the law itself became a separate topic (*locus communis*) did various uses need to be counted.

Luther never saw a need to increase the uses of the law above two and thus create a separate use for believers. In his Galatians commentary of 1535 and in the Smalcald Articles of 1537 Luther continued to count two uses: the political and theological.[67] The modern debate over whether Luther in fact (if not in name) taught a third use of the law reflects later Lutheran controversies and historians' inability to understand the center of his theology.[68] For Luther, the human being encountered the law in the two realms of human existence: *coram Deo* and *coram hominibus*. Thus, there was never any need for more than two uses of the law. In his theology the law never had an independent exist-

---

64. *MSA* 2.1:55–103. Peter Fraenkel, *Testimonia Patrum* (Geneva: Librairie Droz, 1961), was the first to point this out. The section on the law remained unchanged in the revised edition of 1522.

65. *MSA* 2.1:93.

66. *MSA* 1:179–89.

67. See, respectively, *WA* 40:519–20 and *SA* III.ii.1–5 (in *BKS*, 435–36). Only two (of seven) manuscripts of the "Second Antinomian Disputation" of 12 January 1538 ascribe to Luther three uses of the law—clearly a later addition by a Melanchthon student. See *WA* 39.1:485.16–24 and the notes. A third manuscript places this material under a different article.

68. See Werner Elert, "Eine theologische Fälschung zur Lehre vom tertius usus legis," *Zeitschrift für Religions- und Geistesgeschichte* 1 (1948): 168–70. The classic defense of a third use of the law in Luther comes from Wilfried Joest, *Gesetz und Freiheit: Das Problem des tertius usus legis bei Luther und die neutestamentliche Parainese* (Göttingen: Vandenhoeck and Ruprecht, 1951). See the criticism in Rolf Schäfer, *Christologie und Sittlichkeit in Melanchthons frühen Loci* (Tübingen: Mohr/Siebeck, 1961), 120–22.

ence that demanded definition, but it was always a part of the human encounter with God.

The 1527 and 1528 *Scholia* were the first publications in which Melanchthon explicitly defined two functions of the law.[69] The text of Colossians 2:16–17 reads, "Let no one judge you in matters of food or drink or in the distinction of feast days, new moons, or sabbaths, which are a shadow of future things. The body is Christ's." The entire exegetical tradition understood the first part of this text as referring to Mosaic laws. Melanchthon, aware of this tradition, distanced himself from it in comments on the phrase "which are a shadow of future things":

> They interpret "shadow" as *typon*, as if [Paul] said this: "The law does not justify, therefore [its] ceremonies are not necessary," as also Acts 15:5 indicates. What then are ceremonies? *Typoi* of Christ, as the Passover signifies the death of Christ, the ark signifies the church, propitiatory sacrifices Christ, who makes the Father pleased with us. I do not disapprove of this exposition, but it does not explain the nature of the law well enough.[70]

The "they" in this text was in fact Erasmus (relying on Origen and Theophylact), who argued that the point of Colossians was first to defend Christ's two natures and second to demonstrate that Mosaic *ceremonies* were no longer necessary for the Christian. In the context of this passage Erasmus distinguished the Old and New Testaments in terms of shadow and reality (or type and fulfillment). This distinction touched only the ceremonial, not the moral law.

In contrast, Melanchthon insisted that the phrase "shadow of future things" referred to the whole law: "That is, the whole law was given, not to justify, but to signify justification, which was promised through Christ."[71] For him, the Mosaic ceremonies never justified. Thus David and Samuel were justified not by performing ceremonies, but by believing in the justification promised through Christ. Christ, therefore, is the end of the whole law, not just the ceremonies.

Underneath Erasmus's (and Origen's) approach, which related individual ceremonies to later historical events, Melanchthon smelled dangerous allegories that "did not help consciences."[72] Instead, laws and ceremonies were needed because God had chosen the Jews to be a special people who would bear his Word and among whom Christ would

---

69. Hans Engelland, *Melanchthon, Glauben und Handeln* (Munich: Kaiser, 1931), 100–101. When Martin Becker of Decin (Bohemia) charged his pastor, Dominic Beyer, with antinomianism in 1524, Luther, Johann Bugenhagen, and Melanchthon sent a letter to the disputants that implied two uses for the law. See *MBW* 336 (*WA* 15:229).

70. *MSA* 4:252.2–8.

71. *MSA* 4:252.10–12.

72. *MSA* 4:252.25.

be born. Through laws this physical kingdom, distinguished from all other nations, was maintained until the advent of Christ. "A political entity can hardly exist without many laws."[73]

For most exegetes this would have sufficed. However, Melanchthon viewed each individual text of Scripture as a specific case of a general topic or *locus communis*. Thus the fact that in explaining this text he had touched upon the use of law in maintaining government gave him leave to investigate the broader question of the law's functions. So Melanchthon continued, "God wanted the two offices of the law to be as follows."[74]

Here, drawing heavily upon Luther's exposition of Galatians 3 in the sermon on the epistle for New Year's Day, Melanchthon set forth his position. First, God wanted the law to coerce the "carnal human being" (1 Tim. 1:9 and Gal. 3:24). This was his reason for giving laws to the Israelites and to all people: "For this reason God gives magistrates and laws to the nations."[75] The second office of the law is "to inspire terror, to condemn and to humble, so that we may realize that we are sinners and may be driven to seek grace and justification through Christ."[76] Here the proof texts included Romans 3:20 and 11:32. Nevertheless, Melanchthon concluded, the law did not only condemn "but also reminded of the promises concerning Christ."[77] He summarized his remarks by suggesting that any discussion of the law of Moses would be enhanced by teaching that God gave the law for two reasons, "to coerce the flesh and to terrify or humble."[78]

In comments added in 1528 on the rest of Colossians 2:17 ("the body is Christ's"), Melanchthon continued to hammer away at the same points. Christ was not a lawgiver like Moses. David was justified not by works but, as he had stated in Psalm 32, by faith and the nonimputation of sin. To be sure, this faith brought forth obedience: "For there ought to be some exercise of faith in this life."[79] Nevertheless, the law was given not because it justifies, but because God wanted to separate a certain *politeia* from the nations. At this point Melanchthon warned the readers specifically against Origen and others (=Erasmus) who imagine that the Decalog "or, as they say, *opera moralia*" justify.[80] Paul's arguments in Romans show clearly that "opera moralia" do not justify.

---

73. *MSA* 4:253.1–2.
74. *MSA* 4:253.2.
75. *MSA* 4:253.7–8.
76. *MSA* 4:253.9–12.
77. *MSA* 4:253.23–24. In *Scholia* 1528, 47v°, Melanchthon added the words "through all ceremonies."
78. *MSA* 4:253.29–30.
79. *Scholia* 1528, 48(a)r°.
80. *Scholia* 1528, 48(a)v°.

In the late 1520s, then, Melanchthon, as part of a struggle against Erasmus over how to interpret the biblical text in light of justification by faith alone, defined the two uses of the law. For Melanchthon, as for Luther, the Old Testament was no longer simply a shadow cast by future events, and Paul's understanding of Christ as the end of the law could not be reduced to a change in ceremonies. Instead, God used the law to maintain the order and particularity of the Israelites until the coming of Christ, to terrify the sinner, and, as a result of both these functions, to remind us of the promise of Christ.

To answer an opponent who used suspect exegesis to support an emphasis on works and undermined justification by faith alone, two uses of the law sufficed for Melanchthon. Under what circumstances, then, did Melanchthon need a third use? Here modern scholarship has sometimes charged Melanchthon with caving in to his opponents and abandoning Luther's theology,[81] or else it has defended him by arguing that the third use of the law was implicit both in his earlier theology and in Luther's.[82] These approaches overlook the historical moment in which Melanchthon himself switched from two to three uses of the law. By examining that moment, we gain a new perspective on this question.

The Romans commentary of 1532 still described two uses of the law: to restrain the flesh and to accuse the conscience.[83] Unfortunately, fragments of the 1533 lectures on the *Loci* do not include discussion of the law's uses.[84] In the 1534 *Scholia*, however, a clear shift has taken place. To be sure, the printer still included the marginal notation of the 1527 and 1528 editions on Colossians 2:17, "The law has two functions."[85] But in the text Melanchthon now talked of three. In 1527 and 1528 he had written: "As much as the law may have carved out for Moses things that had to be interpreted, it would be just as useful to teach that God gave the law for these two reasons: to coerce the flesh and to terrify or humble."[86] But in 1534 Melanchthon altered this section to read: "As much as the law may have carved out for Moses things that had to be interpreted, it would be just as useful to teach that God gave the law for

---

81. See, for example, Ragnar Bring, *Gesetz und Evangelium und der dritte Gebrauch des Gesetzes in der lutherischen Theologie* (Helsinki, 1943). See also the careful criticism by Schäfer, *Christologie und Sittlichkeit*, 147–57.

82. Engelland, *Melanchthon, Glauben und Handeln*, 424–33; and, for a much more nuanced view, Schäfer, *Christologie und Sittlichkeit*, 116–57.

83. See the excursus "De duplici usu legis" in *MSA* 5:97.23–98.22.

84. *CR* 21:253–332, esp. 294–96.

85. *MSA* 4:253, note on line 2 (=*Scholia* 1528, 47r°): "Legis duo sunt officia."

86. *MSA* 4:253.27–30 (=*Scholia* 1528, 47v°): "Quoties autem aliqua Moisi lex inciderit tractanda, profuerit docere, quod Deus dederit legem propter has duas causas: ad coercendam carnem et ad terrendum seu humiliandum."

these three reasons: to coerce the flesh and to terrify or humble. The third reason pertains to the righteous, that they may practice obedience."[87] To be sure, the technical terms *officia* and *usus* were not employed.[88] But Melanchthon's intent is clear. Moreover, the verbs used demonstrated an important break between the first two "causae" and the third. Whereas Melanchthon defined the first two in the passive ("cohercendam" and "terrendum seu humiliandum"), implying God's active use of the law on human beings, he shifted the third use to the work of the righteous ("exerceant").

Again the forensic nature of justification, as Melanchthon defined it, played a role here. The believer is declared righteous but is left with a remnant of sin. The law, rather than coming to its true end in the gospel, simply has lost its accusatory voice. Being written in the hearts of all, including believers, that law continues to reveal not only the remnants of sin, but the will of God and the contours of Christian obedience. The conscience, made good by God's gracious declaration, must by necessity use the law to please God. No wonder Melanchthon's theology now needed a third use of the law!

The complexities of this expansion in the law's functions appeared most clearly in Melanchthon's comments on Colossians 3:11 ("ubi non est Graecus et Iudaeus"), a text that already in 1527 he had associated with Christian liberty. By 1528 the six pages of the original comments had been expanded to twelve. In 1534 he rewrote two sections of the comments from 1528, cleverly introducing the third use of the law into his discussion and reaffirming the central role played by the law in Christian freedom.

In 1527 and 1528 Melanchthon had defined three different degrees (*gradus*) of Christian freedom. First, Christian freedom means freedom from sin and, for those who have the Holy Spirit ("who rules and governs hearts"), freedom from the power of the devil.[89] Second, Christian freedom means that Christians are not bound to the civil and ceremonial laws of Moses, and hence are free to follow the law of

---

87. *Scholia* 1534, XLVIII.r°: "Quoties autem aliqua Moisi lex inciderit tractanda, profuerit docere, quod Deus dederit legem propter has tres caussas: ad cohercendam carnem, & ad terrendum seu humiliandum. Tertia ad iustos pertinet, ut exerceant obedientiam."

88. For a discussion of earlier traces of the "tertius usus" see Schäfer, *Christologie und Sittlichkeit*, 116–56. (Schäfer contends that Melanchthon's later use of this term, particularly in the 1543 *Loci*, is basically informative.) True, earlier statements of Melanchthon make it clear that there was in his thought fertile ground for this development. However, Schäfer does not deal with the fact that prior to 1534 Melanchthon simply did not speak of a third use of the law. By looking at events surrounding this shift an explanation for its appearance at this time will become clear.

89. *MSA* 4:287.8–10, 15–16 (=*Scholia* 1528, 87v°): "qui regat et gubernet corda."

their own land.[90] The third level of Christian freedom is to know that human traditions neither condemn nor justify.[91] In this context Melanchthon raised the question whether the Decalog had been abrogated. He divided the law into three parts (judicial, ceremonial, and moral) and argued that only the moral law, that is, the Decalog, applied universally. In 1527 he reviewed all the commandments, showed their general applicability, including their use in the New Testament, and concluded with references to natural law and to the two uses of the law.

In 1528 Melanchthon made several additions to the discussion. For one thing, against Agricola he stressed that the promises of God do not contradict the commands.[92] For another, in a section added to attack the recent peasant rebellion, he insisted on obedience to imperial law as a mark of Christian freedom.[93] Third, he defended his use of the threefold division of law by employing language reminiscent of his defense of the threefold division of *poenitentia*.[94] Fourth, in his most extensive rewriting, which dealt with the question of the Decalog, he stressed (against Andreas Karlstadt and others) the efficacy of non-Mosaic law in civil affairs. He also answered a second question, directed at Agricola, whether the Decalog no longer pertained to us because it was part of the political ordinances of Israel. Not only did he differentiate the Decalog from Mosaic ceremonial and political law, he also stressed much more clearly the way the Decalog reflected natural law, which was no more taken away by the gospel than was the sense of sight or hearing. This law always accuses, unless the accusation is taken away by faith in forgiveness of sins on account of Christ. Although the accusation is taken away, the *notitia* of this natural law remains and teaches the righteous, whose faith is not lazy, who continue to live a corporeal existence, and who are being sanctified by the Holy Spirit.[95] As in 1527, to this discussion Melanchthon appended comments on the law's two uses. Despite Agricola's objections he still applied Galatians

90. *MSA* 4:287.30–288.17 (=*Scholia* 1528, 88r°f.). This section was substantially rewritten in 1528. The main point, however, remained the same and matched the discussion on Col. 2:23.

91. *MSA* 4:288.18–31 (=*Scholia* 1528, 92r°). Melanchthon changed the order of his comments in 1528, inserting the question about the Decalog before discussing this third stage.

92. *Scholia* 1528, 88v°, an addition to *MSA* 4:288.11.

93. *Scholia* 1528, 88v°, an addition to *MSA* 4:288.17.

94. *Scholia* 1528, 89r°, an addition to *MSA* 4:288.33.

95. *Scholia* 1528, 90v°f. This line of argument began to approach the category of the third use of the law and, as Schäfer demonstrated in his analysis of the young Melanchthon, focused on the cognitive side of the law. The Christian knows what pleases God. In 1534 Melanchthon rewrote this very section to make room for a third use of the law.

3:24 as well as 1 Timothy 1:9 to the first use, even justifying his use of the term *pedagogus*.[96]

In 1534 Melanchthon reworked this material to include a new degree of Christian freedom and to discuss a third use of the law. First, he rewrote the introduction.[97] The first degree of Christian freedom remained the same, although Melanchthon now stressed how it made the terrified conscience certain and gave it a "firma consolatio." He also mentioned the gift of the Holy Spirit as part of this first degree.

The second degree was completely new and corresponded to Melanchthon's other additions in the *Scholia* of 1534. The first sentence outlined the now familiar themes:

> The second grade of freedom. Although the Decalog remains—because it pertains to obedience, it is necessary (for as we have often said already, the new life is a kind of obedience to God)—nevertheless here again it must be understood that we have this freedom that this obedience is pleasing, not because we may satisfy the law (for we fall far short of the perfection of the law), but because the person, reconciled by trust in the mercy promised on account of Christ, is pleasing.[98]

The complete absence of this degree in 1528 indicates that Melanchthon himself saw this material as new to his theology and as a crucial part of Christian freedom. In fact, Melanchthon then gathered together the familiar texts from Paul (Col. 2:10a; Rom. 6:14; and Gal. 3:13) that in his mind proved that we are freed from the law's accusation but not from obedience to it. Clearly he had formed a new aspect of this *locus communis* on Christian freedom.

The third degree of Christian freedom became in 1534 what had been in 1527 and 1528 the second degree, namely, that believers are free from the ceremonial and judicial laws of Moses. Similarly, the third degree (the freedom to use human traditions) now became the fourth. To the objections raised by Agricola, which by 1528 had been placed between the second and third degrees, Melanchthon now tacked on a discussion of the third use of the law. He rewrote not only the material describing the first two uses of the law, but also his discussion of the end

---

96. This entire section, *Scholia* 1528, 90v°–92r°, bristled with arguments against Agricola's position. See pp. 164–67.

97. *Scholia* 1534, XC.r°–XCI.r°, substituting for *MSA* 4:287.7–30 and *Scholia* 1528, 88r°.

98. *Scholia* 1534, XC.v°: "Secundus gradus. Etsi manet decalogus, quod ad obedientiam attinet, necesse est enim ut saepe iam diximus, nouam uitam esse quandam obedientiam erga Deum, tamen hic rursus sciendum est nos hanc habere libertatem, quod ea obedientia placeat, non quia legi satisfaciamus, procul enim absumus a perfectione legis, sed quia persona placet reconciliata fiducia misericordiae promissae propter Christum."

of the law's *accusatio* but not its *notitia*. He now tied the law's uses much more clearly to natural law: "However, the Decalog is retained as the summary of the law of nature for three reasons":[99]

The Bible passages for the first use of the Decalog ("on account of the unrighteous, so that they may be coerced") are reduced to one: 1 Timothy 1:9. Galatians 3:24 finally became a proof text for the second use of the law ("on account of the preaching of *poenitentia*"), corresponding to Luther's later interpretation of the verse and Agricola's wishes. Melanchthon's approach to this text, however, made it clear that the law was a "pedagogue" in both its first and second uses. The words "in Christum" allowed him to apply the verse to the law's second use.[100] Melanchthon then discussed a third reason for retaining the Decalog, demonstrating the centrality of the law in his theology:

> The third reason for retaining the Decalog is that obedience is required. For although, as I have said, our weakness is forgiven us (because we do not satisfy the law and in the meantime are pronounced righteous on account of Christ), nonetheless obedience is required, as Christ says [Matt. 19:17], "If you want to walk in life, keep the commandments." Likewise [Matt. 5:20], "Unless your righteousness exceeds that of the Pharisees. . . ." Christ also commands love [John 13:34], which is like the summary of the Decalog.[101]

The law coerces (first use); the law terrifies (second use); the law requires obedience (third use). Again the third use stands apart from the others. Whereas the first two uses actually do something to the individual (coerce or accuse), the third use is relatively passive. The believer "is required" to do something, in this case, obey. Hence the third use of the law depends upon the obedience of the human being; the law is used not by God but by the believer.

---

99. *Scholia* 1534, XCIIII.r°f., an addition to *Scholia* 1528, 90v°–92r°: "Retinetur autem Decalogus, tanquam summa legis naturae, propter tres causas." The rewritten material is shorter than what it replaces.

100. Melanchthon went on to say in *Scholia* 1534, XCIIII.r°f., ". . . lege accusantur & perterrefiunt conscientiae, ut Euangelij beneficium quaerant. . . . Lex est paedagogus, et quidem addit [Paulus] in Christum. Nam & disciplina illa & diligentia cohercendi iniustos, ideo necessaria est, ut doceri homines possint, & assuefieri ad cognoscendum Euangelium. Deinde & hoc nomine Lex paedagogus est, quia perterrefacit conscientias, ut Christum quaerant."

101. *Scholia* 1534, XCIIII.v°: "Tertia caussa est retinendi decalogi, ut requiratur obedientia. Etsi enim ut dixi condonatur nobis imbecillitas nostra, quod legi non satisfacimus & interim iusti pronunciamur propter Christum, tamen obedientia requiritur, sicut Christus ait. Si uis in uitam ingredi, serua mandata. Item nisi abundauerit iusticia uestra supra iusticiam Pharisaeorum &c. Praecipit & Christus dilectionem, quae est quasi summa quaedam decalogi."

To some extent the distinctiveness of the third use of the law arises from justification itself. For the justified, as justified, the law can no longer coerce or threaten. If it did continue to work in this way on the justified, Melanchthon might have been led to the position that *opera moralia* could somehow merit salvation. Thus the third use of the law arose in part to *exclude* human works from salvation. However, Melanchthon had also succeeded in putting legal conditions back into the Christian life. The law, far from coming to an end with justification—justification itself being only an "interim" arrangement—is instead firmly established by the gospel, since both at their heart require obedience. Thus Melanchthon concluded his excursus in 1534, "The divine law, written in the minds of human beings, teach[es] that God must be obeyed; moreover, the gospel requires obedience toward God."[102]

The Reasons for Melanchthon's New Formulations

For what reasons did this shift occur in Melanchthon's theology? As Rolf Schäfer and others have pointed out, Melanchthon's focus on the law and its third use actually had its roots in his earliest published theology. Comments made in earlier editions of the *Scholia* supported his later position: works were called necessary, an antinomian view was rejected, and the law was depicted as requiring obedience. But the very fact that Melanchthon somehow felt constrained to change these earlier comments to reflect even more clearly his developing position suggests that something must have happened in the meantime.

A crucial factor is the memory of Melanchthon's encounter with John Agricola. There is little doubt that Agricola's denigration of the Decalog—itself a reaction to Melanchthon's theology—caused Melanchthon to strengthen his defense of the role of the law in the Christian's life. It was no accident that in 1534 Melanchthon replaced polemic against Agricola's position on the law with a discussion of the necessity of good works and the third use of the law.[103] It was also no accident that anonymous theses that circulated during the early phases of the antinomian controversy from 1537 to 1540, in which Agricola and Luther played leading roles, included an attack against Melanchthon.[104]

Melanchthon stressed good works and law for more immediate causes. Two events in Melanchthon's life in 1534 set the stage for his re-

---

102. *Scholia* 1534, XCIIII.v°: "Lex diuina scripta in ipsis hominum mentibus docens obediendum esse Deo. Requirit autem Euangelium obedientiam erga Deum."

103. The comments in *Scholia* 1534, XCIIII.r°f., replaced material from *Scholia* 1528, 90v°–92r°.

104. *WA* 39.1:342–45. These theses cited the commentary on Romans from 1532 favorably, but criticized the Visitation Articles.

writing of the *Scholia*, provided the language found there, and beyond that illumined the very nature of his theological method. First, early in 1534 Archbishop Albrecht of Mainz, to whom Melanchthon had dedicated his commentary on Romans (for which he received a monetary gift), attempted with the assistance of the elector of Saxony, John Frederick, to restart conversations between the Roman and Lutheran parties that had broken down at Augsburg. Melanchthon and Gregory Brück were sent by the elector to Leipzig, where they held discussions with the archbishop's representatives: Michael Vehe, Christopher Türck, and Julius Pflug, who also represented Duke George of Saxony. They met in Leipzig's Paulinerkloster on 29–30 April 1534.

At the conclusion of the meetings, on the afternoon of 30 April, Melanchthon sent a detailed report to the elector, including a copy of the agreement on, among other things, the doctrine of justification.[105] Written by Vehe, it was agreed to by Melanchthon and Brück with reservations. Justification, the document stated, is a matter of God's grace alone and is not merited by contrition, faith, love, or hope. This "Gotteswerk," whereby God justifies us, results first in faith, through which we believe in God who justifies us and cling to his Word and promise of grace. Through faith God effects love (so that we love righteousness and hate injustice) and hope (so that we trust God's mercy, and the frightened conscience receives comfort). Those who teach in this way can rightly say that faith alone justifies; they exclude all merit and confess that we are justified by grace and mercy alone.

The document then described good works:

> However, one must perform good works commanded by God, not because righteousness is not received freely for Christ's sake, but because God has commanded good works, because righteousness and faith cannot remain without good works, and because it is necessary that the sinful desire in our flesh be put to death through good works so that the renewal of the Spirit may increase.[106]

Here was the very language Melanchthon would use in the *Scholia* of 1534. Good works *must* be done. This necessity is not a requisite for justification, which happens—one can hear the Latin here—"gratis propter Christum"; rather, it derives from faith itself and the righteous-

---

105. The Latin version of the agreement, which Melanchthon sent to Luther, is no longer extant. For the German report to the elector, see *MBW* 1433 (*CR* 2:722–26).

106. *CR* 2:723: "Aber gute Werke von Gott gebothen muß man thun, nicht daß Gerechtigkeit nicht umsonst um Christus willen erlangt werde, sondern darum, daß Gott gute Werke gebothen hat, daß auch Gerechtigkeit und Glaube nicht bleiben kann ohne gute Werke, und ist noth, die sündliche Lust in unserm Fleisch mit guten Werken zu tödten, daß die Verneuerung des Geistes zunehme."

ness it receives. Here, too, the renewal of the Spirit and the death of the flesh are no longer simply ways to speak of justification, but have become part of the life of the justified.

But this meeting was not the only attempt at religious rapprochement during 1534. At nearly the same time, as part of his continuing struggle with Emperor Charles V, Francis I of France was attempting to build an alliance with the German evangelical princes against the emperor.[107] For such an alliance to occur, the prior problem of religious division needed to be addressed. Guillaume du Bellay, brother of the bishop of Paris, Jean du Bellay, was dispatched to Germany, where he established contact with Martin Bucer and Melanchthon through an envoy, Ulrich Geiger, a Strasbourg physician. Du Bellay's conversation with Melanchthon in the summer of 1534 resulted in Melanchthon's composing a theological opinion covering many of the areas of dispute between Wittenberg and Rome.

Melanchthon sent his opinion to du Bellay at the beginning of August 1534.[108] Among the topics covered was, of course, justification. Melanchthon made direct reference to the Leipzig discussion and the agreement reached there.[109] He began by describing, in terms also employed in the *Scholia* of 1534, the Scholastic teachings rejected in Leipzig, namely "that human beings can satisfy the law of God; that they can merit forgiveness of sins by the worthiness of their works; that they are righteous, that is, accepted, on account of their own worthiness and fulfillment of the law."[110]

The agreement with the *Scholia* of 1534 went even further. Melanchthon divided the discussion of justification into two parts, remission of sins and the worth of good works. He stated that for the remission of sins "contrition and a change in behavior are necessary; nevertheless forgiveness does not occur on account of the worthiness of our contrition or works, but only on account of Christ by [God's] mercy, which is

---

107. For this section see *Martin Bucer: Études sur la Correspondance avec de nombreux textes inédits*, ed. J. V. Pollet, 2 vols. (Paris: Presses Universitaires de France, 1962), 2:488–527. Melanchthon's work here is put in its larger context by Georg Elliger, *Philipp Melanchthon: Ein Lebensbild* (Berlin: R. Gaertner, 1902), 303–30. Elliger makes the mistake of equating Melanchthon's interest in reform with his humanistic impulses and his personality. This was only partly the case.

108. *MBW* 1467 (*CR* 2:741–75). See also *MBW* 1468 and 1469, cover letters to Bucer and du Bellay.

109. *CR* 2:747/8.

110. *CR* 2:747/8: ". . . quod homines possint legi Dei satisfacere, quod mereantur remissionem peccatorum dignitate suorum operum, quod sint iusti, id est, accepti propter propriam dignitatem et legis impletionem." Given the use of this same language in additions in the 1534 *Scholia*, Elliger's description (p. 319) of Melanchthon's opinion to du Bellay as "eigentümlich" is inaccurate.

grasped by faith, that is, by faith in Christ."[111] This formulation was followed almost word for word in the *Scholia* of 1534.[112] While good works were not excluded, they clearly were not a certain and sufficient cause for remission of sins.

The second part of Melanchthon's discussion of justification, good works, also paralleled comments in the *Scholia*. He confidently proclaimed that all now concede that "human beings fall far short of the perfection of the law."[113] More importantly, the better theologians among his adversaries also conceded "that human beings are chiefly righteous, that is, accepted, by faith (that is, by trust in the mercy promised on account of Christ), and that that beginning of [fulfilling] the law in us is pleasing not because it satisfies the law, but because the person has been reconciled in Christ."[114] These two themes and the language used to express them call to mind the additions to the *Scholia* in 1534: acceptance by faith, which Melanchthon defines as trust in the mercy promised "propter Christum"; and works pleasing to God not because they satisfy the law, but because the person is reconciled in Christ. In the same place, Melanchthon noted that such an understanding of faith and works was necessary to fortify pious minds against despair, yet another point stressed in the *Scholia*.[115] He also declared that "the righteousness of good works or of a good conscience is necessary."[116] The phrase "the righteousness of a good conscience" and the assertion that such works are necessary occur in the *Scholia* as well.

There were also some differences between the *Scholia* and Melanchthon's opinion sent to du Bellay. In the latter Melanchthon stressed that the Holy Spirit is given in the remission of sins, discussed mortification of the old creature and growth in faith, and even argued that the Holy Spirit does not remain in anyone who has committed a mortal sin. He also went as far as to assert that "free choice" aided by the Holy Spirit is active in guarding against such failings.[117] Even this final reintroduc-

---

111. *CR* 2:747/8f.: ". . . necessaria sit contritio et mutatio morum, et tamen remissionem contingere non propter dignitatem nostrae contritionis seu operum, sed tantum per misericordiam propter Christum, quae fide, hoc est, fiducia Christi apprehenditur."

112. *Scholia* 1534, XVII.rº.

113. *CR* 2:749/50: "homines procul absint a perfectione legis." This language was also used in the *Scholia* 1534; see n. 98.

114. *CR* 2:749/50: ". . . quod homines principaliter iustos, id est, acceptos esse fide, hoc est, fiducia misericordiae promissae propter Christum, et quod illa inchoatio legis in nobis placeat, non quia legi satisfaciat, sed quia persona est reconciliata in Christo."

115. *CR* 2:749/50: "Necesse est enim pias mentes contra desperationem praemuniri, et doceri, quomodo placeat haec nostra obedientia."

116. *CR* 2:749/50: "iustitia bonorum operum seu bonae conscientiae sit necessaria."

117. *CR* 2:749/50: "Item [illa conveniunt,] quod liberum arbitrium aliquid agat in cavendis talibus delictis. Item quod adiuvetur a Spiritu sancto, ut caveat talia delicta."

tion of the "liberum arbitrium" into the doing of good works was not far from the one change made on this point in the 1534 *Scholia:* the human mind hears and does not reject the gospel.

The attempts at alliance with the evangelicals of Germany ended in failure for Francis I and his privy councilor, du Bellay. The Affair of the Placards, the change in popes (Clement VII–Paul III), and the shift in political alliances saw to that.[118] Still, Melanchthon's opinion and its striking agreement with the revisions in the *Scholia* of 1534 elucidate some important aspects of his approach to theology. Georg Elliger and J. V. Pollet alike claim that Melanchthon's flexibility sprang from his humanist training and his relation to Erasmus. Elliger even describes the period of Melanchthon's life after the Diet of Augsburg until Luther's death as filled with such "Friedensbestrebungen," almost as if this were a kind of theological principle from which his opinions and activities arose. From such a position it is only a short distance to the charges of "Leisetreterei (treading softly)" that have been leveled in some analyses of Melanchthon's behavior.[119]

A more fruitful approach to Melanchthon's theology in the 1530s opens when we concentrate on his understanding of theological language itself. Throughout his career Melanchthon sought to use definition, that is, the dialectical question "Quid sit?" and subsequent *finitiones*, as the basis for theology. Proper definitions bring clarity and certainty to a topic. When the topic is theological in nature, such clarity and certainty become the basis for clear and certain faith. Without those attributes the uncertain conscience can never attain to the comfort and consolation of the gospel.

The confessional divisions in Europe, especially in their clarified form after the Diet of Augsburg in 1530, provided a perfect opportunity to use accurate definitions in the service of peace in the church. The process of arriving at such definitions was one of continual development, as theologians used the *loci* provided by the Scriptures to attain greater clarity. This development was, of course, hindered by the devil and sinful humanity; nevertheless, God's work in this world through language and logic and the fundamental clarity of his Word provided assurance that theological clarity was being attained. The mind-numbing regularity with which Melanchthon employed certain definitions at certain times in his life—one thinks of "gratis propter Christum per fidem"—shows how wedded he became to this method.

118. In 1535 Melanchthon was issued an invitation to come to Paris (*MBW* 1550 [*CR* 2:855–59]). This, too, never came to pass.

119. The term itself came from one of Luther's descriptions of Melanchthon's work at the Diet of Augsburg in 1530 and was not necessarily negative.

In this light, Melanchthon's encounters with moderate Romanists at Leipzig and from Paris provided test cases for the method upon which he had based the entire theological enterprise. When, in his opinion to du Bellay, Melanchthon described the Leipzig agreement with phrases such as "concerning many things there is convergence among the learned," "all confess," and "some good and prudent men would agree,"[120] he was not simply patronizing the French, nor was he "treading lightly" as if the theological enterprise meant nothing to him.[121] Instead the theological enterprise as he had defined it all along was at stake. Prudent people had to be able to arrive at clear definitions and thus preserve the comfort and effect of the gospel for the church. Otherwise the gospel itself was in jeopardy.[122]

In the case of justification, Melanchthon arrived at his definitions by way of a careful synthesis, a third way between the theology of merit proposed by the Scholastics—John Eck and the authors of the *Confutatio* among them—and the antinomianism of the likes of John Agricola. To eliminate absolutely every notion of merit from the definition of justification, even that of Augustine, Melanchthon narrowed his metaphors to one, the forensic declaration of forgiveness by God "gratis propter Christum." Now there could be no doubt that we are clothed in a righteousness outside ourselves. No merit and no works are involved; we are justified as a gift. The accusation of the law, which demands our righteousness, comes to an end.

However, this definition left Melanchthon and the Reformers open to the charge of antinomianism or libertinism. The charge that had dogged Lutherans from the beginning—that they had no place in their theology for good works—seemed even harder to defend against when insisting upon forensic justification. So while eliminating human works from God's declaration of righteousness, Melanchthon asserted that the law continues in terms of obedience. Here suddenly law and gospel merge into one command: obedience to God. For the totally disobedient conscience, there is justification "gratis propter Christum" that makes the conscience good. For the good conscience, in which still reside the remnants of sin and whose best works are still impure, there is nevertheless divine acceptation of flawed obedience because the person is in Christ. To inform the good conscience and encourage it to obedience, a third use of the law is necessary.

---

120. *CR* 2:747/48: "de multis iam convenit inter doctos"; "omnes fatentur"; "aliqui boni viri et prudentes colloquerentur." There are other such references as well.

121. His attacks on the Scholastic theologians in the same document proved the opposite.

122. This same assumption motivated his students to develop the Formula of Concord a generation later.

At the same time that forensic justification, as Melanchthon defined it, demands obedience, it also demands that the human being play an increased role in salvation. Because justification is an external declaration to be received in faith, the message itself no longer moves the individual to faith. Instead, the individual must hear *and not reject it*. Faith is much more the action of the individual over against both the promise of grace and the command to obey. Thus Melanchthon could speak about the individual's active participation in the process before and after justification. Melanchthon made these theological moves to hold what he considered a middle ground between a theology of merit, which claims that human beings earn salvation "ex puris naturalibus," and a theological determinism, in which the human being is oblivious to God's saving acts. This middle way led in the 1535 *Loci* to insistence that the Word, the Holy Spirit, and the human will are the three causes of salvation. In all of this, Melanchthon's single-minded concern for proper, clear distinctions and definitions in theology brought him to surprising new formulations.

The Effects of Melanchthon's New Formulations

Reaction to Scholastic theologians and memories of his dispute with Agricola, negotiations with open-minded theologians in Leipzig and opinions written for the French king all combined with Melanchthon's own theological predilection for definition to bring about striking changes in the *Scholia* of 1534. What effect did these new formulations have on his contemporaries? Did anyone notice?

The opinion sent to du Bellay resulted in Melanchthon's being invited to Paris. There was no question, too, that some of the changes in the *Scholia*—one thinks particularly of the third use of the law—were refined by Melanchthon in his second edition of the *Loci* and in turn employed by a young French exile, John Calvin, in the first edition of his *Institutes of the Christian Religion*.[123] Melanchthon's understanding of the relation between justification and good works was also reflected in discussions with the Roman party at Regensburg in 1541.[124]

Perhaps the most notable reaction to Melanchthon's new positions on faith and works arose much closer to home, in the person of Conrad Cordatus (1476?–1546).[125] Cordatus, a student at Wittenberg on

123. *CR* 29:50; perhaps Calvin also had access to Melanchthon's commentary on Colossians.

124. Timothy J. Wengert, "The Day Philip Melanchthon Got Mad," *Lutheran Quarterly*, n.s., 5 (1991): 419–33.

125. For this section see Timothy J. Wengert, "Caspar Cruciger (1504–1548): The Case of the Disappearing Reformer," *Sixteenth Century Journal* 20 (1989): 417–41, and the literature referred to there.

and off from 1523, was pastor in the neighboring town of Niemegk. In 1532 he became the first to record Luther's table talk. He was accustomed to walking to Wittenberg in order to attend the lectures of a variety of theological professors. On 24 July 1536 he attended the lecture of a young professor of theology, Caspar Cruciger, Sr. (1504–48), at which he heard that good works were a "conditio sine qua non" for justification.

On 20 August in a now lost letter, which Cruciger never answered, and again on 8 September Cordatus wrote to Cruciger to complain of the lecture.[126] Cruciger's response on 10 September 1536 pointed out that neither he nor anyone he knew ever said that "we are justified by our works as a *causa sine qua non*," but that instead we are justified by faith, Christ being the "causa propter quam."[127] However, Cruciger continued, saying that we are justified "gratis" includes contrition, which in the one being justified is necessary as a "causa sine qua non." Finding this letter unacceptable, Cordatus wrote a third letter on 17 September and came to Wittenberg the same day in order to meet with Cruciger the next morning at 7 A.M.[128] According to Cordatus's own account of the interview, Cruciger admitted that he was Melanchthon's disciple and that the lectures were Philip's.[129] Although there was most likely something of an exaggeration in Cordatus's account, there can be no doubt that at this juncture Melanchthon, too, was implicated in the matter.

When Cruciger counseled that, before doing anything else, Cordatus should wait for Melanchthon's return to Wittenberg (he was in Tübingen to help with the reform of the university there), Cordatus instead stayed in Wittenberg an extra night and gained an audience with Luther the next day (19 September). According to Cordatus, Luther showed him a letter from Nicholas von Amsdorff that was dated 14 September

126. An excerpt is found in *CR* 3:159. In a portion omitted from the *CR*, but found in the original manuscript, Cod. Guelf. 11.10.Aug.2°, 596v°, Cordatus quoted from his sermon for the fourteenth Sunday after Trinity, 1534 (6 September 1534): "So sie [die papisten] also singen, mus ein Christ auch gute wercke thuon, muß ehr gute wercke thun, so rechtfertigt der glaub nicht allein. Vnd die wercke sind aufs wenigste folgende vrsache der gerechtigkeit, ob sie gleich nicht die erste, vnd neheste Vrsach sindt, darzu sagt ein Christ kurtz [?], Ein Christ mus nicht gute wercke thun, sondern ehr thu williglich gute gute [*sic*] wercke."

127. *CR* 3:159–61.

128. Cordatus's account of the meeting is found in *WABr* 7:541f., with several small omissions.

129. *WABr* 7:541: "Hic homo Creutzigerus, de quo omnes studiosi et universitas tota tantum spei conceperat, quantum de ullo alio, postquam diu negaverat se haec dixisse nec dictasse, sed convictus scriptis et dictatis, respondit se esse D. Philippi discipulum, et dictata omnia esse D. Philippi, se ab eo in illam rem traductum et nescire quo modo."

and that referred to rumors that some were teaching the necessity of works for eternal life.[130] Luther claimed that if it came to a dispute he was ready, and, after looking up the meaning of "sine qua non" in Lombard and Occam, insisted that Melanchthon and Cruciger taught the concept most ineptly.[131]

After this meeting things simmered down for a brief time until, on 12 October 1536, Cordatus lodged an official complaint with Johann Bugenhagen, accusing both Cruciger and Melanchthon in this matter. He followed up with another foray into Wittenberg. On 22 October he heard Luther preach at vespers; on the next day he met with Bugenhagen; at 9 A.M. on the morning of 24 October he met with Luther, who was dean of the theological faculty. At that meeting he showed Luther the offending passages from Cruciger's lectures on 1 Timothy and "in Philip's second question on Colossians."[132] Here is evidence that Colossians was involved and that Melanchthon may have been lecturing on that book during this time. It is clear that the problem of the necessity of good works, which forms the basis of the additions to the *Scholia*, was at the heart of this dispute. Cordatus reported that Luther viewed the teaching of the necessity of good works as "the very theology of Erasmus."[133] He also claimed that Luther vowed to investigate the matter with Melanchthon and to force Cruciger to make a public revocation.[134]

As a result of Cordatus's complaint, Luther, as dean, must have written to Melanchthon on behalf of the theological faculty.[135] When the latter returned to Wittenberg, he immediately wrote a letter answering Cordatus's charges.[136] Melanchthon outlined the very shifts in his understanding of justification that we have discussed in detail. First, he insisted that he never taught anything different from what his colleagues taught. Second, he noted that when he realized that many

---

130. *WABr* 7:539–41.

131. *WABr* 7:542. To the charge that he did not understand the meaning of "sine qua non" Melanchthon responded on 1 November in a letter to the Wittenberg theological faculty—*MBW* 1802 (*CR* 3:179–81; *WABr* 7:579–83).

132. Theodor Kolde, ed., *Analecta Lutherana: Briefe und Aktenstücke zur Geschichte Luthers* (Gotha: Perthes, 1883), 264–66: "in 2 quaest ad Collos. philippi." The dispute may have motivated Luther to read and mark his copy of the 1534 *Scholia*. See Ulrich Bubenheimer, "Unbekannte Luthertexte," *Luther-Jahrbuch* 57 (1990): 220–41.

133. Kolde, *Analecta Lutherana*, 265: "ipsissima Theologia Erasmi."

134. Cruciger never recanted, although the later antinomian controversy proves that Luther was capable of forcing colleagues to do so. Cordatus's difficult personality, noted by many of his contemporaries, including Luther himself, makes all of his accounts questionable. In fact, upon returning home that afternoon, Cordatus wrote a letter asking Luther not to question Melanchthon. See *WABr* 7:568–70.

135. The letter is not extant.

136. *MBW* 1802.

understood justification by faith alone to be an infusion of grace—that is to say, he added, not by faith alone—then, starting in the Apology, he decided to be more clear by speaking of gratuitous imputation. "From this arises, as you know, questions: if we are accepted only by mercy, then to what purpose or how is the new obedience required?"[137] Here we have Melanchthon's own admission that the question of good works arose specifically out of his attempt to clarify the doctrine of justification. He argued that many had incorrect ideas about these matters; accordingly, for the young he took "an approach accommodated to teaching (*via ad docendum accommodata*)" that occasionally included "dialectical terminology (*verba dialectica*)."[138] This was, of course, the heart of Melanchthon's theological method. He insisted that he did not praise works falsely and clearly denied that they merited eternal life. He also added that he was not so stupid as not to know what "sine qua non" meant. This concluded his formal defense.[139]

With this letter the dispute in effect came to an end. When, probably on the basis of this letter, Bugenhagen announced in a sermon preached on 8 November 1536 that the dispute was merely over words, Cordatus defended himself in a letter to Luther.[140] By the time of his next letter to Luther, dated 6 December, he requested nothing more than a hearing on his complaints against Cruciger.[141] A week later, in a letter to Luther that was never sent, Cordatus stated that he would be appealing his case directly to the rector, Justus Jonas, and, should that fail, to the elector himself.[142] In fact, Cordatus did appeal to the rector of the university, who met with him in private on 17 December and insisted that he stop all action against Cruciger and Melanchthon. In a letter to Jonas dated 31 December, a chastened Cordatus agreed to end his

137. *WABr* 7:580.18–20: "Inde oriuntur, ut scitis, quaestiones: si tantum per misericordiam sumus accepti, ad quid igitur aut quo modo requiritur nova obedientia."

138. *WABr* 7:580–81.

139. In the other two paragraphs that make up the letter, Melanchthon expressed his willingness to answer the charges publicly and to follow his colleagues' advice. He also defended himself against the charge that several teachers in Wittenberg's grammar school (*paedagogium*) had been unduly influenced by him. In a letter to von Amsdorff at this time he defended his theological method; see *MBW* 1805 (*CR* 3:181f., where Cordatus is mistakenly listed as the recipient).

140. *WABr* 7:600–602. The extant copy of the letter was dated 3 November. Very likely a "1" dropped out, that is to say, the letter was probably written on 13 November.

141. *WA* 7:606–8. On the same day Cordatus wrote, but did not send, a letter to Melanchthon, accusing him of being the source of the error and threatening to bring a case against him. After defending himself against the charge that he had not followed Matthew 18 in his dispute with Cruciger, Cordatus claimed that this letter fulfilled his obligation vis-à-vis Melanchthon; see *MBW* 1819 (*CR* 3:202–4).

142. *WA* 7:615–16.

attacks on Melanchthon.[143] The dispute with Cruciger stopped altogether when Cordatus took a call to Eisleben to replace John Agricola, and when Luther finally addressed the issue in a public dispute in June 1537. There he agreed with Bugenhagen's earlier sermon that it had been a fight over words, but he also insisted that language like "conditio sine qua non" was not always helpful to the untrained. By this time, however, a more serious dispute was brewing between Agricola and Luther over many of the same issues.[144]

With this mention of the antinomian controversy our analysis has come full circle. What had begun in 1527 and carried over into the *Scholia* of 1528 as a debate over *poenitentia*, now reemerged as a full-blown dispute over the nature and benefits of the law. When Agricola arrived in 1537, he inherited some discontented students who, like Cordatus, saw the gospel itself being swallowed up by the law in the teaching of some of the university's theologians. Agricola's sermons caused immediate hostility among some in Luther's inner circle, who had already been put on the defensive by Cordatus's charges. Luther, whose moderate temperament was always inclined to defend his friends, now took the lead in defining the work of the law within the life of the Christian. Differences between his and Melanchthon's solutions to this dilemma would cause their theological heirs a host of divisions over justification, good works, and the uses of the law. At this time, however, they were still united in opposition to Roman legalism and evangelical antinomianism.

---

143. *CR* 3:206–8. In a letter to Melanchthon on 14 April 1537, Cordatus repeated his intention of attacking only Cruciger; see *MBW* 1887 (*CR* 3:341f.). Cordatus tried to convince Melanchthon not to take on his controversy with Cruciger and refused to meet with Melanchthon as long as he was still angry. Melanchthon's response (*MBW* 1889 [*CR* 3:342–46]) continued to insist that he would take the case on himself. Cordatus's glosses on this letter have been preserved in Cod. Guelf. 11.10.Aug.2°, 620r°–22r°.

144. See Greschat, *Melanchthon neben Luther*, 217–42, for a closer description of Melanchthon's part in the controversy. Cruciger received an anonymous threatening letter at this time; see *CR* 3:387. He had actually hoped that Luther would respond to this issue in the Smalcald Articles, of which he was a copyist; see Richard Wetzel, "Caspar Cruciger als ein Schreiber der 'Schmalkaldischen Artikel,'" *Luther-Jahrbuch* 54 (1987): 84–93.

Appendix 1

The Exegetical Works of John Agricola

1. Annotations on the Gospel of Luke

A$_1$. "IN EVAN | GELIVM LVCAE ANNO= | TATIONES IOANNIS | AGRICO-LAE ISLE= | BII. SVMMA SCRI= | PTVRARVM | FIDE TRA= | CTA= | TAE. | [Three dots] | MDXXV." Woodcut, 8°. Colophon: "Auguste Vindelecorum, per Simpertum Ruff. | Anno. XXV. Mense Aprili." 182 + [2 unnumbered] leaves.

A$_2$. "IN EVAN= | GELIVM LVCAE ANNOTA | tiones Ioannis agricolae Islebij, sum | ma scripturarum fide | tractae. | [Petreius's seal] | Norembergae apud Ioan. Petreium. | M.D.XXV." No woodcut, 8°. Colophon: "NOREMBERGAE APVD IOAN | NEM PETREIVM EXCV= | DEBATVR ANNO DO= | MINI M.D.XXV. | MENSE IVLII."

a. "Wie man die Heilig ge- | schrifft lesen/ vnd wess man in der lesung | der Euangelischen histori acht haben/ | Was man darinn ersuchen vnd | forschen soll/ Ain kurtze vnd | Schöne Bericht. | Johannis Agricole Eyßlebenn | zu Wittenberg. | Johannis am 5. | Suochet in der Schrifft/ dann Ir | mainet/ jr habt das leben darinn/ | vnnd Sy ists/ die von mir zeüget. | M.D.XXVI." No woodcut, 4°. Colophon: "Getruckt zuo Augspurg/ durch | Silvann Ottmar/ im jar/ | M.D.XXVI." [13 unnumbered] (+ 1 blank) leaves. This excerpt follows the first edition of 1525.

B. "IN EVAN | GELIVM LVCAE ANNO | tationes Ioannis Agricolae Isle= | bii, iam per autorem ipsum | & locupletatae & | recognitae. | [design] | M.D.XXVI. | HAGENOAE." Woodcut, 8°. Colophon: "Haganae Per Amandum | Farcallium Anno. | M.D.XXVI."

C. "IN LV= | CAE EVANGELIVM, | Adnotationes Iohannis Agri | colae Islebij, bona fide Scri | pturarum tractatae, & | nuper per authorem ip= | sum recognitae ac | restitutae. | Haganoae, per Iohan. Sec. | An. M.D.XXIX." Woodcut, 8°. Colophon: "Haganoae, in aedibus Iohannis Secerij. | Anno M.D.XXIX. | Mense Maio." 225 + [8] leaves.

2. Sermons on Colossians

A$_1$. "Die Epistel an die | Colosser/ S. Pauls/ Zu | Speier gepredigt auff | dem reychstage/ D. Martinum Lu= | ther vbersehen. | Wittemberg | 1527." Woodcut, 8°. Colophon: "Gedrückt Zu Wit= | temberg durch | Simphorian | Reinhart. | Anno. M.D.XXVii." [135] (+ 1 blank) leaves.

A₂. "Die Epistel an I die Colosser/ S. Pauls/ I zuo Speier gepredigt I auff dem Reychs= I tage/ von Joann I Agricola Eyß= I leben. I Durch Doctor Martinum I Luther übersehen. I Wittemberg. I 1527." Woodcut, 8°. No colophon [Augsburg: Philip Ulhart, Sr.]. [151] (+ 1 blank) leaves.

A₃. "Von der Messe vnd I ihrem Canone Magistri Johan= I nis Agricolae Eysleben/ Lhere I vnd schrifft/ Welche er auff dem I Reichstag zu Speyer in der Epistel zu den Collossern I geprediget/ vnd folgend Anno M.D.XXVII. I zu Wittenbergk im Druck offentlich hat I ausgehen lassen/ Dem Interim so er ytzt I hat helffen stellen/ gantz entgegen/ I Daraus sein geyst zuuer= I mercken. I Psalm. cxlj. I HErr behüte meinen mund/ vnd beware meyne lip= I pen/ Neige mein hertz nicht auff etwas böses/ ein I Gottloß wesen zufüren mit den vbelthe= I tern/ Das ich nicht esse/ von dem I das ihnen geliebet. I Hiero. super Esaiam. I Non sic adulandum est Principibus, ut I Sanctarum scripturarum ueritas negligatur." No woodcut, 4°. No colophon [probably printed in Magdeburg]. An excerpt of A₁ or A₂.

3. Scholia on Titus

A. "IN EPIS= I TOLAM PAVLI I AD TITVM I Scholia. I IOAN. AGRICOLA I Islebio Autore. I PHIL. MEL. I οὐδὲκε δαιδάλεος τ[ὸν] Χριστὸν γράψαι I Ἀπελλῆς, I Ἔνθεος ὡς Παῦλος τῷ δ᾽ ἐχάραξε I λόγῳ. I I. K. I Non sic Daedaleus Christum pinxisset Apelles, I Vt sacer hunc Paulus exprimit ore pio." Woodcut, 8°. Colophon: "Vvitebergae apud Georgium I Rhau. M.D.XXX." [68] leaves.

4. Translation of Melanchthon's *Annotations on Romans and 1 and 2 Corinthians*

A. "Auslegung I der Episteln S. I Pauls/ eine an die Rö= I mer vnd zwo an die Co= I rinther/ Philippi Melan= I chthons/ gedeudscht. I Wittemberg. I 1.5.2.7." Woodcut with the initials I. K., 8°. Colophon: "Gedrückt durch Joseph Klug. I zu Wittemberg. Anno. I 1.5.27." 302 + [28] leaves. The prefatory letter of Agricola to Wilhelm Rincken, a coworker in Eisleben, is dated "am tage Fabiani vnd Sebastiani [= January 20] Im M D vnd XXVii."

Appendix 2

Early Catechisms (Additions to the Work of Ferdinand Cohrs)

The roman numerals in the following list reflect Cohrs. The letters for individual editions supplement Cohrs's lists. Those booklets not found in Cohrs are placed at the end and assigned arabic numbers in quotation marks.

XIII. "Eyn buchlin fur die leyen vnd die kinder"
   1. Low German Editions
      g. "Eyn Bö= | keschen vor de | leyen vñ kinder. | De teyn Bade Gades | De löue mitt eyner vth | leggynge. | Dat benedicite vñ gratias | Van der Döpe. | Van demn Sacramente | Van der Bycht. | De duodesche tal mit den | cifern. | Dat titell bökeschenn. | Wittemberch. | 1526." Woodcut, 8°. No colophon [Erfurt: Loorsfeld]. [23] (+ 1 blank) leaves. HAB call no. QuH 169.4 (1); *VD* 16: B 6330.
      h. = *VD* 16: B 6334.
      i. = *VD* 16: B 6337.
      j. = *VD* 16: B 6338
   3. High German Editions
      F. "Eyn buchlin fur | die leyen vnd | kinder. | Wittemberg. | MDXXV." Woodcut, 8°. No colophon [Wittenberg: Nicholas Schirlentz]. HAB call no. QuH 132.7 (5).
   [4. Excerpts]
      2. = B 9113.
XVI. John Agricola's "Elementa pietatis congesta: Christliche Kinderzucht"
   2. German Editions
      A*. = *VD* 16: A 976.
      Cohrs C and E were both printed in Augsburg by Philip Ulhart, Sr.
      F. "Eyn Christliche | Kinderzucht/ in Got= | tes wort vnd lere. | Ausz der Schuol zuo | Eiszleben. | M.D.XXviij." Woodcut, 8°. No colophon. [50] leaves. *VD* 16: A 978.
XX. Philip Melanchthon's "Sprüche"
   2. Low German Editions
      e. "Etlike spro | ke dar jnne dat gan= | tze Christlyke leuent | geuatet ys/ nutlick alle= | wege vor ogen tho heb | bende vnde tho be= | trachtende. | Philippus Mela[n]chthon | M.D.XXvij." Woodcut, 8°. Col-

ophon: "Gedrücket dorch Ludwich Dietz I des 14. dages Februarij." [Rostock or Lübeck.] [12] leaves.

XXI. John Agricola's "Hundertdreißig gemeine Fragestücke"
    2. "Der Hundertsechsundfünfzig Fragestücke"
        I. = *VD* 16: A 990. Colophon: "Gedruckt zu Er= I ffurd durch Melchior Sach- I ssen/ ynn der Archa I Noe."

XXXVII. Martin Luther's "Fünf Fragen vom Abendmahl"
Under this title Cohrs mentions a few examples of a catechism that could have been included in its own right.
    B*. This is a slightly different printing of the volume listed in Cohrs 4:155. "Eyn trostlich I gesprech büchleyn auff I frag vnd antwort gestellet/ I den glauben vnd die lieb be I treffent/ Vnd wie eyner den I andern Christlich vnter= I weysen sol/ gantz nütz I lich zu den artickeln I D. Vrbani Regij I vnd Gretzin I gers. I Wittemberg. I 1525." Woodcut, 8°. No colophon [Wittenberg: Johann Rhau-Grünenberg]. [48] leaves. HAB call no. 1174.8 Th (4).

The following editions are not listed by Cohrs and do not contain Luther's "Five Questions."

    1. High German First Edition (with call numbers from Munich's Staatsbibliothek)
        a. Nuremberg: Jobst Gutknecht, 1524. SB Mün Katech 269.
        b. Nuremberg: J. Gutknecht, 1525. SB Mün Katech 563.
        c. Leipzig: Nikkel Schmitt, 1525. UB Mün 8° Theol 5216.

    2. High German Second Edition (the edition to which Luther's "Five Questions" was later added)
        a. "Ein trostliche di= I sputation/ auff frag vnd I antwort gestellet/ Von I zwayen Handtwercks I mennern/ den Glauben/ I vñ die lieb/ auch andere I Christliche leer betref= I fen/ auch form wie einer I den andern Christenlich I vnderweysen sol/ gantz I nützlich zu den artickeln I Doctoris Vrbani Regij I vnd Gretzingers. I New corrigiert vnd gemert. I 1525." Woodcut, 8°. No colophon [Nuremberg: Jobst Gutknecht]. [60] leaves. HAB call no. Yv 589 Helmst. 8° (3).
        b. "Eyn tröstlich I gesprech büchleyn I auff frag vnd ant= I wort gestellet/ den glauben I vnd die lieb betreffent/ Vnd I wie eyner den andern Chri I stlich vnterweysen soll/ I gantz nützlich zu den I artickeln D. I Vrbani I Regii vnd I Gretzingers. I Wittemberg." Woodcut, 8°. No colophon [Wittenberg: Joseph Klug, 1525 (the date is handwritten at the end of the HAB copy)]. [44] leaves. HAB call no. QuH 169.15 (2).
        c. "Eyn trostliche I Disputation/ auff I frag vnd antwort I gestellet/ den glauben I vñ die lieb betreffent/ I Vñ wie eyner den an= I dern Christlich vnterwey I sen soll/ gantz nützlich tzu I den Artickel D. Vrbani I Regij vnd Gretzin= I gers. I 1525." Woodcut, 8°. Colophon: "1525" [Leipzig: Nikkel Schmidt]. [48] leaves. HAB call no. J 149 Helmst. 8° (2).
        d. HAB call no. 1163.6 Th 8°. The title page is missing. Colophon: "1525" [Leipzig: Jakob Thanner]. 47 (+ 1 blank) leaves.

e. "Eynn trostli= | che Disputation/ | auff frag vnnd ant= | wort gestel-let/ den glauben | vnd die lieb Betreffent. Vñ | wie einer den andern christ | lich vnterweysen sol/ gantz | nuotzlich zu den Artickel D. | Vrbani Regij vñ | Gretzingers. | .1525." Woodcut, 8°. No colophon [Leipzig: Michael Blum]. [43] (+ 1 blank) leaves. HAB call no. Yv 991 Helmst. 8°.

f. Augsburg: H. Steiner, 1526 = SB Mün Katech 563a.

3. Low German Translation of the High German Second Edition

a. "Eyne trostlicke | disputation vp fra= | gen vnd antwort gestel= | let/ den gelouen vnd leve | bedrepende/ vñ wo eyner | den anderen Christlick | vnderwysen schal/ gantz | nütte tho den artikeln D. Vr-bani Regij vnd | Gretzingers. | 1525." Woodcut, 8°. No colophon [Wittenberg: Nicholas Schirlentz]. [82] leaves. HAB call no. QuH 161.18 (2).

b. "Eine trostlike | disputatio/ vp frage | vnde antwort gestel= | let/ den gelouen vnde leue | Belangende vnde wo de ene | den anderen Christlick vn= | derwysen schal/ gans nüt= | lick den artikelen D. Vr= | bani Regij/ vnde | Gretzingers | .1525." Woodcut, 8°. Colophon: "Gedrücket to Lypsick dorch Mychel Blömen." [45] (+ 3 blank) leaves. HAB call nos. Ts 175 (2) and QuH 132.7 (2).

4. High German Third Edition: see Cohrs, "C."

5. Low German Second Edition

a. "Eyne tröstlyke dispu | tatio/ vp frage vnde ant= | wort gestellet/ den gelouen | vnde leue belangende/ vnde | wo de ene den anderen Christ= | lyck vnderwysen schal/ gans | nütlyck tho den artikelen | D. Vrbani Regij/ vnde | Gretzingers. | Tho dem anderen male auerge-seen." Woodcut, 8°. Colophon: "Gedrücket tho Wyttem= | berch dorch Hans Barth | M.D.xxv." [47] (+ 1 blank) leaves. HAB call no. J 238 Helmst. 8° (2).

b. "Eyne tröstlike | disputatio/ vp frage vn | de antwort gestellet/ den | gelouen vnde leue belan= | gende/ vnde wo de eyne | den anderen Christlick vn= | derwysen schal/ gans nüt= | lyck tho den Artikelen | D. Vrbani Regij/ | vnde Gretzin= | gers. | [design] | Tho dem anderen mal auergeseen." Woodcut, 8°. Colophon: "Gedrucket tho Wittem= | berg dorch Hans Barth yn dem | iär dusent vyffhundert se= | uen vnde twyndich etc." [44] leaves. HAB call nos. J 611 Helmst. 8° and 918.14 Th. (2).

c. "Eine tröstlike | disputatio/ vp frage vn= | de antwort gestellet/ den | gelouen vnde leue belan= | gende/ vnde wo de eine den an= | deren Christlick vnderwisen | schal/ gantz nüttlick tho | den Artikelen D. Vr= | bani Regij/ vnde | Gretzingers. | [design] | MDXXVIII." Woodcut, 8°. No colophon [Magdeburg: Hans Barth]. [47] (+ 1 blank) leaves. HAB call nos. TS 170 (2) and J 151 Helmst. 8° (3).

"1". George Rauth's "Die Siebzehn Hauptartikeln der ganzen Schrift"

A. "Die Siebenze= | hen heupt Arti= | ckel/ der gantz= | en schrifft/ die do ey= | nem Christlichen | menschen | Seher | tröstlich zu wissen sind. | Georgius Raut. | Wittemberg. M.D.xxv." Woodcut, 8°. No colophon

[Wittenberg: Joseph Klug]. [39] (+ 1 blank) leaves. HAB call no. Ts 176 (2); *VD* 16: R 427.

B. "Die Sieben | zehen hewbtartickel/ der | gantzen schrifft/ die | einem Christli= | chen menschen | seher tröst= | lich | zu wissen sind. | Georgius Raut. | Wittemberg. | 1525." Woodcut, 8°. No colophon except "Ubersehen durch | Steph. Rodt." [Wittenberg: Johann Rhau-Grunenberg.] HAB call no. S 149b Helmst. 8° (5); *VD* 16: R 428.

C. "Die siebentze | hen hawbt Artickel/ der gan= | tzen schrifft/ die eynem Christ | lichen menschen seer | tröstlich zu wiss= | en sind. | New corrigirt | durch Stephanum Rodt | Wittemberg | .1525." Woodcut, 8°. No colophon [Leipzig: Michael Blum]. HAB call no. J 41 Helmst. 8° (14); *VD* 16: R 426.

D. "Die Sybenze= | hen Haubt arti= | ckel der gantzen schrifft/ | aym yeden Christ | lichenn men= | schenn seer | tröstlich | zuo wis | sen. | Georgius Raut zuo Tresen. | M.D.XXVI." Woodcut, 8°. No colophon [Augsburg: Simprecht Ruff]. 37 + [4] (+ 1 blank) leaves. *VD* 16: R 427.

"2". For Urbanus Rhegius's "Eine Erklärung der Zwölf Artikel," see *VD* 16: R 2024–56.

"3". For Benedict Gretzinger's "Ein unüberwindlich Beschirmbüchlein von Hauptartikeln . . . der göttlichen Lehre," see *VD* 16: G 3248–68.

Appendix 3

The Printing History of the Latin Version of Philip Melanchthon's Visitation Articles

A$_1$. "ARTI= I CVLI DE QVIBVS I EGERVNT PER VISI= I tatores in regiones Saxoniae. I Wittembergae I 1527." Woodcut with "N S" in shield, 8°. Colophon: "Excusum Wittembergae, per I Nicolaum Schirlentz. I Anno. I 1227 [*sic*]." [19] (+ 1 blank) leaves.

A$_2$. "ARTI= I CVLI DE QVIBVS I EGERVNT PER I VISITATORES I in regione Saxo= I niae. I Wittem bergae I 1527." Woodcut same as A$_1$, 8°. Colophon: "Excusum VVittembergae, per I Nicolaum Schirlentz I Anno. I 1527." [16] leaves. Clearly an improved version of A$_1$.

A$_3$. "ARTICV= I LI, DE QVIBVS EGE I runt Visitatores in re= I gione Saxoniae. I Anno, M.D.XXVII." No woodcut, 8°. Colophon: "1527." [23] (+ 1 blank) leaves. Text based on A$_1$, but lacking the prayer after Amen (cf. *CR* 26:28). Published in Basel by Johannes Froben.

A$_4$. "ARTI= I CVLI DE QVI= I BVS EGERVNT I PER VISITA I tores in regione Saxoniae." Woodcut, 8°. No colophon. [18] leaves, with the following printer's numbers: [], A2, [], [], A5, [], [], [], B, B2, [], [], B9, [], [], [], [], []. The initials and woodcut seem to indicate a Dutch provenance for this printing: Antwerp, Deventer, or Zwolle, probably 1527 or 1528.

B$_1$. "ADVERSVS I ANABAPTISTAS PHILIPPI ME= I lanchthonis Iudicium. I ITEM I An Magistratus iure poßit occidere Anabaptistas, I Iohannis Brentij Sententia. I ITEM I Articuli, inspectionis Ecclesiarum I Saxoniae, emendati." No woodcut, 8°. [68] leaves. Identified by Josef Benzing, *Bibliographia Haguenovienne* (Baden-Baden: Koerner, 1973), 81, no. 91, as Haguenau: Johannes Setzer, 1528. Cf. Walter Köhler, *Bibliographia Brentiana* (Berlin: Schwetschke and Son, 1904), 305, no. 645.

Bibliography

Primary Sources

Aquila, Caspar. "Wider den spöttischen Lügner vnd vnverschempten verleumbder D. Eßlebium Agricolam. Nötige verantwortung/ vnd Ernstliche warnung/ Wider das Interim. APOLOGIA M. CASPARIS AQVILAE Bischoff zu Salfeldt. M.D.XLVIII." Magdeburg, 1548.

Die Bekenntnisschriften der evangelisch-lutherischen Kirche. 10th ed. Göttingen: Vandenhoeck and Ruprecht, 1986.

Bucer, Martin. *Martin Bucer: Études sur la Correspondance avec de nombreux textes inédits.* Edited by J. V. Pollet. 2 vols. Paris: Presses Universitaires de France, 1962.

Buchwald, Georg. "Lutherana: Notizen aus Rechnungsbüchern des Thüringischen Staatsarchivs zu Weimar." *ARG* 25 (1928): 1–98.

Bugenhagen, Johann. *Annotationes . . . in Epistolas Pauli, ad Galatas, Ephesios, Philippenses, Colossenses, Thessalonicenses primam & secundam, Timotheum primam & secundam, Titum, Philemonem, Hebraeas.* 2d ed. Basel: Adam Petri, 1525.

———. *Dr. Johannes Bugenhagens Briefwechsel.* Edited by Otto Vogt. Hildesheim, 1966 reprint.

Cohrs, Ferdinand. *Die evangelischen Katechismusversuche vor Luthers Enchiridion.* Vol. 1: *Die evangelischen Katechismusversuche aus den Jahren 1522–1526.* Vol. 2: *Die evangelischen Katechismusversuche aus den Jahren 1527–1528.* Vol. 3: *Die evangelischen Katechismusversuche aus den Jahren 1528–1529.* Vol. 4: *Undatierbare Katechismusversuche und zusammenfassende Darstellung.* Berlin: A. Hofmann, 1900–1902.

Förstemann, Karl Eduard, ed. *Album Academiae Vitebergensis.* 2 vols. Leipzig, 1841.

———. *Neues Urkundenbuch zur Geschichte der evangelischen Kirchen-Reformation.* Hamburg, 1842.

Grimm, Jacob, and Wilhelm Grimm, eds. *Deutsches Wörterbuch.* Leipzig, 1873.

Handbuch zur Kinder- und Jugendliteratur. Edited by Theodor Brüggemann with Hans-Heino Ewers. 2 vols. Stuttgart: J. B. Metzler, 1982, 1987.

Jonas, Justus. *Der Briefwechsel des Justus Jonas.* Edited by Gustav Kawerau. 2 vols. Halle: O. Hendel, 1884.

Kolde, Theodor, ed. *Analecta Lutherana: Briefe und Aktenstücke zur Geschichte Luthers.* Gotha: Perthes, 1883.

Luther, Martin. *Luthers Werke. Kritische Gesamtausgabe.* [*Schriften.*] 65 vols. Weimar: H. Böhlau, 1883–1993.

―――. *Luthers Werke. Kritische Gesamtausgabe. Bibel.* 12 vols. Weimar: H. Böhlau, 1906–61.

―――. *Luthers Werke. Kritische Gesamtausgabe. Briefwechsel.* 18 vols. Weimar: H. Böhlau, 1930–85.

―――. *Luthers Werke. Kritische Gesamtausgabe. Tischreden.* 6 vols. Weimar: H. Böhlau, 1912–21.

―――. *Martin Luther: Briefwechsel.* Edited by Ernst Ludwig Enders. 19 vols. Frankfurt and Leipzig, 1884–1932.

―――. *Martin Luther: Studienausgabe.* 5 vols. to date. Berlin: Evangelische Verlagsanstalt, 1979–.

Melanchthon, Philip. *Annotationes . . . in Epistolam Pauli ad Romanos unam. Et ad Corinthios duas.* 2d ed. Strasbourg: J. Herwagen, 1523.

―――. *Annotationes, oder Anzeygung . . . über die Andern Epistel S. Pauli zuo den Corinthiern verteütscht.* Nuremberg: H. Hergot, 1524.

―――. *Auslegung der Episteln S. Pauls eine an die Römer vnd zwo an die Corinther . . . gedeudscht.* Translated by J. Agricola. Wittenberg: J. Klug, 1527.

―――. *Corpus Reformatorum. Philippi Melanthonis opera quae supersunt omnia.* Edited by Karl Bretschneider and Heinrich Bindseil. 28 vols. Halle: A. Schwetschke and Sons, 1834–60.

―――. *Melanchthons Briefwechsel: Kritische und kommentierte Gesamtausgabe.* Edited by Heinz Scheible. 10 vols. to date. Stuttgart–Bad Cannstatt: Frommann-Holzboog, 1977–.

―――. *Melanchthons Werke in Auswahl.* [*Studienausgabe.*] Edited by Robert Stupperich. 7 vols. Gütersloh: Gerd Mohn, 1951–75.

―――. *Philippi Melanchthonis epistolae, iudicia, consilia, testimonia aliorumque ad eum epistolae quae in corpore reformatorum desiderantur.* Edited by Heinrich Bindseil. Halle: Gustav Schwetschke, 1874.

―――. *Supplementa Melanchthoniana.* 4 vols. Leipzig: Rudolf Haupt, 1910–26.

―――. *Der unbekannte Melanchthon: Wirken und Denken des Praeceptor Germaniae in neuer Sicht.* Edited by Robert Stupperich. Stuttgart: Kohlhammer, 1961.

Müller, Joseph, ed. *Die Deutschen Katechismen der Böhmischen Brüder.* Berlin: A. Hofmann, 1887.

Novum Testamentum Latine. Edited by Eberhard Nestle. 11th edition. Stuttgart: Württembergische Bibelanstalt, 1971.

Reu, John Michael. *Quellen zur Geschichte des kirchlichen Unterrichts in der evangelischen Kirche Deutschlands zwischen 1530 und 1600.* 4 vols. in 9. Gütersloh: C. Bertelsmann, 1904–35.

Rhau, Georg, ed. *HORTVLVS ANIMAE. Lustgarten der Seelen: Mit schönen lieblichen Figuren.* Wittenberg: Georg Rhau, 1548.

Roth, Stephen. "Stadtschreiber M. Stephan Roth in Zwickau in seiner literarisch-buchhändlerischen Bedeutung für die Reformationszeit." Edited by Georg Buchwald. *Archiv für Geschichte des deutschen Buchhandels* 16 (1893): 6–246. Reprinted as *Zur Wittenberger Stadt- und Universitäts-Geschichte in der Reformationszeit: Briefe aus Wittenberg an M. Stephan Roth in Zwickau.* Edited by Georg Buchwald. Leipzig: G. Wigand, 1893.

Sehling, Emil, ed. *Die evangelischen Kirchenordnungen des XVI. Jahrhunderts.* Aalen: Scientia, 1979 reprint.

Seidemann, J. K. "Schriftstücke zur Reformationsgeschichte." *Zeitschrift für die historische Theologie* 44 (1874): 116f.

Verzeichnis der im deutschen Sprachbereich erschienenen Drucke des XVI. Jahrhunderts. 19 vols. to date. Stuttgart: Anton Hiersemann, 1983–.

Secondary Sources

Bagchi, David V. N. *Luther's Earliest Opponents: Catholic Controversialists 1518–1525.* Minneapolis: Fortress, 1991.

Barton, Peter F. "Die exegetische Arbeit des jungen Melanchthon 1518/19 bis 1528/29: Probleme und Ansätze." *ARG* 54 (1963): 52–89.

Biundo, Georg. *Kaspar Aquila: Ein Kämpfer für das Evangelium in der Pfalz, in Sachsen und Thüringen.* Grünstadt/Pfalz: Verein für Pfälzische Kirchengeschichte, 1963.

Brecht, Martin. *Martin Luther.* 3 vols. Translated by James Schaaf. Minneapolis: Fortress, 1985–93.

Bring, Ragnar. *Gesetz und Evangelium und der dritte Gebrauch des Gesetzes in der lutherischen Theologie.* Helsinki, 1943.

Bubenheimer, Ulrich. "Unbekannte Luthertexte." *Luther-Jahrbuch* 57 (1990): 220–41.

Ebeling, Gerhard. *Luther: An Introduction to His Thought.* Philadelphia: Fortress, 1970.

Edwards, Mark. *Luther and the False Brethren.* Stanford, Calif.: Stanford University Press, 1975.

Elert, Werner. "Eine theologische Fälschung zur Lehre vom tertius usus legis." *Zeitschrift für Religions- und Geistesgeschichte* 1 (1948): 168–70.

Elliger, Georg. *Philipp Melanchthon: Ein Lebensbild.* Berlin: R. Gaertner, 1902.

Engelland, Hans. *Melanchthon, Glauben und Handeln.* Munich: Kaiser, 1931.

Forde, Gerhard O. *The Law-Gospel Debate.* Minneapolis: Augsburg, 1969.

Fraenkel, Peter. *Testimonia Patrum: The Function of the Patristic Argument in the Theology of Philip Melanchthon.* Geneva: Librairie Droz, 1961.

Geyer, Hans-Georg. *Von der Geburt des wahren Menschen.* Neukirchen-Vluyn: Neukirchener Verlag des Erziehungsvereins, 1965.

Grane, Leif. *Modus loquendi theologicus: Luthers Kampf um die Erneuerung der Theologie (1515–1518).* Leiden: E. J. Brill, 1975.

Green, Lowell. *How Melanchthon Helped Luther Discover the Gospel.* Fallbrook, Calif.: Verdict, 1980.

Greschat, Martin. *Melanchthon neben Luther: Studien zur Gestalt der Rechtfertigungslehre zwischen 1528 und 1537.* Witten: Luther, 1965.

Hammann, Gustav. "Nomismus und Antinomismus innerhalb der wittenberger Theologie von 1524–1530." Ph.D. diss., Friedrich Wilhelms Universität, 1952.

Hartfelder, Karl. *Philipp Melanchthon als Praeceptor Germaniae.* Berlin: A. Hofmann, 1889.

Hausammann, Susi. *Buße als Umkehr und Erneuerung von Mensch und Gesellschaft*. Zurich: Theologischer Verlag, 1974.

Hendrix, Scott. *Luther and the Papacy: Stages in a Reformation Conflict*. Philadelphia: Fortress, 1981.

Holl, Karl. "Die Rechtfertigungslehre in Luthers Vorlesung über den Römerbrief mit besonderer Rücksicht auf die Frage der Heilsgewißheit." In *Gesammelte Aufsätze zur Kirchengeschichte*, 1:124–29. 3d ed. 3 vols. Tübingen: J. C. B. Mohr/Paul Siebeck, 1923.

Joest, Wilfried. *Gesetz und Freiheit: Das Problem des tertius usus legis bei Luther und die neutestamentliche Parainese*. Göttingen: Vandenhoeck and Ruprecht, 1951.

Junghans, Helmar. *Der junge Luther und die Humanisten*. Göttingen: Vandenhoeck and Ruprecht, 1985.

Kawerau, Gustav. *Johann Agricola von Eisleben: Ein Beitrag zur Reformationsgeschichte*. Berlin: Wilhelm Hertz, 1881.

Kjeldgaard-Pedersen, Steffen. *Gesetz, Evangelium und Buße: Theologiegeschichtliche Studien zum Verhältnis zwischen dem jungen Johann Agricola (Eisleben) und Martin Luther*. Leiden: E. J. Brill, 1983.

Koch, Ernst. "Johann Agricola neben Luther: Schülerschaft und theologische Eigenart." In *Lutheriana: Zum 500. Geburtstag Martin Luthers von den Mitarbeitern der Weimarische Ausgabe*, edited by Gerhard Hammer and Karl-Heinz zur Mühlen, 131–50. Cologne and Vienna: Böhlau, 1984.

Koehn, Horst. "Philip Melanchthons Reden: Verzeichnis der im 16. Jahrhundert erschienenen Drucke." *Archiv für Geschichte des Buchwesens* 25 (1984): 1277–1495.

Kolb, Robert. *Confessing the Faith: Reformers Define the Church, 1530–1580*. St. Louis: Concordia, 1991.

———. "Historical Background of the Formula of Concord." In *A Contemporary Look at the Formula of Concord*, edited by Robert Preus and Wilbert Rosin, 12–87. St. Louis: Concordia, 1978.

———. "Philipp's Foes, but Followers Nonetheless: Late Humanism among the Gnesio-Lutherans." In *The Harvest of Humanism in Central Europe*, edited by Manfred P. Fleischer, 159–77. St. Louis: Concordia, 1992.

Krumwiede, Hans-Walter. *Zur Entstehung des landesherrlichen Kirchenregiments in Kursachsen und in Braunschweig-Wolfenbüttel*. Göttingen: Vandenhoeck and Ruprecht, 1967.

McGrath, Alister. *Luther's Theology of the Cross*. New York: Blackwell, 1985.

Manschreck, Clyde. *Melanchthon: The Quiet Reformer*. New York and Nashville: Abingdon, 1958.

Maurer, Wilhelm. *Der junge Melanchthon zwischen Humanismus und Reformation*. 2 vols. Göttingen: Vandenhoeck and Ruprecht, 1967, 1969.

Mehlhausen, Joachim. "Der Streit um die Adiaphora." In *Bekenntnis und Einheit der Kirche: Studien zum Konkordienbuch*, edited by Martin Brecht and Reinhard Schwarz, 105–28. Stuttgart: Calwer, 1980.

Meijering, E. P. *Melanchthon and Patristic Thought: The Doctrines of Christ and Grace, the Trinity and the Creation*. Leiden: E. J. Brill, 1983.

Meyer, Johannes. *Historischer Kommentar zu Luthers Kleinem Katechismus.* Gütersloh: C. Bertelsmann, 1929.

Neuser, Wilhelm H. *Der Ansatz der Theologie Philipp Melanchthons.* Neukirchen-Vluyn: Verlag des Erziehungsvereins, 1957.

Oberman, Heiko A. *The Harvest of Medieval Theology: Gabriel Biel and Late Medieval Nominalism.* Durham, N.C.: Labyrinth, 1983 reprint.

———. *Werden und Wertung der Reformation.* 2d ed. Tübingen: J. C. B. Mohr [Paul Siebeck], 1979.

Peters, Albrecht. "Die Theologie der Katechismen Luthers anhand der Zuordnung ihrer Hauptstücke." *Luther-Jahrbuch* 43 (1976): 7–35.

———. *Kommentar zu Luthers Katechismen.* 5 vols. Göttingen: Vandenhoeck and Ruprecht, 1990–94.

Quere, Ralph. *Christum cognoscere: Christ's Efficacious Presence in the Eucharistic Theology of Melanchthon.* Nieuwkoop: B. De Graaf, 1977.

Reu, John Michael. *Dr. Martin Luther's Small Catechism: A History of Its Origin, Its Distribution and Its Use.* Chicago: Wartburg, 1929.

Rogge, Joachim. *Johann Agricolas Lutherverständnis: Unter besonderer Berücksichtigung des Antinomismus.* Berlin: Evangelische Verlagsanstalt, 1960.

Schäfer, Rolf. *Christologie und Sittlichkeit in Melanchthons frühen Loci.* Tübingen: J. C. B. Mohr/Paul Siebeck, 1961.

———. "Melanchthons Hermeneutik im Römerbriefkommentar von 1532." *Zeitschrift für Theologie und Kirche* 60 (1963): 216–35.

Scheible, Heinz. "Luther and Melanchthon." *Lutheran Quarterly,* n.s., 4 (1990): 317–39.

———. "Melanchthons Bildungsprogramm." In *Lebenslehren und Weltentwürfe im Übergang vom Mittelalter zur Neuzeit,* edited by Hartmut Boockmann et al., 233–48. Göttingen: Vandenhoeck and Ruprecht, 1989.

———. "Melanchthons Brief an Carlowitz." *ARG* 57 (1966): 102–30.

———. "Philip Melanchthon (1497–1560): Melanchthons Werdegang." In *Humanismus im deutschen Südwestern: Biographische Profile,* edited by Gerhard Schmidt, 221–38. Sigmaringen, Germany: Jan Thorbecke, 1993.

Schneider, John R. *Philip Melanchthon's Rhetorical Construal of Biblical Authority: Oratio sacra.* Lewiston, N.Y.: Edwin Mellen, 1990.

Schwarzenau, Paul. *Der Wandel im theologischen Ansatz bei Melanchthon von 1525–1535.* Gütersloh: C. Bertelsmann, 1956.

Stupperich, Martin. *Osiander in Preussen: 1549–1552.* Berlin: De Gruyter, 1973.

Stupperich, Robert. "Die Rechtfertigungslehre bei Luther und Melanchthon 1530–1536." In *Luther and Melanchthon in the History and Theology of the Reformation,* edited by Vilmos Vajta, 73–88. Philadelphia: Muhlenberg, 1961.

Trusen, Winfried. *Um die Reform und Einheit der Kirche: Zum Leben und Werk Georg Witzels.* Münster: Aschendorff, 1957.

Wengert, Timothy J. "Caspar Cruciger (1504–1548): The Case of the Disappearing Reformer." *Sixteenth Century Journal* 20 (1989): 417–41.

———. "Caspar Cruciger Sr.'s 1546 'Enarratio' on John's Gospel: An Experiment in Ecclesiological Exegesis." *Church History* 61 (1992): 60–74.

———. "The Day Philip Melanchthon Got Mad." *Lutheran Quarterly*, n.s., 5 (1991): 419–33.

———. "'Fear and Love' in the Ten Commandments." *Concordia Journal* 21 (1995): 14–27.

———. *Human Freedom, Christian Righteousness: Philip Melanchthon's Exegetical Dispute with Erasmus of Rotterdam*. New York: Oxford University Press, 1998.

———. "Melanchthon's Biblical Commentaries." In *Philip Melanchthon (1497–1560) and the Commentary*, edited by M. Patrick Graham and Timothy J. Wengert. Sheffield: Sheffield Academic Press, 1997.

———. *Philip Melanchthon's "Annotationes in Johannem" in Relation to Its Predecessors and Contemporaries*. Geneva: Librairie Droz, 1987.

———. "Wittenberg's Earliest Catechism." *Lutheran Quarterly*, n.s., 7 (1993): 247–60.

Wetzel, Richard. "Caspar Cruciger als ein Schreiber der 'Schmalkaldischen Artikel.'" *Luther-Jahrbuch* 54 (1987): 84–93.

Wiedenhofer, Siegfried. *Formalstrukturen humanistischer und reformatorischer Theologie bei Philipp Melanchthon*. 2 vols. Frankfurt am Main: Peter Lang, 1976.

Scripture Index

Subject Index

227

Timothy J. Wengert is professor of the history of Christianity, The Lutheran Theological Seminary at Philadelphia. He is the author of numerous scholarly articles, *Philip Melanchthon's "Annotationes in Johannem" in Relation to Its Predecessors and Contemporaries* (Droz) and *Human Freedom, Christian Righteousness: Philip Melanchthon's Exegetical Dispute with Erasmus of Rotterdam* (Oxford). His Ph.D. degree is from Duke University.